The Battle of the Greasy Grass/Little Bighorn

In June of 1876, the U.S. government's plan to pressure the Lakota and Cheyenne people onto reservations came to a dramatic and violent end with a battle that would become enshrined in American memory. In the eyes of many Americans at the time, the battle of Little Bighorn represented a symbolic struggle between the civil and the savage. Known as the Battle of the Greasy Grass to the Lakota, the Battle of the Little Bighorn to the people who suppressed them, and as Custer's Last Stand in the annals of popular culture, the event continues to captivate students of American history.

In *The Battle of the Greasy Grass/Little Bighorn*, Debra Buchholtz narrates the history of the battle and critically examines the legacy it has left. In five concise chapters, bolstered by government documents, newspaper articles, and eyewitness accounts, Buchholtz shows how the battle continues to shape the way we understand indigenous peoples, the Wild West, and the history of America.

For additional documents, images, and resources please visit *The Battle of the Greasy Grass/Little Bighorn* companion website at:

www.routledge.com/cw/criticalmoments

Debra Buchholtz is a lecturer in the Geography and Anthropology department at California State Polytechnic University

Critical Moments in American History

Edited by William Thomas Allison

The Assassination of John F. Kennedy
Political Trauma and American Memory
Alice L. George

The Battle of the Greasy Grass/Little Bighorn
Custer's Last Stand in Memory, History, and Popular Culture
Debra Buchholtz

The Battle of the Greasy Grass/ Little Bighorn

Custer's Last Stand in Memory, History, and Popular Culture

Debra Buchholtz

Routledge
Taylor & Francis Group

NEW YORK AND LONDON

First published 2012
by Routledge
711 Third Avenue, New York, NY 10017

Simultaneously published in the UK
by Routledge
2 Park Square, Milton Park, Abingdon, Oxon OX14 4RN

Routledge is an imprint of the Taylor & Francis Group, an informa business

Library of Congress Cataloging in Publication Data
Buchholtz, Debra.
    The battle of the Greasy Grass / Little Bighorn : Custer's last stand
    in memory, history, and popular culture / by Debra Buchholtz.
    p. cm.
    Includes bibliographical references and index.
    1. Little Bighorn, Battle of the, Mont., 1876. 2. Cheyenne Indians—
    Wars, 1876. 3. Dakota Indians—Wars, 1876. 4. Indians in popular culture.
    5. Indians of North America—Public opinion. 6. Custer, George A.
    (George Armstrong), 1839–1876—Public opinion. 7. Public opinion—
    United States. I. Title.
    E83.876.B93 2012
    973.8′2—dc23

ISBN: 978-0-415–89558-3 (hbk)
ISBN: 978-0-415–89559-0 (pbk)
ISBN: 978-0-203–11678-4 (ebk)

Typeset in Bembo and Helvetica Neue
by Florence Production Ltd, Stoodleigh, Devon

Contents

Series Introduction		vi
List of Figures		vii
Acknowledgments		viii
Timeline		ix
1	Road to War	1
2	Battle of the Greasy Grass/Little Bighorn	36
3	Aftermath	72
4	Reverberations	101
5	The Battle in Memory and History	131
	Documents	151
	Notes	203
	Bibliography	210
	Index	215

Series Introduction

Welcome to the Routledge *Critical Moments in American History* series. The purpose of this new series is to give students a window into the historian's craft through concise, readable books by leading scholars, who bring together the best scholarship and engaging primary sources to explore a critical moment in the American past. In discovering the principal points of the story in these books, gaining a sense of historiography, following a fresh trail of primary documents, and exploring suggested readings, students can then set out on their own journey, to debate the ideas presented, interpret primary sources, and reach their own conclusions – just like the historian.

A critical moment in history can be a range of things – a pivotal year, the pinnacle of a movement or trend, or an important event such as the passage of a piece of legislation, an election, a court decision, a battle. It can be social, cultural, political, or economic. It can be heroic or tragic. Whatever they are, such moments are by definition "game changers," momentous changes in the pattern of the American fabric, paradigm shifts in the American experience. Many of the critical moments explored in this series are familiar; some less so.

There is no ultimate list of critical moments in American history – any group of students, historians, or other scholars may come up with a different catalog of topics. These differences of view, however, are what makes history itself and the study of history so important and so fascinating. Therein can be found the utility of historical inquiry – to explore, to challenge, to understand, and to realize the legacy of the past through its influence of the present. It is the hope of this series to help students realize this intrinsic value of our past and of studying our past.

William Thomas Allison
Georgia Southern University

Figures

2.1	Campaign Map	43
2.2	Greasy Grass/Little Bighorn Battlefield Map	59
4.1	Indian Memorial	125
4.2	7th Cavalry Memorial	128
5.1	Crow Scouts on the Greasy Grass/Little Bighorn Battlefield	139

Acknowledgments

This volume incorporates results from research conducted in archives around the United States and on or near the Little Bighorn Battlefield National Monument. Funding was generously provided by the University of Minnesota Graduate School and Department of Anthropology, the American Philosophical Society's Phillips Fund for Native American Research, the Autry Institute for the Study of the American West at the Autry Museum of Western Heritage, and The British Academy.

A special word of thanks is due to the many residents of and visitors to the Greasy Grass/Little Bighorn area who graciously shared their thoughts with me and answered my seemingly endless questions. National Park Service staff at the Little Bighorn Battlefield National Monument and the Harper's Ferry Center have gone out of their way to be of assistance, often at relatively short notice. Many thanks to them and to the knowledgeable and always helpful Magdalene Medicine Horse Moccasin, former archivist at the Little Big Horn College Archives.

Timeline

1803	Louisiana Purchase
1804–1806	Lewis and Clark Expedition
1851	First Fort Laramie Treaty
1861–1865	Civil War
1862	Santee Sioux (Minnesota) Uprising
November 29, 1864	Sand Creek Massacre
1866	Custer and the 7th Cavalry posted to Fort Riley, Kansas
1866–1868	Red Cloud's War
1868	Second Fort Laramie Treaty
November 27, 1868	Battle of the Washita
1873	Panic of 1873 and recession
1873	Custer and the 7th Cavalry posted to Ft. Abraham Lincoln, Dakota Territory
1874	Custer's Black Hills Expedition
Fall 1875	Allison Commission tries to buy the Black Hills; Lakota refuse to sell
December 3, 1875	Lakota and Cheyenne "wanderers" ordered back to their reservations
January 31, 1876	Deadline for the Lakota and Cheyenne to return to their reservations
February 1, 1876	Off-reservation Indians certified hostile; matter handed to War Department
March 1, 1876	Crook's Wyoming column departs Fort Fetterman, Wyoming Territory
March 17, 1876	Colonel Reynolds attacks Cheyenne camp on the Little Missouri River
April 3, 1876	Gibbon's Montana column departs Fort Ellis, Montana Territory
May 17, 1876	Terry's Dakota column departs Fort Lincoln, Dakota Territory
May 29, 1876	Crook's Wyoming column departs Fort Fetterman again
June 4–7, 1876	Sitting Bull's Sun Dance
June 10–17, 1876	Reno reconnoiters the area between the Powder and Tongue rivers
June 16, 1876	Lakota and Cheyenne move into the Little Bighorn valley
June 17, 1876	Rosebud Battle, or the Battle Where the Sister Saved Her Brother
June 22, 1876	Custer and the 7th Cavalry leave the camp on Yellowstone

June 25, 1876	Battle of the Greasy Grass/Little Bighorn
June 26, 1876	Lakota and Cheyenne break camp and move off
June 27, 1876	Gibbon and Terry relieve besieged remnants of the 7th Cavalry
July 4, 1876	American Centennial
July 6, 1876	Sherman and Sheridan receive confirmation of Custer's defeat and death
1876–1877	Army harasses off-reservation Indians throughout the fall and winter
May 6, 1877	Crazy Horse and his followers surrender
May 7, 1877	Sitting Bull and his followers cross into Canada
September 5, 1877	Crazy Horse killed
1879	First memorial to the 7th Cavalry erected on Last Stand Hill
August 1, 1879	Custer Battlefield designated a national cemetery of the 4th class
July 1881	Present granite memorial to the 7th Cavalry erected on Last Stand Hill
July 19, 1881	Sitting Bull surrenders at Fort Buford
December 7, 1886	National Cemetery of Custer's Battlefield Reservation established
1890	White granite headstones placed to mark where the soldiers fell
December 16, 1890	Sitting Bull killed
December 29, 1890	Wounded Knee Massacre
April 14, 1926	Reno-Benteen Battlefield acquired
January 7, 1940	National Park Service assumes responsibility for the battlefield
March 22, 1946	Battlefield renamed the Custer Battlefield National Monument
December 10, 1991	Battlefield renamed the Little Bighorn Battlefield National Monument
December 10, 1991	Congress authorizes an Indian memorial at the battlefield
May 31, 1999	First red granite headstone placed to mark where a warrior was killed
June 25, 2003	Indian memorial dedicated at Little Bighorn Battlefield National Monument

CHAPTER 1

Road to War

INTRODUCTION

On June 25, 1876, Lieutenant Colonel George Armstrong Custer and the U.S. 7th Cavalry, with the help of Crow and Arikara scouts, found and attacked a Lakota (Sioux) and Cheyenne village on the west bank of the Little Bighorn River in Montana Territory. With its tribal circles swelled by Lakota and Cheyenne Indians who had left their reservations that spring to socialize and hunt with friends and relatives still roaming the northern Plains, the village was much larger than anyone expected. Historians estimate it contained seven thousand people, including as many as two thousand men of fighting age. At the first sign of attack, warriors from the village scrambled to defend their families and homes. By the end of the day Custer and everyone under his immediate command lay dead on the bluffs above the north end of the sprawling village. Meanwhile, the remnants of the 7th Cavalry—troops commanded by Major Marcus Reno and Captain Frederick Benteen and those escorting the slow-moving pack train—reunited on a hilltop just over four miles upstream. Warriors held them under siege there for the rest of that day and most of the next. In all, 263 soldiers and attached civilians died in the battle, 210 of them under Custer's immediate command. Another sixty were wounded but more than four hundred survived. Estimates of Lakota and Cheyenne fatalities run from thirty to three hundred with most credible sources putting their death toll at the lower end of the range.

Late in the afternoon on June 26 Lakota and Cheyenne lookouts detected more troops approaching from the north and the village hastily decamped southward, leaving behind a scattering of household goods and other possessions. Although the Lakota and Cheyenne had won a major victory, any celebration was muted by grief for the loved ones killed or wounded in the battle. Besides, as modern interpreters are keen to note, they may have won the battle but they had already lost the war to preserve their traditional ways of life, something many people in the village already realized. Within just a few weeks the army fielded the largest troop deployment since the Civil War to track them down. Within a year most of the Cheyennes and Lakotas involved in the battle, including Crazy Horse and his followers, had returned to the agencies. Once there, they were forced to relinquish their nomadic lifestyles forever and accept settled life on reservations. Sitting Bull and his followers crossed over the border to Grandmother's Land (Canada) in the spring of 1877. Over the next few years they trickled back south in small groups and surrendered. Sitting Bull finally capitulated in 1881.

Dubbed Custer's Last Stand by the press of the day and celebrated as such by American popular culture ever since, most non-Indians now remember the fight as the Battle of the Little Bighorn. Many Native Americans, however, adopt the nomenclature of their ancestors who were in the village at the time. They call it the Battle of the Greasy Grass, a label derived from the Lakota name for the river. These contrasting designators—Custer's Last Stand, Battle of the Little Bighorn, Battle of the Greasy Grass—signal remarkably different ways of telling the story and understanding the events that led up to the battle and what happened afterwards. They also reflect differences in how people experienced the battle and suffered its consequences. Even now the battle means different things to different people. An appreciation of that is key to understanding what happened, the consequences for those involved, and the battle's changing image in popular culture. But more than just mark dissimilarities in how differently situated people experienced and now remember the battle, these distinct labels offer a route to understanding why this relatively minor series of events became a critical moment in American history.

How the battle story is told has continually changed in response to new evidence and the fluctuating needs of diverse segments of a society undergoing rapid change. Ambiguities, contradictions, and unknowns riddle the story. Different eyewitnesses saw different parts of the action or the same parts from different vantage points. Many participants reported their observations years later, which allowed time for memories to fade or be swayed by other accounts. Fearing reprisals, most Lakotas and Cheyennes hesitated to tell their story at all. To protect themselves or curry favor, some told their white interrogators only what they thought they wanted to hear. Moreover, the questions the interviewers posed inevitably derived from their own preconceived notions of what had happened and thereby shaped the responses they got. Many Native American eyewitnesses shared their accounts through translators, some of whom intentionally or inadvertently mistranslated their words. Certain 7th Cavalry survivors recounted their experiences in ways that advanced a particular interpretation or cast a more positive light on some of their comrades than others. A few even told their stories in different ways at different times. Some scholars have speculated that the survivors "closed ranks" to protect the reputation of the regiment or held back information that reflected poorly on Custer out of respect for his wife. Over the years, scores of people falsely claimed to be "sole survivors" and offered their own fabricated battle accounts. It is for these reasons that eyewitness accounts and other sources often contradict one another.

Despite the huge and still growing body of literature on the battle, including dozens of eyewitness accounts by Native Americans and soldiers and excellent contributions by archaeologists, many unknowns remain and always will. Historians constantly grapple with such issues. But, in this particular case, the discrepancies fuel ongoing and sometimes acrimonious popular debate and controversy and give rise to a seemingly endless parade of new analyses and fictionalized accounts. And because so many of the battle details remain open to interpretation and dispute, different stakeholders—and that is exactly what they are, individuals and groups with "shares" or "vested interests" in the battle story—enjoy wide latitude in how they tell the story and often do so in ways that advance their own interests.

The timing of the battle is also noteworthy. While the Lakota and Cheyenne were fighting Custer's 7th Cavalry out on the northern Plains, elsewhere in the country people were gearing up to celebrate the nation's one-hundredth birthday. Back from recession and with the post-Civil War period of Reconstruction (1865–1877) officially over, the newly reunited nation was brimming with optimism, at least in theory. High-ranking officials such as General William Tecumseh Sherman (Commanding General of the Army) and General Philip Sheridan (head of the Department of the Missouri) were gathered in Philadelphia, where the celebration centered on the blockbuster Centennial Exhibition. From there Sherman, Sheridan, and other officials quickly dismissed as implausible rumors of the 7th Cavalry's defeat and Custer's death that began circulating just after the festivities climaxed on the Fourth of July. When more credible sources confirmed those rumors two days later, the American people were stunned. But should they have been?

The clouds of war had been massing for years—even decades—and anyone paying attention could easily see that peoples like the Lakota and Cheyenne not only stood in the way of America's putative manifest destiny to "overspread the continent" but had been paying a heavy price for the country's westward expansion. Some of them had long responded to threats to their lands, livelihoods, and ways of life with armed resistance and they had fought hard, for they had everything to lose. All spring Indian agents had been reporting that disgruntled Lakotas and Cheyennes were leaving their reservations in greater numbers than ever to join bands of roamers led by such stalwart traditionalists as Sitting Bull (Hunkpapa Lakota), Crazy Horse (Oglala Lakota), and Two Moon (Northern Cheyenne). By early summer even casual readers of the national press should have had an inkling of at least some of the links in the chain of events that culminated on the banks of the river with two names, the Little Bighorn and Greasy Grass.

The specific context in which the battle occurred and how it was initially reported and later re-presented are key to making sense of the continually evolving story and the ways diversely situated stakeholders have understood it at particular junctures. The Greasy Grass/Little Bighorn battle has long captured the attention of a growing cohort of amateur historians. Representing all fifty states and many foreign countries, these individuals pour over the massive body of literature on it. They scour eyewitness accounts, oral history, and primary documents in search of new insights into exactly what happened, how, where, when, and why. Many of them belong to organizations dedicated to the study of this and related battles. Some publish narrowly focused analyses of aspects of the battle. Others critically, almost gleefully, analyze everything their colleagues write. Hundreds congregate in the battlefield vicinity each year over the late June battle anniversary to rehash what happened. A few dress in Cavalry uniforms and take part in one of two battle reenactments staged at that time. The minutiae that so fascinates them is readily available elsewhere, contributes little to our understanding of the context in which the battle occurred and its subsequent ramifications, and, consequently, falls outside the scope of this volume. Nonetheless, readers interested in such fine-grained detail will find the references cited and appended documents a useful starting point. The intense and enduring interest in the battle manifested by these so-called Custer buffs indicates the prominence the battle has attained in American history and popular culture and will be explored in later chapters.

There are many organizations devoted to study of the Greasy Grass/Little Bighorn battle. Foremost amongst them is Friends of the Little Bighorn Battlefield, a group established in 1996 to support the Little Bighorn Battlefield National Monument. Others include the Custer Battlefield Museum & Historical Association, Little Big Horn Associates, the Custer Battlefield Preservation Committee, and the Custer Association of Great Britain. Members of the Order of the Indian Wars also take a strong interest in this particular battle.

From the outset, the Greasy Grass/Little Bighorn battle meant different things to different people. What exactly those things are has changed in step with prevailing social, political, and economic conditions, a thread that runs through this book. In 1876, for example, most (but not all) Americans of European descent understood the battle as the tragic outcome of a clash between civilization and savagery. They glorified Custer and his men as heroes who valiantly sacrificed themselves for the good of the nation. On the eve of World War II many Americans embraced Errol Flynn's Custer in the film *They Died with their Boots On* as a model for how American soldiers should face death fighting for American ideals. But then in the Vietnam era many younger Americans and civil rights activists came to see the battle as the archetype of what, in their eyes, were racist and genocidal wars fought by the United States in pursuit of global dominance. *Little Big Man*, the 1970 film starring Dustin Hoffman in the title role, popularized that view. More recently the battle has been reduced to an almost inevitable outcome of a "clash of cultures."[1] That view is perhaps most evident in the story told by the National Park Service (NPS) at the Little Bighorn Battlefield National Monument. Yet, despite important patterns like these, no consensus view of the battle has ever developed. Furthermore, one must remember that abstract concepts like "civilization," "savagery," and "cultures" don't clash, people do.

At any given point, differently situated groups and individuals have understood and used the battle in profoundly different ways. By incorporating and contextualizing the competing voices and discordant memories suggested by the distinct ways of labeling the battle already noted, this book aims to convey the contingency of history. As will become evident, how such events are remembered is influenced by conditions in the present as well as those at the time. Because of its ironic timing and the mystery that shrouds it to this day, the Greasy Grass/Little Bighorn battle gives itself readily to diverse interpretations, thus making it an ideal vehicle for illustrating how past events are continually reconstituted to reflect current sensibilities and to serve present ends and future objectives. That historical facts can be assembled and reassembled in many different ways in support of different and sometimes conflicting analyses, interpretations, and agendas is an important yet often difficult point for history readers to grasp.

The Battle of the Greasy Grass/Little Bighorn has long fascinated the American public. This book goes beyond the usual battle narrative to ask why and to explore the battle's far-flung implications and ramifications. It begins in the present chapter by locating the battle within the complex social, cultural, political, and economic milieu in which it occurred. This establishes the historical background and contextualizes the political and strategic calculations behind the army's campaign to force the Lakota and Cheyenne roamers onto reservations as well as the logic and motivations that underpinned Lakota and Cheyenne resistance. Chapter 2 narrates the battle as it unfolded, starting with the War Department orders that paved the way for a military campaign against the off-reservation Lakota and Cheyenne. Chapter 3 describes what happened to parties from both sides after the battle, how they responded, and the battle's longer-term consequences for them. How the American public, including so-called Friends of the Indian groups, understood and reacted to those events is noted at relevant points throughout this and the next chapter. Chapter 4 periodizes remembrance of the event. It not only traces the continuing reverberations and ramifications of the battle but links specific iterations of the story to social, political, and economic conditions at particular points in time. By describing the contexts in which it has been remembered and memorialized in this way, the volume begins to unravel how and why the Greasy Grass/Little Bighorn battle, which was relatively minor by then recent Civil War standards, attained such prominence in American history and culture. The final chapter critically evaluates scholarly and other treatments of the battle, considering both the end products and the primary sources that went into their creation. It also looks at battlefield interpretation at the national monument in relation to a pair of battle reenactments staged nearby and briefly explores the meanings they asserted and politics they enacted. This clearly illustrates how even today the battle story is used to advance competing agendas.

U.S. WESTWARD EXPANSION

In 1803 the United States acquired the vast swath of territory known as the Louisiana Purchase from France and thus doubled its land base. The 828,200 square mile expanse stretched from the Mississippi River to the Rocky Mountains and from the Gulf of Mexico to the present-day Canadian border. Soon thereafter President Thomas Jefferson commissioned Merriwether Lewis and William Clark to lead an expedition up the Missouri River. The Corps of Discovery, as it was called, had several objectives, all of them in aid of the new nation's westward expansion. Besides attempting to locate the Northwest Passage, a non-existent waterway then believed to connect the Missouri River to the Pacific Ocean, Lewis and Clark were tasked with describing the flora, fauna, and geography of the region, surveying its exploitable resources and potential for economic development, and asserting American dominion over its indigenous peoples. Between 1804 and 1806 the Lewis and Clark expedition crossed and re-crossed the northern Plains. During that time, it encountered many Native groups, including the Lakota, Cheyenne, Crow, and Arikara, peoples destined to feature in the Greasy Grass/Little Bighorn story.

But Spanish, French, and British soldiers, explorers, traders, and missionaries preceded Lewis and Clark and their influences had already altered the balance of power on the Great Plains and effected significant cultural change. Contrary to popular imagery, the Plains Indians did not always have horses. Horses did not exist in the Americas prior to their introduction by Spanish conquistadors. Plains groups acquired them in the 1700s through trade with and theft from indigenous peoples to the south and west who had acquired them directly or indirectly from the Spanish herds. By the middle of the eighteenth century most Plains tribes were mounted. That led to changes in their residence patterns and subsistence strategies, altered their involvement in the fur trade, and influenced inter-tribal warfare. With the acquisition of horses they became even more reliant on the American bison, or what is commonly but less accurately called the buffalo. Not only did the buffalo provide them with food to eat and hides to trade for European goods, they fashioned clothes, tipi covers, and household implements from the skins, bones, horns, and other parts of the animal.

Around that time they also began to obtain guns through French and British traders situated to their north and east. Indigenous peoples furthest east acquired guns first, which gave them a temporary advantage in warfare and hunting for the fur trade. The French and British traders had other enticing goods on offer, which created new wants and needs that drew the tribes deeper into French, British, and (later) American controlled trading networks and thereby disrupted the traditional networks. Most tribes hunted or trapped for furs to trade but some traded finished goods and foodstuffs. For a time, tribes like the Arikara and Crow were strategically positioned and powerful enough to control and profit from the flow of goods by acting as middlemen. They vigorously defended that role while tribes like the Lakota strategically disrupted trade to their rivals.

Smallpox, scarlet fever, measles, and other European diseases to which Native American peoples lacked immunity followed the same routes as horses, guns, and trade goods. Wave after wave of disease—what historians call "virgin soil epidemics"—affected some groups more than others. In 1780 a smallpox epidemic swept across the Plains killing over half the members of those tribes it struck. Other epidemics followed and each further weakened the tribes affected. In the summer of 1837 the *St. Peter* steamed up the Missouri River loaded with goods for the fur trade. The boat also inadvertently carried smallpox. People at stops along the way were infected and from there the disease spread rapidly from tribe to tribe. Because they lived in close proximity to one another, the village Indians were the most seriously affected; nomadic peoples, who lived in more open spaces and could disperse quickly, suffered fewer deaths. The sedentary Mandan, Arikara, and Hidatsa were hardest hit. Demographic sociologist Russell Thornton estimates that only about half the Arikara and Hidatsa survived.[2] The Mandan numbered 1,600–2,000 before the disease struck; just over a hundred remained after it had run its course. The Crow, who had already suffered heavy losses in previous waves of disease, lost a third of their remaining population in the 1837 epidemic. That further undermined their already tenuous geopolitical position and would later influence their strategic decision-making. Many of the nomadic Lakotas had been inoculated, consequently the Lakota suffered far fewer losses than other tribes, which further tilted the balance of power in their favor.

American westward expansion created upheaval throughout the Plains and beyond. White settlement breached the Appalachian Mountains in the early 1700s. In its relentless advance, it drove the Native inhabitants of the newly appropriated lands into territories occupied by other peoples, thereby setting in motion a domino effect. Many of the displaced groups already had guns, which rendered them more powerful than those upon whose lands they encroached. As a result, they dislodged tribes such as the Cheyenne and Lakota from their homelands and pushed them westward into lands already occupied by other indigenous peoples.

Even after pressure from the dislocated eastern tribes abated and all the Plains tribes had guns and horses, settlers continued to disrupt tribal life. In 1843 emigrants in search of their manifest destiny in the far west began to cross the Plains on the Oregon Trail. By 1845 the flow had become a steady stream. The next year the United States acquired all of the disputed Oregon Country south of the 49th parallel. After gold was discovered in California in 1848 people literally flooded westward along the Oregon Trail. Further south traffic on the Sante Fe Trail increased after Mexico transferred California, Colorado, and most of the rest of the territory between the Rio Grande River and the Pacific Ocean to the United States under the terms of the Treaty of Guadalupe Hildago. This marked the end of the War with Mexico (1846–1848), a conflict triggered by the U.S. annexation of Texas.

Ten years later gold was discovered in the Pikes Peak area of Colorado. That sent droves of optimistic prospectors southwest on the Sante Fe Trail. One historian estimates that 18,847 emigrants crossed the Central Plains en route to Utah and the West Coast between 1840 and 1848. That number rose to 52,500 in 1850 and 70,000 in 1852.[3] By 1860 approximately 296,259 emigrants had traipsed westward through Indian territory. Then, in 1862, gold was discovered in what would soon become Montana Territory, which caused thousands of fortune seekers to rush northwest on the Bozeman Trail. Meanwhile land-hungry white farmers were beginning to till the soil across the Plains while others were making their way to the fertile valleys of Oregon. In 1863 work began on the first transcontinental railroad, further exacerbating the situation. Known as the Union Pacific Railroad or the Overland Route, it sliced through the heart of Indian country, as would its successors.

Such incursions inevitably created tension between the Indians and whites, in no small part because the newcomers killed the game, disrupted buffalo migration patterns, and destroyed other resources upon which the Indians depended. When the Indians resisted or retaliated, the emigrants demanded and got military intervention. Soon a cycle of violence developed: frustrated warriors attacked settlements, wagon trains, and stage coaches in revenge for real and perceived injustices inflicted upon them and their peoples by whites and the settlers and army responded with force. The ensuing loss of Indian lives and possessions, coupled with growing food shortages and heightened frustration, provoked new rounds of retaliation and counter-retaliation.

The degree to which the Plains Indians relied on the buffalo cannot be overestimated nor can their anger over the wasteful slaughter of the animals by non-Indians be exaggerated. Army and government officials had long recognized the Indians' dependence on the buffalo as a vulnerability and exploited it by encouraging civilians and soldiers to hunt for meat and sport. In 1867 General Philip Sheridan assumed command of the Division of the Missouri, which encompassed the Plains. Later that year the Fort Laramie Treaty (see Documents) established the Great Sioux Reservation in Dakota Territory. It also granted the Lakota the right to hunt in the unceded territory west of the reservation "so long as the buffalo may range thereon in such numbers as to justify the chase." While an important clause to the Indians, it was perceived as a minor concession by the government negotiators, who expected the rapidly dwindling herds to soon vanish and planned to hurry the process along. Writing about the Indians in a letter to General Sherman later that fall, Sheridan proposed that the "best way for the government now is to make them poor by the destruction of their stock, and then settle them on the lands allotted to them."[4] It was a strategy of total war familiar to Sherman, the soon-to-be Commanding General of the Army remembered for slashing and burning his way through rebel fields and food stores during the Civil War. As such, it put to rest his qualms over granting the Lakota permission to hunt outside the reservation borders.

> Hide-hunters killed an estimated 7.5 million buffalo between 1872 and 1874. After stripping them of their hides, they usually left the carcasses to rot where they fell.

But it took more than the army to wipe out the buffalo. In the end it was the hide-hunters that finished off the herds. After a Pennsylvania tannery developed a way to convert buffalo hides into commercial grade leather in 1871 the price for hides skyrocketed, prompting hide-hunters to flock to the Plains. By the mid 1870s the great buffalo herds of the central Plains were gone; by the early 1880s the herds from the northern Plains were also gone. The Plains tribes were devastated and demoralized. Plenty Coups, a Crow leader, told his biographer that "[w]hen the buffalo went away the hearts of my people fell to the ground, and they could not lift them up again. After this nothing happened. There was no singing anywhere."[5] Sitting Bull, the Hunkpapa Lakota holy man at the center of the Greasy Grass story, said that "[a] cold wind blew across the prairie when the last buffalo fell—a death-wind for my people."[6]

INDIGENOUS PEOPLES OF THE NORTHERN PLAINS

Throughout the nineteenth century the Lakota, Cheyenne, and Crow roamed the Plains in search of game and other resources upon which they depended. But they hadn't always done so. Each group has oral traditions that refer to an earlier time when they had very different lifeways and made their homes in the woodlands west of the Great Lakes or in the forests and on the rolling prairies of the upper Mississippi River drainage. Ample archaeological and historical evidence exists to support this oral history. Ancestors of the people now known as the Crow were the first to move out on to the Plains on a full-time basis. Pressed by better armed Native peoples dislocated by white settlement in the east and lured by the plentiful game and new economic opportunities created by the fur trade to the west, the Cheyenne and Lakota followed them in the late seventeenth and early eighteenth centuries. These were slow migrations into lands already occupied by other tribes and they were completed in stages punctuated by conflict. Along the way new tribal subdivisions developed as constituent groups peeled off to follow their own routes westward and new rivalries and inter-tribal alliances formed based on conflicting and shared interests.

Like many Native American groups, the Crows refer to themselves by a different name than that used by their enemies, government officials, and most non-Indians. They call themselves *Apsáalooke* ("Children of the Long Beaked Bird," a reference to a bird no longer seen in Crow Country). Early fur traders and explorers mistranslated this word as "Crow," which is what the *Apsáalooke* are still called in English. The Crow sometimes also refer to themselves *Biiluke* ("On Our Side"), a term that invokes their common ancestry and language as well as shared spiritual beliefs, forms of social organization, and cultural practices.

According to Crow tradition and archaeological and linguistic evidence, the Crow and Hidatsa once constituted a single people.[7] Their ancestors hunted, gathered, and fished in the boreal forests north and west of Lake Superior long before Europeans arrived on the scene. Gradually they migrated westward until they reached the Missouri River area of what is now North Dakota. There they established sedentary villages and grew beans, corn, squash, and other crops. Evidence suggests that around 1500 small groups of hunters began to move out onto Plains in search of game. Eventually some of them no longer returned to the Missouri River villages to live and began to think of themselves as a separate people. They became the *Ashalahó* ("Many Lodges") or Mountain Crow. Some time later another group broke off from the Hidatsa. Crow oral history attributes this split to a dispute over the distribution of meat. These people became the *Binneassiippeele* ("Those Who Live Amongst the River Banks") or River Crow. A third division, the *Eelalapíio* ("Kicked in the Bellies") or *Ammitaalasshé* ("Home Away from the Center"), formed out of the Mountain Crow. Together these three divisions constituted the *Apsáalooke*, as they still do.

The first Europeans the Crows met were probably the La Vérendrye brothers, a pair of French fur traders from Montreal they encountered in 1743. The brothers called the Crows the *Beaux Hommes* ("handsome men"); the Crows called the Europeans *Baashchíile* ("people with yellow eyes"). More than sixty years later they met another French fur trader from Montreal named François Antoine Larocque. He also found them striking. His journal entry for June 25, 1805, describes a large band of splendidly dressed Crow men that paraded into the Hidatsa village he was visiting.[8] He spent the rest of the summer traveling with them in an attempt to secure their participation in the fur trade on behalf of his employer, the British Northwest Company. According to Larocque, the River Crow habitually hunted north of the Yellowstone valley in the upper Missouri River area and the Mountain Crows hunted south of Yellowstone, with the main body favoring the area around the Bighorn and Absaroka mountains. The Kicked-in-the-Bellies roamed the Powder River country of what is now southeastern Montana and northeastern Wyoming, an area that includes the Bighorn and Little Bighorn rivers. The three divisions maintained close contact. They traded, visited back and forth, and cooperated to defend their families and hunting grounds.

Except for stealing a few horses and a relatively minor clash between the army and a small group of young Crows led by Sword Bearer in 1887, the Crows have always maintained peaceful relations with the whites. They signed their first treaty with the U.S. government in 1825. It was a pledge of friendship. In 1851 they joined with other Plains tribes in signing a treaty at Fort Laramie, which the Senate never ratified. The 38.5 million acres demarcated as Crow territory in that treaty encompassed most of their traditional hunting grounds and constitutes what modern Crows call Crow Country. On the east it was bounded by the Powder River, on the north by the Missouri and Musselshell rivers, on the west by the headwaters of the Yellowstone River, and on the south by the Wind River Mountains. The Fort Laramie Treaty of 1868 diminished Crow holdings by about 30 million acres and subsequent agreements and Executive Orders further reduced them to just 2.2 million acres. Despite these assaults on their land base, the Bighorn and Little Bighorn valleys have always remained within the federally recognized boundaries of Crow territory.

Although a series of treaties, agreements, and Executive Orders clearly demarcated the borders of Crow Country, the Crows had to fight hard to defend their game-rich lands from incursions by the Lakota, Cheyenne, and other tribes. As the nineteenth century wore on, the buffalo herds were shrinking and consolidating in the Powder River country south of Yellowstone valley. Weakened by population losses through warfare and European diseases like smallpox, the Crow had grown so vulnerable that some white observers predicted their imminent demise as a people. Like other small tribes, the biggest threat they faced came from neighboring groups, not the whites. Consequently, the Crow's cooperation with the U.S. government, including the enlistment of Crow warriors as army scouts against the Lakota and other rival groups, must be understood as a strategic decision. Plenty Coups told Frank B. Linderman that the "decision was reached, not because we loved the white man who was already crowding other tribes into our country, or because we hated the Sioux, Cheyenne, and Arapahoe, but because we plainly saw that this course was the only one that might save our beautiful country for us."[9]

The Arikara also played a key part in the Greasy Grass/Little Bighorn story. When Europeans first met them, they lived in earthlodge villages in the lower Middle Missouri region, as they had for several hundred years. Along with the Mandan and Hidatsa further upstream, the Arikara served as middlemen in long-standing inter-tribal trade networks, hunted buffalo, and grew corn, beans, squash, and other crops. By the early nineteenth century, the French, British, and American fur trades were undermining their role in the traditional networks. Tensions heightened and in 1823 violence broke out between them and American fur traders under William Ashley that left more than a dozen white men dead. The U.S. government responded by sending a punitive expedition against the Arikara. It was led by Colonel Henry Leavenworth and accompanied by hundreds of Lakotas. After several days of shelling by the troops and peace negotiations, the Arikara slipped away and sought refuge with the Mandan and Hidatsa. From then on they had a reputation as hostile to whites. But that changed after the fur trade collapsed in the late nineteenth century. They then began to actively support government attempts to subdue the Lakota by serving as mail carriers, hunters, and scouts. Arikaras accompanied Custer on his 1874 expedition to the Black Hills and to the Little Bighorn two years later. Bloody Knife, Custer's favorite scout, was half Arikara. He was also half Lakota, which suggests the complexities inherent in Plains Indian identity politics.

By the time of the Ashley affair, massive population losses due to smallpox and depredations by the Lakota and other tribes were already forcing the Mandan, Hidatsa, and Arikara to consolidate their villages. After another devastating epidemic in 1845, the Mandan and Hidatsa established Like-a-Fishhook village for self-defense. Still harassed by the Lakota, the disease-weakened Arikara joined them there in 1862. By then all three had lost most of their population and along with it much of their traditional knowledge. Many of their social, political, and economic structures had also been destabilized, including their roles as middlemen in inter-tribal trading networks. Still culturally distinct and politically autonomous peoples, the federal government treated the three tribes as affiliated for administrative purposes. An Executive Order signed in 1870 redefined the boundaries of their territory and established the Fort Berthold Reservation for them.

The Cheyenne were living in what is now central Minnesota when they first appeared in the written record.[10] Use of the word Cheyenne as a tribal designator probably originated at that time as a mistranslation of what other Native peoples called them. A 1678 French map located the *Chaiena* east of the Mississippi River. Sieur de La Salle, a French trader who met them in 1680, called them the *Chaa* while the Dakota, then their neighbors, labeled them *Shahiyena* or *Shahiela* ("people who talk differently," "foreigners," or "aliens"). Regardless of the specific derivation of the name, that is not how the Cheyenne referred to themselves. Then as now, they called themselves *Tsistsistas*, which translates into English as "human beings" or "the people." This contrast between what outsiders called them and how they referred to themselves reflects a pattern of distinction and ethnocentrism typical of groups across the region.

When Europeans first met the Cheyenne they lived in small villages and subsisted by hunting, gathering, harvesting wild rice, and fishing. During the eighteenth century the Ojibwe and Assiniboine, who had already acquired guns, forced them south and west on to the prairies. Some Cheyenne bands became nomadic buffalo hunters. Others settled in earthlodge villages along watercourses in present-day North Dakota and started to grow crops. As soon as they obtained horses they abandoned their villages, where they had been vulnerable to attack from the Lakota and to smallpox and other European diseases. As they moved out on to the Plains they adopted the lifeways of mounted buffalo hunters but tailored them to their own cultural patterns. By the early 1800s the sedentary and nomadic bands had reunited and were hunting in the Black Hills area. There they encountered the Sutai, a culturally similar people who spoke a mutually intelligible language. The two groups became allies and by 1820 the Sutai constituted a distinct band within the Cheyenne tribe. Throughout this period the Cheyenne fought the Crow, Wind River Shoshoni, and other neighboring peoples, whose hunting grounds they encroached upon as Lakota territorial expansion pushed them south and west.

Around 1830 some Cheyennes swung north in their migration while others moved south into present-day Nebraska and Colorado, where they fought different tribes and formed new alliances. Despite the divergence, members of the two divisions remained in close contact. In the 1840s the Cheyenne came into increasing conflict with settlers streaming across the frontier in search of better lives and with whites working to open the region for economic exploitation. That conflict prompted the army to establish new forts in the area, including Fort Laramie in 1849. It was there that two years later U.S. government negotiators forged an ineffectual treaty with several Plains tribes.

The 1851 Fort Laramie Treaty had two main objectives: (1) to stop inter-tribal warfare by defining the boundaries between the Cheyenne, Arapaho, Crow, Lakota, Arikara, and other participating tribes; and (2) to ensure safe passage across the Plains for non-Indians. As in most treaties, the tribes agreed to relinquish land in exchange for monetary compensation, farm animals and implements, and regular distributions of food and clothing. They also agreed to become sedentary farmers and to allow roads to be built for the movement of troops and emigrants through their territories. The treaty contained other pledges and promises aimed at securing peace between the Indians and whites, nearly all of which proved unrealistic and were soon broken. One enduring consequence of the treaty was the lumping together of the southern Cheyenne and Arapaho for administrative purposes. Thereafter the northern and southern Cheyenne existed as distinct legal and political entities.

As settlers and soldiers flowed through Indian territory they killed or drove off the game and destroyed other resources upon which the Cheyenne and their neighbors depended. Faced with starvation, frustrated Cheyennes harassed the wagon trains and settlements for food and other goods. In 1857 Colonel Edwin V. Sumner attacked White Antelope's band of Cheyenne on the Solomon River in retaliation for Cheyenne raids against settlements on the Platte. Other Cheyennes clashed with troops along the Oregon Trail. The ongoing cycle of violence claimed innocent victims on both sides. William Bent, a trader who had married into the Cheyenne tribe and acted as Indian Agent for the federal government, summed up the situation as follows:

> A smothered passion for revenge agitates these Indians, perpetually fermented by the failure of food, the encircling encroachments of the white population, and the exasperating sense of decay and impending extinction with which they are surrounded . . . A desperate war of starvation and extinction is imminent and inevitable, unless prompt measures shall prevent it.[11]

The 1861 Fort Wise Treaty sought to end the conflict. In it the Southern Cheyenne agreed to give up lands defined as theirs by the 1851 Fort Laramie Treaty. In return, they were to receive a much smaller tract on Sand Creek in southeastern Colorado, monetary compensation, goods, and farm implements. Acting on their own initiative, six Peace Chiefs signed the treaty on behalf of the entire tribe. Black Kettle was one of them. Because the influential Dog Soldiers would not acknowledge the treaty and most other Cheyennes refused to settle on the reservation, the situation remained largely unchanged. To further complicate matters, resources on the new reservation proved inadequate to meet their most basic subsistence needs and starvation seemed likely.

Tensions continued to mount. In 1862 the Homestead Act unleashed a new stampede of settlers into Indian country, which provoked more raids. That same year frustrated Santee (Dakota Sioux) struggling to survive on greatly diminished lands with grossly inadequate resources rose up in Minnesota. The Sioux or Minnesota Uprising claimed more than four hundred non-Indian and an unknown number of Santee lives and resulted in massive property damage. Of the 303 Santee initially sentenced to death, President Abraham Lincoln ordered 38 hanged in what remains the largest mass execution in the history of the country. Most of those executed were probably innocent. What the press of the day called the Minnesota Massacre fueled the fears of whites living in or traveling through Indian country. It was within that context and largely abandoned by the army, which was busy fighting the Civil War (1861–1865), that the Territorial Governor of Colorado took matters into his own hands. In 1864 he raised a militia to put an end to the Indian raids menacing his jurisdiction.

On November 29 the 3rd regiment of Colorado Volunteers attacked and destroyed Black Kettle's sleeping village on Sand Creek. Leading the 700-strong regiment was Colonel John M. Chivington, who had long called for "extermination of the red devils." Confident that they were free from danger, the band had settled on Sand Creek after reporting to Major Scott Anthony at Fort Lyon in an attempt to secure peace. While the Cheyenne death toll remains controversial most scholars agree that it was about 150 people and that most of the dead were women, children, or elderly. Many more Cheyennes were wounded. The militia suffered minimal casualties and afterwards paraded through the streets of Denver brandishing scalps and other gruesome war trophies. Black Kettle survived and continued to champion peace.

In 1867 the government forged another treaty with the Southern Cheyenne, Arapaho, and other southern Plains tribes. Like its predecessors, the Medicine Lodge Treaty aimed to bring peace to the region, this time by assigning the tribes to reservations. To that end the Southern Cheyennes were first moved to a small reservation in Kansas and then to Indian Country in what is now Oklahoma. Many refused to go; others went but left again when the promised provisions weren't forthcoming. Some warriors resumed their raiding, which brought out the army. This is where Lieutenant Colonel George Armstrong ("Autie") Custer and the 7th Cavalry enter the story.

In 1866, with the Civil War over and the army free to deal with the so-called Indian problem, Custer and the newly formed 7th Cavalry were posted to Fort Riley, Kansas, from where they patrolled the southern Plains. In the fall of 1867, after abandoning his duties to see his wife, Custer faced a court-martial on charges of misconduct and being absent without leave. The military court convicted him and suspended him from duty and rank without pay for one year. But before his sentence had expired General Philip H. Sheridan recalled him to lead the 7th Cavalry in a winter campaign against the southern Arapaho and Cheyenne. At dawn on November 27, 1868, Custer's troops attacked Black Kettle's village on the Washita River in Oklahoma. Despite the American and white flags that flew over Black Kettle's tipi to signal his "friendly" status, the soldiers killed him and a large number of other Cheyennes, most of them women and children. They also completely destroyed the village and its large pony herd and took fifty-three women and children prisoner. Among the

George Armstrong Custer (1839–1876)

George "Autie" Armstrong Custer was born on December 5, 1839, in New Rumley, Ohio to Mary Ward and Emanuel Henry Custer. Emanuel was a farmer and a blacksmith. The couple had four other children, all younger than George: Thomas, Boston, Margaret, and Nevin. Emanuel also had several children from a previous marriage. For most of his adolescence, George lived with his sister Margaret and her husband James Calhoun in Monroe, Michigan. The Custer family—or what some of his contemporaries called the "Custer clan"—was close knit. Three of the Custer brothers—George, Thomas, and Boston—would die together in the Greasy Grass/ Little Bighorn battle along with brother-in-law James Calhoun and nephew Harry Armstrong "Autie" Reed. Eighteen-year-old Harry was the only son of half-sister Lydia and David Reed.

After finishing school in Monroe, Custer attended Hopewell Normal College in Ohio and then briefly worked as a school teacher. Although from a family of staunch Democrats, the ever ambitious Custer managed to persuade his Republican congressman to secure him an appointment to the United States Military Academy in West Point, New York. He matriculated to West Point in 1858 and graduated at the bottom of his class in 1861, a year early due to the start of the Civil War. During his three years at the academy he accumulated a shocking number of demerits.

Custer began active duty as a second lieutenant in the 2nd Cavalry. He joined his regiment just in time for the First Battle of Bull Run and afterwards was reassigned to the 5th Cavalry, where he served on the staff of Major General George B. McClelland. His dazzling rise through the ranks of the Civil War army had begun. Many scholars and amateur historians attribute his career successes to a combination of daring, a knack for making the right friends at the right time, skillful political jockeying, and what came to be known as "Custer's luck." After capturing the first Confederate battle flag of the war, Custer was promoted to the temporary rank of captain and became McClelland's aide-de-camp. By then he was adept at the fine art of self-promotion, had taken to wearing flamboyant uniforms of his own design, and was well on his way to becoming the darling of the Union press. Brevet promotion followed brevet promotion as Custer charged across the major Civil War battlefields. In June 1863, just before the Battle at Gettysburg, Major General Alfred Pleasonton promoted him to brigadier general of the volunteers. At twenty-three years of age, he was one of the youngest generals in the Union Army. Custer personally received General Robert E. Lee's flag of truce at Appomattox Court house and was present when the surrender was signed. Major General Philip Sheridan was so impressed with his role in winning the war that he presented the table upon which the surrender papers were signed to Custer's wife Libbie as a gift. By then Custer held the brevet rank of major general of volunteers.

While their paths had already crossed, Custer formally met Elizabeth "Libbie" Clift Bacon, the daughter of Daniel Bacon, a prominent Monroe judge, in November of 1862. Because of Custer's inferior social standing as the son of a farmer and blacksmith, Judge Bacon initially opposed his courtship of his daughter. Only after Custer was promoted to brigadier general did Libbie's father warm to the idea of him as a son-in-law. Custer and Libbie married in February 1864 and thereafter Libbie gamely followed him from post to post. The couple remained together until Custer was killed in the Greasy Grass/Little Bighorn battle but had no children. Libbie never remarried.

Nearly all wartime promotions were temporary, so when Custer was mustered out of the volunteer army at the end of the Civil War, he reverted to his permanent rank of captain in the 5th Cavalry of the regular army. Despite the official change of rank and reduction in pay, it was permissible, even conventional, for people to continue to address him by his wartime rank of general. Custer's first post after the Civil War was reconstruction duty in Texas. It was then that he started to write in earnest. In 1867 he was promoted to the rank of lieutenant colonel and awarded command of the newly created 7th Cavalry, which was posted to Fort Riley, Kansas. In 1873 Custer and the 7th Cavalry were transferred to the just established Fort Abraham Lincoln near Bismarck in Dakota Territory. It proved to be the last post for Custer and many of the enlisted men and officers.

hostages was a beautiful young woman named Monasetah (also known as Me-o-tzi).

Rumors later circulated that Custer took Monasetah into his tent after the battle and developed a relationship with her that lasted for several months. The Cheyenne believe that he fathered a child by her during that time and claim that Monasetah and the fair-haired boy, named Yellow Bird, were in the village on the Greasy Grass when the 7th Cavalry attacked it eight years later. Although it seems certain that some sort of relationship developed between Custer and the young woman, there is conflicting evidence regarding its exact nature, including some that suggests she was already pregnant when they met.

Custer faced strong criticism over the Washita attack. Because so many of the Cheyenne dead were non-combatants, Friends of the Indian groups and certain other people called the battle a "massacre" and condemned him for it. Others disagreed and praised him for a great victory, a difference of opinion that continues to this day. Custer claimed that he had followed a raiding party back to the village. While that may be true, it is not certain that the raiders were members of Black Kettle's band. Other criticisms focused on the fate of Major Joel Elliott and his men. The seventeen-man detachment had chased after a group of Indians fleeing Black Kettle's camp and not yet rejoined the regiment when a large contingent of warriors from nearby camps began massing and Custer ordered a withdrawal. Weeks later the badly mutilated bodies of the missing soldiers were found where they had been surrounded and killed by the Indians. Several officers, and perhaps none more so than Captain Frederick Benteen, strongly believed that the 7th Cavalry should have remained in the area until the detachment was found. They blamed Custer personally for the deaths. The issue created rancor in the ranks that persisted to the Little Bighorn and beyond.

In the early spring of 1869 Custer met with the Cheyenne to try to quell the hostilities peaceably by persuading them to surrender. He smoked a peace pipe with Stone Forehead, the Cheyenne Keeper of the Sacred Arrows. Afterwards Stone Forehead tipped the ashes from the pipe on to Custer's boots and warned him that if he ever broke his promise of peace with the Cheyenne he would become like those ashes. Seven years later Custer would break that promise and die on the Greasy Grass/Little Bighorn.

Organized resistance by the Southern Cheyenne effectively ended the next year with the defeat of the Dog Soldiers at Cherry Creek, Colorado. The southern bands finally surrendered in 1875. Some Southern Cheyennes joined the Northern Cheyenne, who continued their resistance and did so in increasingly close cooperation with the Lakota.

When Europeans first met them, the loose alliance of tribes called the Sioux lived west of the Great Lakes.[12] In the mid-seventeenth century their territory stretched from the forests and prairies of the Mississippi and Minnesota river drainages to the Missouri River. Those in the east subsisted by hunting buffalo and other game, gathering wild rice, and growing corn while those further west relied more heavily on the buffalo. To the north and east the Sioux were bordered by the Ojibwe (also known as Chippewa or Anishenaabe), a people with whom they had once been allies. The fur trade had undermined that relationship and the two groups were now rivals who fiercely contested choice hunting grounds. The term "Sioux" originated in this period. It derives from the Ojibwe name for them: *Na-towe-ssiwa* or *Nadouwesou* (variously translated into English as "adder" or "people of an alien tribe"). French fur traders adopted the name and shortened it to its final syllable, thus arriving at "Sioux."

As they do today, the Sioux recognized three divisions—the Dakota, the Yankton-Yanktonai, and the Lakota—which together comprised *Oceti Sakwin* ("the Seven Council Fires"). The *Mdewakantonwan* (Mdewakanton), *Wahpetonwan* (Wahpeton), *Wakpekute* (Wahpakute), and *Sisitonwan* (Sisseton) comprised the Dakota or Santee, the easternmost division. The *Ihanktonwan* (Yankton) and *Ihanktonwanna* (Yanktonai) constituted the middle division, also known as the Nakota or Yankton. The *Tetonwan* (Teton or Lakota) were the westernmost division. Dakota, Nakota, and Lakota also refer to the different dialects each division spoke, with Dakota and Nakota often lumped together as Dakota. The *Tetonwan* ("people of the Plains") were further subdivided into seven bands: *Sichá?gu* (Brulé or

Burned Thighs), *Oglála* (Oglala), *Itázipcho* (Sans Arc or No Bows), *Húʔkpapʔa* (Hunkpapa), *Mnikʔówožu* (Miniconjou), *Sihásapa* (Blackfoot Sioux), and *Oóhenuʔpa* (Two Kettles). Although closely allied, each band was politically autonomous and had a distinct sense of identity. Members of all seven Lakota bands took part in the Battle of the Greasy Grass, as did a few Yankton and Santee.

Warfare with the Ojibwe had forced most of the Sioux on to the prairies beyond the Mississippi by the 1730s. Pushed from behind by their enemies and lured forward by new economic opportunities, they gradually drifted south and west after the receding buffalo herds. Soon they were rich in horses, which intensified their buffalo-hunting culture pattern. For many years the Lakota division, which featured most prominently in the Greasy Grass battle, hunted buffalo in the summer, hunted and trapped for the fur trade in the winter, and attended trade fairs in the spring. Eventually, however, they came to concentrate their energies almost entirely on buffalo hunting. Lakota territorial expansion into the northern and central Plains, shaped in part by the migratory patterns of the remaining buffalo herds, continued into the mid 1800s, when it was curtailed by the territorial aspirations of the United States.

By the early 1800s the main reasons the Lakota and other tribes fought were to acquire horses and to gain access to prime hunting grounds, the later being increasingly important as the buffalo herds shrank. Inter-tribal warfare was a serious business that stemmed not from deeply ingrained cultural impulses or ancient animosities but from political and economic calculations rooted in the material conditions of the day.[13] It was also deadly. Throughout the eighteenth century the Lakota population had been growing owing to a high birth rate and a relatively low disease-induced death rate. Meanwhile, epidemics had continued to weaken their rivals through population loss and the cultural upheaval that caused. The Lakota took advantage of the situation, trading or raiding at will. They also strategically disrupted their rivals' trading relationships and attempts to form alliances. By the beginning of the nineteenth century the Lakota dominated the Missouri River area and were expanding into the game-rich Plains to the south and west. This brought them into increasing conflict with the Crow.

In the 1840s the Lakota joined the Cheyenne and Arapaho in harassing travelers on the Oregon Trail. That most of the ten thousand Indians who attended the 1851 Fort Laramie treaty negotiations were Lakota, Cheyenne, and Arapaho indicates just how powerful that alliance had become. When Black Hawk (Oglala) addressed the gathering, he defended Lakota territorial expansion as no different than what the Americans had been doing for a long time. He explained that "these lands once belonged to the Kiowas and the Crows, but we whipped those nations out of them, and in this we did what the white men do when they want the lands of the Indians."[14] By the end of the treaty negotiations it was clear that the Lakota and the Americans were the main powers to contend with in the region. Given that, the tendency to depict peoples like the Crow and Arikara as traitors or white collaborators is short-sighted. Like the Lakota, they were making strategic decisions based on their own tribal needs and loyalties.

Conflict erupted between the Lakota and U.S. soldiers in 1854. On August 17 a Minneconjou killed and slaughtered a cow from a Morman wagon train halted near Fort Laramie, Wyoming. Two days later soldiers from the 6th Infantry led by Lieutenant John Lawrence Grattan entered the Lakota camp to arrest the man responsible. Shots fired by the soldiers killed Conquering Bear, a Brulé chief. The Lakota responded in kind. Lieutenant Grattan and twenty-nine other soldiers died in what the press dubbed the Grattan Massacre. Predictably, the army launched a punitive expedition against the Lakota. It delivered its retribution just over a year later, when troops commanded by Brigadier General William S. Harney attacked a band of Brulé led by Little Thunder at Ash Hollow near Blue Water Creek in present-day Nebraska. The soldiers killed eighty-six Lakotas and took seventy women and children prisoners. Clashes between the Lakota and the army occurred with increasing frequency thereafter.

Hostilities escalated after gold was discovered in Montana in 1862. In 1864, the year of the Sand Creek Massacre, failed prospector John Bozeman blazed a shortcut to the Montana gold fields in an attempt to profit from the miners if not from mining. The Bozeman Trail cut through Lakota hunting grounds. In an effort to protect people traveling on it from attack, the army established Fort Reno (1864) and Fort Phil Kearny (1866) in northern Wyoming and Fort F.C. Smith (1866) on the Big Horn River in Montana. The new forts further incensed the Lakota. On August 29, 1865, General Patrick Connor attacked a group of Arapahoes in an attempt to drive them away from the trail. The next year Lakotas led by Red Cloud (Oglala) and aided by Cheyennes launched a sustained assault against the forts and travelers on the Bozeman Trail. On December 6 they attacked a woodcutting detail outside Fort Phil Kearny and on December 21 they led Captain William Fetterman and his command into an ambush. Fetterman had once bragged that he could ride through the entire Sioux nation with eighty men; he and his entire eighty-man detachment died that day. A mysterious Oglala warrior named Crazy Horse played a key role in both attacks, as he would in the Greasy Grass fight ten years later. In July 1867 Congress authorized President Andrew Johnson to send a Peace Commission to negotiate a treaty with the Plains tribes in an attempt to stop the hostilities and start them on the road to civilization.

Meanwhile the attacks continued. In August Lakota and Cheyenne warriors attacked hay cutters near Fort Smith and wood cutters and their military escort outside Fort Keary. Further south Cheyennes led by Spotted Wolf destroyed a Union Pacific train. Other attacks followed.

The Peace Commission met with northern Plains tribes at Fort Laramie in the spring of 1868. It signed treaties with the Crow, various Lakota bands, the Yankton, and the Northern Cheyenne and Arapaho. Among other provisions, the treaties redefined the boundaries between

---

Crazy Horse (ca. 1840–1877)

Crazy Horse (or *Tasunke-Witko* in Lakota) was born in the early 1840s on the Belle Fourche River near sacred Bear Butte at the edge of the Black Hills. His father was Crazy Horse, a holy man, and his mother was Rattling Blanket Woman. When he was a boy his name was *Cha-O-Ha* ("In the Wilderness" or "Among the Trees") but most people called him Curly or Light Hair, nicknames that referred to his unusual hair color and texture. When he grew older and had proven himself as a warrior, his father honored him by giving him his own name, Crazy Horse, a common Lakota practice. Thereafter Crazy Horse's father went by the name of *Wagwula* ("Worm"). Crazy Horse died on September 5, 1877, after a soldier bayoneted him in the back during a guardhouse struggle at Fort Robinson, Nebraska. His family buried his body in a place that remains secret to this day. Because Crazy Horse would let no one take his picture, there are no known photographs of him.

Crazy Horse married three times. His first marriage was controversial. He had long had strong feelings for Black Buffalo Woman, who was already married to a man named No Water. When Crazy Horse finally invited her to accompany him on a buffalo hunt, she left her husband and did so, as was her right. Despite that, No Water followed the couple and tried to kill Crazy Horse but only succeeded in shooting him in the jaw. After carefully considering the matter, the tribal leaders decided that No Water should pay compensation to Crazy Horse for shooting him. But because he had caused so much trouble by taking another man's wife, they also stripped Crazy Horse of his coveted title of Shirt Wearer. The Shirt Wearer title signified a man's ability to lead war parties and raids and was thus considered a great honor. Crazy Horse then married Black Shawl Woman, who had helped nurse him back to health after No Water wounded him. They had a daughter together whom they named They Are Afraid of Her. The little girl died at the age of three from a "white man's disease," possibly cholera. Crazy Horse was devastated. Black Shawl Woman died some time later, probably of tuberculosis. Crazy Horse again remarried. His third wife, a half French and half Cheyenne woman, outlived him but had no children.

As he was growing up, Crazy Horse quickly developed a reputation among his people as a shrewd and courageous warrior committed to the traditional way of life. He was also kind, humble, and generous, as one would expect of an Oglala leader. By the age of thirteen he had stolen his first horses from the Crow and by twenty he had led his first war party. He was present in the village when Grattan's men killed Conquering Bear and were then annihilated. Afterwards Crazy Horse began to have visions. Eventually he undertook a successful *Hanblecheyapi* (Vision Quest) in the Black Hills. During his fast, a spirit being came to him with instructions on how to prepare himself for war, protect his pony, and conduct his life more generally. The advice was good and Crazy Horse was never again wounded in battle, despite the many opportunities afforded by his daring exploits in the conflict-ridden 1860s and 1870s.

Crazy Horse distinguished himself in Red Cloud's War. In December 1866 he and a handful of other warriors decoyed Captain William J. Fetterman's command into an ambush near Fort Phil Kearny. As a result, all the soldiers were killed. The next summer he took part in the Wagon Box fight, again near Fort Phil Kearny. This time the whites were able to fend off the attack. In 1868, a treaty was signed at Fort Laramie that brought an end to Red Cloud's War, resulted in the closure of the Bozeman Trail, and installed most of the Lakota bands on reservations. Crazy Horse did not sign the treaty nor did he acquiesce to reservation life. Thereafter he led a band of so-called non-treaty Indians, who continued to roam the northern Plains in search of buffalo and other game.

During the 1870s Crazy Horse developed increasingly close ties with Sitting Bull's people and the non-treaty Cheyenne. By the time 1876 rolled around he was a mature, respected, and seasoned warrior with a proven track-record, which prompted many younger men to follow him. He was also an uncompromising champion of the traditional way of life and remained steadfastly opposed to either negotiating with the *wasichus* or settling on reservations. Throughout the late winter and spring of 1876 Crazy Horse and his followers harassed the soldiers and settlers along the Yellowstone and in the Powder River country. They also helped other bands who had been attacked by the soldiers. Crazy Horse played a prominent role in the June 17 attack on General Crook's column on the Rosebud and then again in the Greasy Grass battle a week later. Throughout the following winter he and his followers alternated between fighting the soldiers and fleeing from them. Finally, the hardships caused by the army's relentless pursuit forced Crazy Horse to admit defeat. On May 6, 1877, he led his starving band into Fort Robinson and surrendered. They soon settled into the routine of reservation life.

the tribes and established the Great Sioux Reservation in Dakota Territory. It also granted the Lakota permission to hunt in the vaguely defined unceded territory between the western reservation border and the crest of the Big Horn Mountains so long as sufficient buffalo remained there. Red Cloud refused to negotiate until the army closed and withdrew its soldiers from the forts along the Bozeman Trail. Rendered a relatively painless concession by an extension of the Union Pacific that had opened a new supply route to Montana, the government relented. He finally signed the treaty in November after forts Reno, Kearny, and Smith were dismantled, thus bringing an end to Red Cloud's War. Some historians describe this as a great victory for the Lakota; others dismiss it as a government stalling tactic.

PLAINS INDIAN CULTURE

Although sometimes depicted as an ancient way of life, nineteenth-century Plains Indian culture—or what some people call the Buffalo Culture—developed out of earlier cultural forms in response to processes set in motion by European colonization. As they moved west, the Crow, Sioux (and especially the Lakota division), and Cheyenne encountered new peoples and entered environments that presented different challenges, constraints, and opportunities. Each group adapted by adopting subsistence practices and technologies better suited to their altered circumstances and by adjusting their social, political, and economic arrangements to better meet their changing needs. To support their evolving ways of life and to address the new uncertainties they faced, they also modified other aspects of their cultures, including their worldviews, religions, and material cultures.

There was inevitably a sharing of ideas, practices, and technologies amongst the migrating peoples and between them and the new peoples they encountered. This led to the development of that configuration of traits anthropologists call Plains Indian culture. Although the mounted buffalo-hunting lifestyle commonly associated with the Plains Indians can be described in terms of shared traits, each group refashioned those traits according to their own cultural imperatives and in light of their pre-existing cultural patterns. The resulting differences are subtle but significant. Three interrelated constellations of traits are particularly relevant to the Greasy Grass/Little Bighorn story: those pertaining to the nomadic life of mounted buffalo-hunters, to their spiritual life, and to Plains Indian warfare.

Although the Lakota, Cheyenne, and Crow hunted buffalo long before they acquired horses, the horse enabled them to do so in a different and, for a while at least, more reliable and efficient way. Horses quickly became an integral part of their cultures. They valued horses and riding skill and maintained large herds. The animals also constituted a form of wealth and the ability to steal and give them away served as routes to prestige. They changed how the Plains Indians conducted war and created new reasons for individuals to fight. Reliance on the horse led the different groups to modify their subsistence strategies and aspects of their social and political organization to better articulate with a nomadic way of life. As they shifted from the mixed economies that had supported their earlier ways of life in the east to economies focused more narrowly on communal buffalo-hunting, they adjusted their ways of reckoning descent, residence patterns, band structures, and forms of decision-making and leadership. Each group came to feature horses prominently in their myths, stories, and songs. They also developed rituals to protect the health and fertility of their horses and to enhance their speed, endurance, and performance.

Their material cultures also changed. Items like clay pots were abandoned as no longer practical and replaced by more transportable alternatives. The Indians also shortened their bows to make them more usable on horseback. Particularly well suited to their nomadic lifestyle was the tipi, a conical structure made of buffalo hides stretched over a framework of poles. As homes, they were dry, warm in the winter, and cool in the summer. They could also be erected and dismantled quickly and transported easily. Once reliant on dogs to help transport their possessions, the Indians now loaded their belongings and even small children and the elderly or infirm onto travois, which trailed behind their horses as they moved camp. They assembled these v-shaped racks by lashing together their tipi poles.

Anthropologists describe the nineteenth-century Plains Indians as animists: they believed that all things have a spirit. Most groups believed in a singular Great Spirit, or what the Lakota call *Wakan Tanka*. Besides the Great Spirit, which has power over everything, their universes were populated by a pantheon of lesser spiritual beings and animated by a variety of spiritual forces. Particular individuals could also be w*akan* ("blessed" in Lakota) or what English-speakers call holy or medicine men and women. Sitting Bull, for example, was *wakan*; so was Crazy Horse, but in a different sort of way. Both men had special powers that set them apart from others. Some people who were *wakan* could heal the sick. Others received special insights from the spirit world regarding the future or the movement of game. Some were particularly adept at interpreting dreams and visions.

Objects could also be imbued with special powers. Such objects could benefit particular individuals, perhaps by contributing to their success in warfare or to their good health, or they could benefit the whole tribe. Individuals took great care of their "medicine" objects, handling them as instructed in dreams and visions. Most tribes stored their sacred objects in medicine bundles, which had to be handled in ritually prescribed ways. The Cheyenne, for example, had a Sacred Medicine Hat Bundle, the proper care of which was essential to tribal well-being.

The Plains Indians had two main ways of courting the intercession of the spirit world in their everyday affairs. They were the Vision Quest and the Sun Dance. Although found in nearly every Plains tribe, these rituals varied widely in their specifics. The Vision Quest, or what the Lakota called *Hanblecheyapi* ("crying for a vision"), was an individual undertaking. In most Plains Indian cultures it constituted an important rite of passage from adolescence to adulthood, particularly for aspiring young warriors. It was a way of acquiring what the Crow call *baxbe* ("power") and a Guardian Spirit, or what the Cheyenne call a *maiyunahu'ta* ("Spirit Who Told me in Sleep"). After a period of instruction and purification, the quester would go alone to a remote place, where he (or occasionally she) would spend several days fasting, crying, and praying for a vision. To demonstrate their sincerity and to induce the Great Spirit to take pity on them, they would sometimes cut off pieces of flesh or a finger joint as an offering. If an individual received a vision, it could define his or her direction in life and establish a special relationship with a spiritual power, winning its blessing, guidance, and assistance in times of need.

Oftentimes visions contained instructions on how to prepare special amulets and paint oneself for war or songs to sing to evoke power and taboos to respect. Crazy Horse once received such instructions in a vision. Just how important strict adherence to them was can be gleaned from a 1930 interview with Red Feather, the younger brother of his first wife.[15] Speaking of Crazy Horse, Red Feather reported:

> The enemy killed his saddle horse under him eight times but
> they never hurt him badly. During war expeditions he wore a little
> white stone with a hole through it on a buckskin string slung over
> his shoulder. He wore it under his left arm. He was wounded
> twice when he first began to fight but never since after he got
> the stone.

In the same vision in which he was advised to wear the stone, Crazy Horse was instructed to paint a zigzag lightning bolt down his cheek and white spots resembling hail stones on his body and on his horse before going into battle. Despite his frequent displays of daring, Crazy Horse was never again wounded in battle.

In contrast to the Vision Quest, the Sun Dance was a collective undertaking. Although invariably a time of fasting, prayer, healing, and special rituals, each tribe performed the ceremony in its own way and for its own reasons. Each also attributed its own meanings to it. Conducted in early summer, the Sun Dance was (and still is) one of the most sacred ceremonies of the Lakota and many other Plains tribes. With its elaborate symbolism of the universe and the place of humans within it, the Sun Dance was a powerful means of connecting with the spirit world. Central to the several day long ritual was a prolonged period of fasting, self-sacrifice, and suffering that tested the dancer's commitment and fortitude. The Cheyenne, who called it the Medicine Lodge, viewed it as a time of tribal renewal and revitalization. Despite its significance for the whole group, individuals who sacrificed themselves and suffered in the Sun Dance lodge did so for many different reasons. Young men often did so to demonstrate their courage and stamina and to acquire spiritual power. As Sitting Bull did shortly before the Greasy Grass battle, older men sometimes sought prophetic visions through fasting, exhaustion, and self-torture in the Sun Dance lodge. In some tribes individuals sacrificed themselves to assuage their grief over the death of a loved one or to fulfill a vow to the Great Spirit.

Plains Indian warfare has been widely misunderstood. Scholars have often reduced it to a game-like individual quest for status, prestige, and wealth or attributed it to some sort of deep-seated cultural instinct. Such depictions ignore the historical and material roots of warfare and, consequently, fail to generate useful insights or to withstand closer scrutiny. They also imply that warriors fought because they were inherently aggressive. Quite to the contrary, warriors fought because they had to. To understand Plains Indian warfare and its cultural elaboration one must distinguish between individual and tribal motivations for fighting. Individuals may have fought or raided for honor, prestige, and wealth in horses or to advance their political careers but tribes almost always fought because their survival as a people depended on it. They fought to defend their lands and resources against outside threats or to expand their territories and, by extension, their resource bases. That individuals gained prestige and personal advancement through warfare does not mean that fighting was optional for them. As in the case of the Crow, skilled warriors were key to group survival. W.W. Newcomb argues that

> warfare was not caused by "a sportive urge" or by the desire to play a "game" or even by the desire to attain social standing; these are the ways in which warfare was made to look attractive to the individual, not the causes of it. The Plains cultures were warlike because they had to be.[16]

Warfare was not about killing or defeating the enemy; it was about achieving geopolitical and economic objectives in a rapidly changing environment.

Warfare was nonetheless a culturally elaborated and integrated part of tribal life. Elaborate rituals and belief systems supported and rewarded the risks young men were encouraged to take. Non-Indians had difficulty making sense of several aspects of Plains Indian warfare, including its hit-and-run tactics and lack of formal leadership. Only rarely did tribes launch the large-scale assaults so familiar to military strategists. More common were raids, lightning strikes, and ambushes. Once in battle, each warrior fought how and for as long he (or, occasionally, she) saw fit and was usually intent on amassing war honors and thereby achieving personal glory. War parties sometimes used group tactics but only rarely did they operate according to a grand strategy, in part because they lacked a formal command structure. Individuals might initiate raids or take a leading role in a particular battle but they lacked real authority. Whatever influence they exerted derived from their persuasiveness, personal attributes, and reputation for success.

Perhaps more than anything else, the Plains Indian practice of counting coup perplexed the white soldiers. For many warriors, gaining prestige through public displays of bravery was an end in itself and that was best accomplished by counting coup. Counting coup entailed successfully challenging the enemy; it did not necessarily involve wounding or killing the enemy, which were considered easier and less risky alternatives. The Crow, for example, recognized four types of coup: touching a live enemy, taking an enemy's weapon in hand-to-hand combat, stealing a picketed horse from an enemy camp, and leading a successful war party. The Lakota and Cheyenne placed greatest emphasis on touching a live enemy, sometimes with a special coup stick. Warriors who counted coup were entitled to recite their feats at public gatherings and enjoyed enhanced status.

GRANT ADMINISTRATION

After he signed the 1868 Fort Laramie Treaty, Red Cloud never again waged war against the United States or anyone else but the treaty nonetheless failed to end the hostilities. Other Lakotas, most notably Hunkpapas led by Sitting Bull and Oglala followers of Crazy Horse, had refused to participate in the treaty negotiations altogether. In the years that followed, they stepped up their struggle against white incursions into what they considered their homelands. But with the establishment of Dakota, Montana, and Wyoming territories in the 1860s, the completion of the Transcontinental Railroad in 1869, the naming of Yellowstone as the country's first national park in 1872, and work commencing on the Northern Pacific Railroad that same year, it was increasingly evident that the federal government intended to claim the northern Plains for white settlement.

The Lakota, Cheyenne, and Crow were not the only ones under pressure. With its population growing at a much faster rate than its land base, the United States was feeling the strain of over-crowding. In 1790 there were less than four million people in what was then the continental United States. That equated to about 4.6 people per square mile.[17] By 1870 there were 13.4 people per square mile and within just a decade that figure had risen to 16.9. Some of that growth was due to the country's relatively open immigration policy. Between 1820 and 1840 there were 742,564 recorded new arrivals to the country. The next two decades witnessed the arrival of more than 4.3 million immigrants followed by upwards of 5.1 million between 1860 to 1880.[18] In the 1830s fewer than 0.9 percent of the people in the United States were foreign born; by 1880 roughly 13.3 percent of the population originated elsewhere. The highest numbers came from Germany and Ireland followed by the United Kingdom and Canada. Not only did these newcomers clamor for land to farm, the swelling populations of the eastern industrial centers needed food to eat.

As was the case for the different Plains Indian groups, a set of shared cultural assumptions underpinned and shaped American behavior throughout this period. Most Americans, for example, believed that it was their manifest destiny, if not Christian duty, to claim and productively exploit the empty interior of the continent. The term "manifest destiny" derived from an article by John O'Sullivan published shortly after the war with Mexico ended.[19] In it he defended the annexation of Texas on the grounds that it was America's "manifest destiny to overspread the continent allotted by Providence for the free development of our yearly multiplying millions." While he was merely articulating a long-held assumption that the country was divinely ordained to spread from "sea to shining sea," his elegant phrasing aptly reflected public sentiment and stuck. It also masked a major problem: popular perceptions notwithstanding, the lands in question were neither vacant nor unused. They were home to hundreds of thousands of indigenous peoples divided into scores if not hundreds of polities distinguished from one another by elaborate belief systems and political, economic, and social structures adapted to their particular environments. And those peoples had no intention of relinquishing their lands, at least not without a good fight.

The 1868 election of Ulysses S. Grant as president ushered in a new era in the administration of Indian affairs. In his 1869 inaugural address, Grant declared that "proper treatment of the original occupants of this land—the Indians" was "deserving of careful study." Stating that he would "favor any course toward them which favors their civilization and ultimate citizenship," he clearly indicated the direction his Indian policy was to take.

Grant's Peace (or Quaker) Policy emphasized acculturation, or the gradual merging of Native Americans into American society. It was an approach that originated in the idealism of the reconstruction era and assumed that once Native Americans learned the language, values, habits, and practices of the American mainstream they would peacefully join the body politic. To promote that civilizing agenda, Grant distributed administrative responsibility for the Indian agencies amongst several religious denominations and appointed a board of commissioners to oversee their work.

By the early 1870s, Congress was fed up with the high cost of administering Indian affairs and looking for new options. The 1871 Indian Appropriations Act contained provisions that made Indians wards of the government rather than members of sovereign nations as was previously the case and ended treaty-making with the tribes. In his State of the Union Address that year, Grant praised the progress made thus far:

> Through the exertions of the various societies of Christians to whom has been in trusted the execution of the policy . . . many tribes of Indians have been induced to settle upon reservations, to cultivate the soil, to perform productive labor of various kinds, and to partially accept civilization. They are being cared for in such a way, it is hoped, as to induce those still pursuing their old habits of life to embrace the only opportunity which is left them to avoid extermination.

He then asked Congress to make "liberal appropriations to carry out the Indian peace policy, not only because it is humane, Christian like, and economical, but because it is right." Despite Grant's upbeat assessment, things were not going to plan.

Living conditions for the reservation Indians were deplorable. Food and everyday essentials were in short supply and of poor quality and housing was inadequate. Non-treaty Lakotas and Cheyennes continued to raid settlements, attack travelers and work crews, and fight rival tribes. In the summer of 1872 General David Stanley led an expedition up the Yellowstone River valley to survey a route for the Northern Pacific Railroad. Sitting Bull and his warriors attacked it on August 14. Two months later they attacked another survey crew and then a nearby fort. In response, the army dispatched Custer and the 7th Cavalry to Dakota Territory to help protect the railroad and the settlers. They joined Stanley's 1873 Yellowstone Expedition. In August they clashed with a band of Lakota warriors near the Tongue River; it was Custer's first military engagement with the Lakota. At the end of the expedition, the 7th Cavalry returned to Dakota Territory to the newly established Fort

Abraham Lincoln. Situated opposite Bismarck on the west bank of the Missouri River, it would headquarter the 7th Cavalry for the next several years and serve as home to Custer, his wife Libbie, two of his brothers, his sister and brother-in-law, and for a while his nephew.

In 1873 most industrialized economies lapsed into a recession triggered by a worldwide fall in demand for silver. The silver market collapse had a particularly strong knock-on effect in the United States, where much of the silver was mined. Until then the United States had backed its currency with both silver and gold. With its controversial passage of the Coinage Act of 1873, Congress de-monetized silver and the country adopted an exclusive "gold standard," which led investors to question the stability of the American currency. That, coupled with over-expansion of the post-Civil War economy led by the railroad boom, set the stage for the Panic of 1873. Jay Cooke & Company, financial backers of the Northern Pacific Railroad, filed for bankruptcy in September of that year setting off a wave of bank closures and bankruptcies that caused the New York Stock Exchange to shut down for ten days. Many more businesses failed over the next few years and unemployment rose to 14 percent by 1876. The economy was clearly in need of a stimulus.

It is no coincidence, then, that General Philip Sheridan, commander of the Division of the Missouri, in consultation with General Alfred Terry, commander of the Department of Dakota, and partly in response to Custer's own urgings, ordered a military expedition to the Black Hills in 1874. Its critics alleged that the decision was motivated by rumors of gold but its officially stated objectives were to locate a spot to build a fort, to find a route through the hills, and to collect scientific data. Those may have been its official aims but members of the expedition also harbored other expectations. Lieutenant James Calhoun, Custer's brother-in-law, wrote in his diary:

> It is supposed in the vicinity of the Black Hills there are vast treasures of immense wealth. That rich mines await the industry of the hard-working miner. That precious metals invite discovery, and that in the bottoms of the many streams, and other parts of this domain, large deposits of gold are to be found.[20]

On July 2, 1874, Custer set out from Fort Lincoln at the head of a 1,000–1,200 member force. Captain William Ludlow of the Corps of Engineers, a geologist, paleontologist George Bird Grinnell, two "practical miners," five reporters, photographer William Illingworth, and President Grant's son Frederick accompanied it. The expedition found ample evidence of Indians but encountered no resistance. More ominously, the civilian experts discovered gold, which Custer duly reported to the Assistant Adjutant General of the Department of Dakota. Aided by an overly enthusiastic press that announced "gold at the grassroots," rumors of gold in far greater quantities than actually found quickly spread, thus triggering a new Gold Rush, this time to the Black Hills.

Under the provisions of the 1868 Fort Laramie Treaty, the Black Hills belonged to the Lakota. They call them *Pahá Sápa*. *Pahá Sápa* was—and continues to be—one of their most sacred places. It is the center of their universe and a place imbued with great spiritual power. It was where many of their young men went and still go to seek visions. The abundant and reliable resources found there once led Sitting Bull to describe the area as his people's "food pack." The Cheyenne also held the Black Hills, or what they called *Mo'ohta-vo'honáaeva*, sacred, as they still do. It was in a cave at nearby Bear Butte that *Maiyun*, a personification of the Great Spirit, gave the great Cheyenne culture hero, Sweet Medicine (*Mutsoyef*), the four Sacred Arrows (*Mahuts*) that symbolize the tribe's collective existence. Because the Custer expedition set in motion a chain of events that culminated in the taking of *Pahá Sápa* from them, the Lakota labeled its route the Thieves Road.

Despite promises made in the 1868 Fort Laramie Treaty, no one asked the Lakota for permission before the 7th Cavalry trampled into their sacred hills and the army made only feeble attempts to keep gold-crazed prospectors out afterwards. Acting under the pretext of preserving peace between the Indians and the prospectors, the federal government decided to lease or buy the Black Hills from the Lakota. A commission headed by Senator William B. Allison met with the Lakota in September 1875 to negotiate the deal. Eventually the commission offered them $6 million for the Black Hills. That as many as twenty thousand Indians had gathered for the negotiations, most of them Lakotas (but some Cheyennes and Arapahoes as well), indicates the strength of opposition to the proposal. In the end, the Lakota refused to relinquish their sacred *Pahá Sápa*.

Less than six weeks after the failed negotiations, Secretary of the Interior Zachariah Chandler, Assistant Secretary of the Interior Benjamin Cowen, and Secretary of War William Belknap met with President Grant, General Sheridan, and General Crook to discuss the matter. Grant informed those gathered that he was going to authorize military action against the non-treaty Indians. A few days later E.C. Watkins of the Indian Bureau submitted a report on the state of affairs on the Lakota reservations. It indicated that the Indians were angry over the deplorable conditions on the reservations, including the lack of food, and that many were leaving to join Crazy Horse and Sitting Bull. On December 3, Secretary Chandler ordered an ultimatum to be issued to Sitting Bull and the other wanderers demanding that they return to the reservations by the end of January or "be deemed hostile." Not all of the bands received the orders before the deadline expired and most of those that did were not inclined to comply. On February 1 Secretary Chandler turned the matter over to Secretary of War William Belknap. A week later Sheridan notified generals Crook and Terry that the War Department had ordered military action against the Indians.

Meanwhile, Grant was increasingly preoccupied with his own political problems. In February 1876 the *New York Herald* published an article that alleged that Secretary Belknap had been profiting from the award of potentially lucrative traderships (exclusive licenses to buy, sell, and distribute food and supplies on reservations and posts) in the west. It also implicated Orvil Grant, the president's brother. Custer got drawn into the fray. He had experienced the consequences of the graft first-hand, since it resulted in the under-provisioning of soldiers and reservation Indians alike with over-priced and poor quality food and supplies. In the past he had unsuccessfully tried to draw attention to the matter and he now strongly believed that the shortages were driving Indians away from the reservations and into the camps of Sitting Bull and Crazy Horse. With impeachment proceedings already under way against him, Belknap resigned on March 2. Hester Clymer, chairman of the committee investigating the scandal, nonetheless refused to let the matter drop and subpoenaed Custer to testify.

Custer went before the Clymer Commission on March 29. Based on his personal experiences and observations of corruption in the army and post traderships, his testimony was devastating. President Grant was furious at what he perceived as personal attacks by Custer against his own brother and close personal friends. Custer was summoned to testify again. Anxious to return to his command, which was already preparing for the rapidly approaching campaign against the off-reservation Indians, he appealed to his superiors. General Sherman eventually granted Custer permission to return to Fort Lincoln but advised him to meet with the president first. When Grant refused to see him, Custer left without final authorization from either him or the War Department. He arrived in Chicago on May 3 to find a member of Sheridan's staff waiting at the train station to arrest him. General Terry intervened on Custer's behalf and managed to secure his release to return to his command. However, to punish him, it was decided that Terry would have overall command of the Dakota column during the upcoming campaign. Custer would only command his own regiment. It was May 10 before Custer got back to Fort Lincoln to assume command of the 7th Cavalry. By then the campaign was six weeks behind schedule.

About ten million people, or the equivalent of roughly a fifth of the country's population, attended the Centennial Exposition. In conjunction with the Department of the Interior, the Smithsonian Institution created a living exhibit of the indigenous peoples of the continent. It included more than three hundred Native Americans from fifty-three tribes.

On July 4, 1876, the nation would celebrate its one-hundredth birthday. To mark the occasion and to draw a line under the divisive Civil War and the nation's more recent economic woes, the United States staged a pretentious Centennial Exposition in Phila-delphia. President Grant officially opened it on May 10, the same day Custer arrived back at Fort Lincoln. An unambiguous asser-tion of the country's cultural and industrial progress, the exposition housed more than sixty thousand exhibits in two hundred or so buildings. On display were magnificent inventions ranging from the massive Corliss steam engine to smaller combustion engines and Bell's newly patented telephone. That America's awe-inspiring technological advances were situated amidst exhibits from many other countries must surely have erased any lingering doubts the public may have had about the way forward and a newly reunited America's place in the world. Meanwhile, out on the Plains, the army was setting out in pursuit of the Lakota and Cheyenne wanderers who had failed to report to the reservations as ordered. Conceived as a mop-up operation aimed at securing the region for white settlement, the campaign ended abruptly with the 7th Cavalry's now legendary defeat on the Greasy Grass/Little Bighorn.

News of the debacle and Custer's death would break in Philadelphia on July 6, just two days after the triumphal climax of the centennial festivities. It would shatter the carefully crafted illusion and highlight that all was not well in the republic. The Civil War was a receding memory and Reconstruction officially over, but tensions remained between the North and South. Many issues stemming from the war and the abolition of slavery awaited resolution. The country also needed more space to accommodate its now rapidly growing population. White settlers rushed west in search of their manifest destiny only to find vast swaths of the lands they coveted still claimed by the Indians. It was also a presidential election year and things were going badly for Ulysses S. Grant, the out-going Republican president, and hence for his party. Despite decades of treaty, policy, and law making, the so-called Indian problem remained in the spotlight. Indians and white settlers still clashed with alarming regularity, making it evident that Grant's Quaker Policy had not achieved its civilizing objective after all. On May 29 Grant announced he would not seek a third term in office. By the time the six-month long exposition closed Custer would be dead and the nation would be in political deadlock following an inconclusive presidential election.

CHAPTER 2

Battle of the Greasy Grass/Little Bighorn

COMMISSIONER'S ULTIMATUM

Things moved quickly after the November 3 meeting at which President Grant informed his key cabinet members and generals that he planned to authorize military force against the off-reservation Indians. Six days later Commissioner of Indian Affairs Edward Parmelee Smith and Secretary of the Interior Chandler, whose department included the Indian Bureau, received a report on the western Sioux (Lakota) from Indian Inspector E.C. Watkins. Chandler immediately forwarded the report to Secretary of War Belknap. In it, Watkins noted that the reservation Indians were increasingly unhappy about their living conditions. As for those wandering beyond the reservation boundaries, the "true policy, in my judgment," he declared, "is to send troops against them in the winter, the sooner the better, and whip them into subjection. They richly merit punishment for their incessant warfare, and their numerous murders of white settlers and their families, or white men wherever found unarmed."[1] While the action he advocated merely echoed the decision already made, his harsh words clearly reflect the tone and tenor of the anti-Sioux sentiment so widespread in official ranks at the time. Planning for a winter campaign against the non-treaty Indians was already quietly under way. But, at the insistence of the Indian Bureau, the roamers were to be given one last chance to turn themselves in before those plans were put into motion and made public. The delay frustrated General Sheridan but the Indians' refusal to take advantage of the opportunity offered them, which surprised no one, only served to further justify military action. It also helped mitigate political fall-out and silence objections voiced by Friends of the Indian groups in the aftermath.

On December 3 Secretary Chandler ordered the Commissioner of Indian Affairs to issue an ultimatum to Sitting Bull and his followers. The Commissioner complied, dispatching Indian runners to find and inform the off-reservation Indians "that unless they shall remove within the bounds of their reservation (and remain there) before the 31st of January next, they shall be deemed hostile and treated accordingly by the military force." The message failed to reach all of the bands by the deadline and virtually none of those it did reach heeded the warning. It is highly unlikely that any of the rest would have complied either had they received the ultimatum. Some scholars argue that the deep snows and frigid temperatures of the harsh Plains winter made it nearly impossible for them to return to the reservations with their families and possessions by the end of January and hence factored in their non-compliance. It is more likely, however, that they ignored the warning for the same reasons they continued to resist white incursions into their territory. In issuing the ultimatum the Grant administration may have secured the political legitimacy it needed for military action but it had also served warning to the off-reservation Lakota and Cheyenne that soldiers were coming.

The deadline came and went and the non-treaty bands remained at large. On the first day of February Secretary Chandler handed the matter over to Secretary Belknap and the War Department "for such action on the part of the Army as you may deem proper under the circumstances."[2] The Sioux Campaign of 1876 was under way.

ROAD TO THE LITTLE BIGHORN: U.S. ARMY

A week after the Secretary of the Interior certified the wanderers in the unceded territory "hostile" and turned the matter over to the War Department, General Sheridan sent confidential telegrams to generals George Crook and Alfred Terry notifying them that he had been authorized to commence operations against the Indians. Crook, the Omaha-based commanding officer of the Department of the Platte, and Terry, the St. Paul-based commanding officer of the Department of Dakota, were at the heart of Sheridan's plan to field the strongest possible force against the recalcitrant Indians. Terry, as the senior officer and head of the Department of Dakota, was to have overall command in the field. As initially conceived by Sheridan, what came to be known as the Sioux Campaign (and later the Centennial Campaign) was to be a winter campaign. Three loosely coordinated columns, two from the Department of Dakota and one from the Department of the Platte, would converge on the non-treaty Indians thought to be wintering in the Powder River country of southeastern Montana. One column would approach from the east departing Fort Lincoln in Dakota Territory. Another would approach from the west out of Fort Ellis in Montana Territory. The third would come up from Fort Fetterman in Wyoming Territory. The combined force would total about twenty-five hundred soldiers and attached personnel. If all went according to plan, the three prongs would trap the Indians between them in a pincer movement.

Based on Indian Bureau estimates, Sheridan reckoned that he faced a total Indian fighting force of between five hundred and eight hundred warriors widely scattered amongst the winter camps. He derived those figures from an assumption that altogether the camps contained about three thousand people housed in four hundred to five hundred tipis. That was probably a fairly accurate estimate for that particular moment in time but the situation was fluid. More and more Lakotas and Cheyennes would join the camps as frustrations mounted, conditions on the reservations deteriorated, and the spring hunting and ceremonial season approached. Regardless of might happen come spring, Sheridan and his generals were confident that their troops could deal with any force thrown at them. Moreover, Sheridan strongly believed that large groups of Indians could not remain together for more than a few days because they could not feed themselves. Generally speaking, that was true. Their pony herds quickly exhausted the grazing land, their hunting parties depleted or frightened away the game, and their cooking fires burned through the fuel at hand. The larger the village, the more quickly all that happened. Sheridan's real concern, and one that Custer would share, was that the soldiers would either not find the Indians or the Indians would scatter before they could launch an attack. Past experience suggested that both were very real possibilities.

Although limited in scope, troops from Gibbon's command undertook the first maneuver of the campaign. On February 22 a small detachment under Major James Brisbin rode out of Fort Ellis on a mission to relieve civilians besieged by Lakota and Cheyenne warriors at the Fort Pease trading post near the mouth of the Big Horn River. That situation quickly resolved, the soldiers rejoined their comrades at Fort Ellis.

Only the Wyoming column headed by General "Three Stars" Crook himself got into the field before spring arrived. His force of about eight hundred infantry and cavalry left Fort Fetterman in early March. On March 16 Crook ordered Colonel Joseph J. Reynolds to take a detachment in pursuit of a group of Cheyenne hunters his scouts had detected. Reynolds followed the hunters to Old Bear's village on the Powder River. The detachment attacked at dawn, scattering its residents, setting fire to the tipis, and capturing the pony herd. Warriors from the village quickly regrouped and counter-attacked. Rather than hold his position, Reynolds withdrew his troops and rejoined the main column, letting the warriors recapture their ponies in the process. Cold and disappointed with the outcome of his sole encounter with his quarry, Crook retreated to Fort Fetterman to resupply. Critics later castigated Reynolds for losing his nerve and retreating unnecessarily and found scant reason to praise Crook. Reynolds was eventually court-martialed over his performance that day. Convicted of dereliction of duty, he was suspended from rank and service for a year. President Grant commuted the sentence but Reynolds never returned to service.

> The Lakota called Crook "Three Stars" because of the insignia he wore on his shoulders. Prior to the Sioux War, Crook campaigned against the Snakes and Paiutes in the Northwest (1864–1868) and the Tonto Apaches and Yavapais in Arizona (1872). In 1882 he unsuccessfully tried to bring in Geronimo and the Chiricahua Apaches. Despite the reputation he built as an Indian fighter, Crook had great sympathy for Native Americans and spoke out against their unjust treatment.

Meanwhile Terry's two columns, delayed by winter storms and Custer's political difficulties in the east, had yet to leave their posts. The Montana column led by Colonel John Gibbon finally left Fort Ellis on April 3. Comprised of the 2nd Cavalry and 7th Infantry, the addition of 50 or so Crows would soon bring its numbers up to about 475. Terry's other column did not depart Fort Lincoln until May 17. It marched out with General Terry in command and Custer at the head of the 7th Cavalry. Besides the 7th Cavalry, the Dakota column included two companies of the 17th Infantry, a company of the 6th Infantry to guard the supply wagons, a detachment of the 20th Infantry to tend three rapid-firing Gatling guns, and thirty-five Arikara scouts, including Custer's friend Bloody Knife. Mark Kellogg, a newspaper reporter on assignment from the *New York Herald*, accompanied it. He stuck close to Custer until the last fatal moments. In all, about nine hundred officers and enlisted men plus a large number of civilian support personnel rode out of Fort Lincoln that day. Re-outfitted for battle, Crook's column left Fort Fetterman again on May 29. By then Sheridan's winter campaign had become a summer campaign. Soon his calculations of the strength of the opposing force would no longer hold true for as spring blossomed into summer a stream of newcomers from the reservations would swell the villages.

Gibbon's column headed east from Fort Ellis to the Yellowstone River with orders to locate and engage the non-treaty Indians. Lieutenant James H. Bradley, Gibbon's chief of scouts, detoured to the Crow agency to recruit scouts. Among them were Half Yellow Face, Hairy Moccasin,

White Man Runs Him, White Swan, Curley, and Goes Ahead. These six men would later ride to the Little Bighorn with Custer. For the next few weeks the Montana column patrolled the north bank of the Yellowstone to prevent the Indians from crossing over and escaping. During that time, Gibbon's the scouts found ample evidence that the non-treaty Lakota and Cheyenne were nearby. In early May a Lakota raiding party made off with the Crow scouts' horses, causing the Crows, now afoot, a great deal of embarrassment and anguish. As the month wore on, Lakota and Cheyenne warriors periodically attacked groups of hunters and scouts from the column. Then on May 16 a scouting party led by Lieutenant Bradley discovered an Indian camp on the Tongue River. Gibbon made several attempts to move his command across the flood-swollen river but gave up after some horses drowned. A week later the column suffered its first casualties when two soldiers and a civilian were killed and scalped while away from camp hunting. Bradley's scouts located the Indians again on May 27. This time they were in the Rosebud valley just eighteen miles away from Gibbon's position. Although in regular communication with General Terry, Gibbon neglected to share this vital piece of intelligence with him. As a result, Terry continued to search in vain for the Lakota and Cheyenne wanderers.

With the regiment band playing *The Girl I Left Behind Me*, the Dakota column rode out of Fort Lincoln on May 17. Custer's wife, Elizabeth Bacon Custer ("Libbie"), accompanied it. Libbie was at her husband's side as they rode past the children and distraught wives the scouts, enlisted men, and officers were leaving behind, some of them forever. As they got out on to the prairie she had a strange experience, which she recounts in *Boots and Saddles*.

> As the sun broke through the mist a mirage appeared, which took up about half the line of cavalry and thenceforth for a little distance it marched, equally plain to the sight on the earth and in the sky. The future of the heroic band, whose days were even then numbered, seemed to be revealed and already there seemed a premonition in the supernatural translation as their forms were reflected from the opaque mist of the early dawn.[3]

That evening the paymaster paid the troops so they could settle their debts with the regiment sutler. The next morning Libbie and Custer said their farewells and the paymaster escorted Libbie back to the fort.

Despite enduring unseasonably foul weather, the Dakota column had a relatively uneventful journey to the Yellowstone. Following up on reports that Sitting Bull was on the Little Missouri River, Terry sent a detachment with Custer on what proved to be a fruitless reconnaissance. Still ignorant of the whereabouts of Sitting Bull and his followers, the column reached the confluence of the Powder and Yellowstone rivers on June 8. The next day Terry met with Gibbon and only then learned that his scouts had sighted villages on the Tongue and in the Rosebud valley. Where the Indians were now was anyone's guess but Terry reasoned they would be found in the upper Little Bighorn valley. To confirm that they had not circled back, he sent Major Marcus Reno with six companies of the 7th Cavalry to examine the Powder and Tongue valleys before rejoining the command at the mouth of the Tongue. Reno's detachment departed camp on the Yellowstone on June 10. Afterwards Terry focused his attention on establishing a supply depot at the mouth of the Powder, which he staffed with his own infantry, three infantry companies from Fort Buford, and the dismounted cavalry. By then Captain Grant Marsh had arrived with the *Far West*, a steamer the army had chartered to support the campaign. Terry sent Custer on to the mouth of the Tongue with the rest of the regiment and followed on board the *Far West*.

Custer departed on June 15. The regiment encountered no problems en route to the Tongue but something did happen that first day that made the scouts and some of the troopers uneasy. They came upon a Lakota campsite from the previous winter. In it, they found a human skull and nearby a cavalry uniform. According to Red Star, one of the Arikara scouts, "all about him were clubs and sticks as if he had been beaten to death. Custer stood still for some time and looked down at the remains of the soldier."[4] A bit further on they came to a Lakota burial ground. Perhaps to avenge the death of the trooper, Custer and his men desecrated the graves. One burial scaffold held a man who appeared to have distinguished himself in battle. Custer ordered Isaiah Dorman, his African American interpreter, to pull the body down. Dorman eventually threw it in the river. Red Star said that he later saw Dorman fishing and assumed he was using pieces of flesh off the body for bait. Boston Custer wrote to his mother about the incident. He told her that her grandson, Autie Reed, had retrieved a bow and arrows and a nice pair of moccasins from the scaffold. As he stood on the battlefield less than two weeks later looking down at the bodies of those involved, Lieutenant Godfrey remembered their behavior that day. Interpreter Fred Gerard, who had also witnessed the incident, wondered if their deaths were divine retribution for their desecration of the Lakota graves.

When Reno found no fresh evidence of Indians in the Tongue or Powder river valleys, he violated his orders and crossed over to the Rosebud. The recent campsites he found there led him to conclude that about four hundred tipis of Indians were in the area. That equated to eight hundred or so warriors, a number comparable to Sheridan's initial and Bradley's more recent estimates. They did not, however, lead him to conclude that the camps had united. Reno followed the trail long enough to verify its generally westward bearing then returned to the Yellowstone as ordered. Terry received Reno's report on June 19 and was enraged to discover that the major had disobeyed his orders. Nonetheless, Reno's observations supported Terry's suspicions that the Indians would be found in the upper Little Bighorn valley. Acting on that assumption, Terry moved his staging point further west along the Yellowstone to the mouth of Rosebud Creek. Custer, already bristling over the fact that Terry had dispatched Reno and not him—an officer of superior rank with a proven track record—to reconnoiter the area to the south, also objected to Reno's breach of orders. He complained that had the Indians detected Reno's troops they would have certainly scattered and thus scuppered the whole campaign. Even then Crook and the Wyoming column were discovering just how wrong Custer was.

On June 17, the day Reno rejoined Terry's command, Crook was in trouble. He had left Fort Fetterman on May 29 with a fully equipped contingent of more than a thousand men drawn from the 2nd and 3rd Cavalry and 4th and 9th Infantry. When he reach the headwaters of the Tongue he went into camp to await his scouts. It was there that a band of Cheyenne scouts—or "wolves" as many Plains tribes called them—tried to run off his horses. After a week in camp more than 260 Crows and Shoshonis arrived to join the regiment. The Wyoming column then moved on. On the morning of June 17, Crook halted his command on Rosebud Creek to make coffee. Soon hundreds of Lakota and Cheyenne warriors led by Crazy Horse swooped down upon them. Had not the Crows and Shoshonis succeeded in holding back the onslaught until the soldiers got organized, the outcome would have been disastrous. As it was, when the Lakota and Cheyenne finally withdrew six hours later, Crook retained possession of the field but had not won what one might call an outright victory. The fight had more or less ended in stalemate.

> Because Crazy Horse refused to have his photo taken no images of him are known to exist. Despite that, a mountain in the Black Hills of South Dakota is slowly being blasted away to form Crazy Horse Memorial, a mammoth statue of a mounted warrior purported to be him.

With wounded to care for, his munitions and rations nearly depleted, and more than a bit unnerved by the Indians' unprecedented and persistent attack, Crook returned south to his supply depot on Goose Creek, where he remained until early August. Although Crook's troops were fighting for their lives only forty miles up

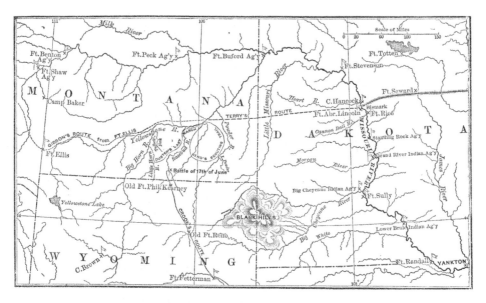

Figure 2.1 Campaign Map. Date unknown. Courtesy of the Buffalo Bill Historical Center, Wyoming, USA; Vincent Mercaldo Collection, VM0013.

the very valley Reno was reconnoitering that day, Reno had no inkling of it. Nor did Terry hear about it or learn that Crook had withdrawn from the field until after the Little Bighorn fight. Consequently, Terry did not know two things Crook had learned: first, that the scattered winter villages had united and, second, that the Lakota and Cheyenne were in a combative mood and no longer inclined to flee at the first sign of soldiers.

On the morning of June 21, Terry dispatched a courier with a message informing Sheridan of his revised plan. Custer, it said, would take the 7th Cavalry up the Rosebud then cross over to the Little Bighorn and work his way downstream. Meanwhile Gibbon, accompanied by Terry, would reverse course along the Yellowstone and ferry his troops across it on the *Far West*. Once on the south bank, he would move up the Big Horn to the mouth of the Little Bighorn. Terry did not say so in his dispatch but he expected Custer to catch up with and attack the Indians and Gibbon to block their escape northward. Late that afternoon, Terry summoned Gibbon, Custer, and Major Brisbin (Gibbon's cavalry chief) to a conference aboard the *Far West*. Together they worked out the timing and details of the plan, assuming as always that the Indians would run if given a chance. Because no one really knew where the Indians were, the plan had a degree of flexibility built into it.

It was agreed that Custer and the 7th Cavalry would move out the next day. On the morning of June 22, Custer received the written orders Terry had dictated to E.W. Smith, his adjutant general, the night before. They instructed him to move up the Rosebud until he determined the direction taken by the trail Reno had discovered. Even if it swung west toward the Little Bighorn, as Terry expected, Custer was to continue south to the Tongue before veering off in that direction himself. All the while he was to take steps to ensure that the Indians did not escape past him to the south or southeast. Meanwhile, Gibbon would move his command to the upper end of the Little Bighorn valley, where Terry expected it to be in position by June 26. He would accompany Gibbon. If all went to plan, the two forces would trap the Indians between them. Terry also ordered Custer to examine the upper part of Tullock's Creek and send George Herendeen, a white scout, through to him with a report of his findings. More controversially, Terry wrote:

> It is, of course, impossible to give you any definite instructions in regard to this movement, and were it not impossible to do so the Department Commander places too much confidence in your zeal, energy, and ability to wish to impose upon you precise orders which might hamper your action when nearly in contact with the enemy. He will, however, indicate to you his own views of what your action should be, and he desires that you should conform to them unless you shall see sufficient reason for departing from them.

Terry's orders to Custer would fuel endless and often acrimonious debate between the pro-Custer and anti-Custer camps: did Custer disobey orders? Focusing on the first sentence just quoted, which appears to give Custer leeway to deviate from the orders almost at will, Custerphiles would argue "No, he did not." Focusing on the last sentence, which seems to require Custer to obey Terry's orders unless events on the ground made it impossible to do so, Custerphobes would argue "Yes, he did." Almost certainly crediting him with far too much foresight, a few would read into Terry's orders an attempt by him to have it both ways and thereby cover himself in any eventuality.

TRAIL TO THE GREASY GRASS: LAKOTA AND CHEYENNE

The Lakota and Cheyenne followed their own event-filled route to the river they call the Greasy Grass. They had, as predicted, wintered in the Powder

General Terry's Orders to Custer

Camp at Mouth of Rosebud River, Montana Territory, June 22nd, 1876.
Lieut.-Col. Custer, 7th Cavalry.

Colonel:

The Brigadier-General Commanding directs that, as soon as your regiment can be made ready for the march, you will proceed up the Rosebud in pursuit of the Indians whose trail was discovered by Major Reno a few days since. It is, of course, impossible to give you any definite instructions in regard to this movement, and were it not impossible to do so, the Department Commander places too much confidence in your zeal, energy, and ability to wish to impose upon you precise orders which might hamper your action when nearly in contact with the enemy. He will, however, indicate to you his own views of what your action should be, and he desires that you should conform to them unless you shall see sufficient reason for departing from them. He thinks that you should proceed up the Rosebud until you ascertain definitely the direction in which the trail above spoken of leads. Should it be found (as it appears almost certain that it will be found) to turn towards the Little Horn, he thinks that you should still proceed southward, perhaps as far as the headwaters of the Tongue, and then turn towards the Little Horn, feeling constantly, however, to your left, so as to preclude the possibility of the escape of the Indians to the south or southeast by passing around your left flank. The column of Colonel Gibbon is now in motion for the mouth of the Bighorn. As soon as it reaches that point it will cross the Yellowstone and move up at least as far as the forks of the Big and Little Horns. Of course its future movements must be controlled by circumstances as they arise, but it is hoped that the Indians, if upon the Little Horn, may be so nearly inclosed by the two columns that their escape will be impossible.

The Department Commander desires that on your way up the Rosebud you should thoroughly examine the upper part of Tullock's Creek, and that you should endeavor to send a scout through to Colonel Gibbon's column, with information of the result of your examination. The lower part of the creek will be examined by a detachment from Colonel Gibbon's command. The supply steamer will be pushed up the Bighorn as far as the forks if the river is found to be navigable for that distance, and the Department Commander, who will accompany the column of Colonel Gibbon, desires you to report to him there not later than the expiration of the time for which your troops are rationed, unless in the meantime you receive further orders.

Very respectfully, Your obedient servant,
E. W. Smith,
Captain, 18th Infantry, Acting Assistant Adjutant-General.

River country. As always, they settled in small villages in sheltered spots along watercourses, living on stores stockpiled in the warmer months and whatever game their hunters could kill. There were a hundred or so tipis of Cheyennes along with some Lakotas in Old Bear's village when Colonel Reynolds attacked it on March 17 (see Two Moon's account in Documents). After the warriors drove the soldiers off, the now destitute band made its way to the Little Powder River, where they joined Crazy Horse's village on March 24. Although they had already heard that soldiers were coming, the Reynolds attack drove home the immediacy of the threat. The combined village then moved further north to join Sitting Bull, who was camped on the Powder River. Word of the ultimatum and the Reynolds attack spread, prompting more and more bands to unite in self-defense.

As enough tender spring grasses emerged to sustain their pony herds, the Lakota and Cheyenne slowly followed the game west from the Powder River to the Tongue and then on to the Rosebud. It was warriors from their camp on the Tongue who discovered Gibbon's column and stole the Crow scouts' horses. Even as the village moved on from there, Lakota and Cheyenne wolves kept an eye on the Montana column and warriors continued to harass its scouting and hunting parties as opportunities arose to do so. This alone should have alerted Gibbon to their militant frame of mind but it didn't. Other wolves followed the movements of the Wyoming column and from time to time tried to stampede its horses. On June 9, a small Cheyenne party led by Little Hawk fired into Crook's camp on the Tongue and had a go at the horses. They failed to run them off and galloped away after a brief skirmish. By now, most of the Lakotas and Cheyennes wintering in the unceded territory had united; friends and relatives from the reservations had yet to join them.

After a successful buffalo hunt in what the Lakota call the Moon of the Ripening Chokecherries, Sitting Bull decided that, although a bit early yet, it was a good time to hold a Sun Dance. The four-day ceremony took place June 4–7 at the sacred Deer Medicine Rocks in the Rosebud valley. While only Hunkpapas took part in the ritual, the other Lakotas and Cheyennes watched with great interest. Sitting Bull himself entered the Sun Dance lodge, where Jumping Bull, his adopted brother, cut fifty pieces of skin from each arm. This was the "scarlet blanket" he had promised *Wakan Tanka* in exchange for a vision and help. Sitting Bull then danced around the center pole crying. He prayed that his people would live in peace with everyone, have plenty of food to eat, and live unmolested in their own territory. After hours of dancing, crying, praying, and continually gazing upward, he stopped and stood motionless staring at the sky. He had received a vision. Others lowered him to the ground and he recounted his vision to those gathered around him. In it he had seen a great many horses and soldiers falling upside down into a village. That only a few people in the village were upside down indicated to him a great victory was at hand. A voice also had spoken to him. It said "I give you these because they have no ears" and warned that his people must not take anything from the dead soldiers. The powerful vision lifted everyone's spirits and bolstered their confidence.

After the Sun Dance, the Lakota and Cheyenne followed a buffalo herd discovered by their wolves west toward the Greasy Grass. By now friends and relatives were streaming in from the reservations, as they did every summer. But this year, angry over government pressure to sell their sacred Black Hills and the Commissioner's ultimatum and frustrated by the food shortages and corruption they faced on their reservations, more of them were arriving than ever before. It was a time of reunion, celebration, socializing, and ritual but it was also a time of great concern because the soldiers were never far from their minds. The now rapidly growing procession crossed over the divide between the Rosebud and Greasy Grass valleys on June 16 and set up camp on the upper fork of Reno Creek. Just as the women were putting up their tipis, Little Hawk (Northern Cheyenne) and his wolves, who had once again been out checking on Crook's column, returned to report that the soldiers were headed toward the Rosebud.

The chiefs met in council to consider the matter. A consensus reached, they sent the camp criers through the various tribal circles to announce their decision: do nothing unless the soldiers attack. Excitable young Lakotas and Cheyennes, newly empowered by Sitting Bull's prophetic vision, ignored the decision. The Cheyenne warrior Wooden Leg told his biographer, Thomas B. Marquis,[6] that

> as darkness came on we slipped away. Many bands of Cheyenne
> and Sioux young men, some with older ones rode out up the
> south fork toward the head of Rosebud Creek. Warriors came
> from every camp circle. We had our weapons, war clothing,
> paints, and medicines.

With the exodus of the warriors accomplished, the chiefs relented. Sitting Bull, Crazy Horse, and other more seasoned warriors prepared themselves for battle and joined those already en route to the Rosebud.

Early on the morning of June 17, hundreds of Lakota and Cheyenne warriors raced up the valley headlong into Crow and Shoshoni scouts patrolling at the periphery of Crook's inopportune bivouac. Sitting Bull, arms still inflamed and useless after his sacrifice in the Sun Dance lodge, did not fight but rode amongst the warriors exhorting them to have

Sitting Bull (ca. 1830–1890)

Sitting Bull (or *Tatanka-Iyotanka* in Lakota) was born on the Grand River in what was to become Dakota Territory. His parents were Sitting Bull and Her-Holy-Door. Initially his family named him Jumping Badger but most people called him *Slon-He* ("Slow") because of his deliberate and unhurried manner. As he approached adulthood his father transferred his own name, Sitting Bull, to him. Many years later, when circumstances finally forced him to relinquish his traditional way of life and settle down on the Standing Rock Reservation, Sitting Bull made his home on the Grand River near the spot where he was born. It is there that Lakota police officers killed him, his son Crow Foot, and several supporters during a botched arrest attempt in the early morning hours of December 15, 1890. The incident, which occurred at the height of the Ghost Dance panic, was an attempt to curtail Sitting Bull's support of the new movement. Several policemen also died that day. A Lakota police officer named Red Tomahawk allegedly fired the gunshot to the head that killed Sitting Bull. Immediately afterwards his body was hauled away and buried in a simple grave at Fort Yates on the Standing Rock Reservation. In the 1950s it was moved to Mobridge, South Dakota, and reburied under a granite shaft.

Sitting Bull was a respected holy man, brave warrior, good father, fine singer, strong leader, and fearless defender of Lakota lands and traditional lifeways. Despite his menacing reputation, he did not necessarily hate whites. He went on his first raid in his early teens. It was against the Crow. Many other raids and fights followed but he didn't clash with American soldiers until he was about thirty. His first armed encounter with them came in June 1863, when soldiers retaliating for the Santee uprising in Minnesota attacked a camp he was in. The next year Sitting Bull fought soldiers again at Killdeer Mountain. From then until the late 1870s he led or participated in a great many attacks against soldiers, forts, settlers, railroads, and travelers in the Missouri River country. Sitting Bull belonged to the Brave Heart warrior society and the Silent Eaters, a group dedicated to safeguarding the welfare of his people.

Sitting Bull had several wives. Two died before they had children but he fathered many children with his last two wives, Four Robes and Seen-By-the-Nation. His favorite children were probably his son Crow Foot and his daughter Standing Holy. Sitting Bull's own father was killed by the Crow in 1859. From then until she died in 1884, Sitting Bull's widowed mother enjoyed a place of honor in his lodge.

Although Sitting Bull was widely feared by whites during the Indian wars, there were those who knew him who spoke highly of him. Mrs. Fanny Kelly spent her five months as a Hunkpapa captive living in Sitting Bull's tipi. After her ordeal, she described him as a gentle, well-respected man who was kind to his wife and children. Sitting Bull and his wife had treated her like a guest, she said. As a result, "they both have a very warm place in my heart."[5] Catherine Weldon, a Christian missionary and teacher at Standing Rock, echoed Mrs. Kelly's sentiments and described Sitting Bull as a steadfast patriot. The Ashcrofts, Sitting Bull's white neighbors on the Grand River, also spoke highly of him. They considered him one of their oldest and best friends. Those who met him on tour with Buffalo Bill found him approachable, warm, and congenial. Yet even after he died non-Indians who didn't know him continued to vilify him.

courage. The battle raged all morning and into the afternoon. According to Wooden Leg,[7] "there were charges back and forth. Our Indians fought and ran away, fought and ran away. The soldiers and their Indians and scouts did the same. Sometimes we chased them, sometimes they chased us." Clearly these were not Indians who planned to flee at the first sign of soldiers; they were angry warriors committed enough to bring the fight to the army. Thirteen Lakotas were killed that day and one Cheyenne; many more were wounded. Crook lost nine soldiers and one scout. Another twenty-three soldiers and seven scouts sustained wounds.

White historians call this the Battle of the Rosebud but the Cheyennes remember it as the Battle Where the Sister Saved Her Brother. Chief Comes in Sight, a Northern Cheyenne known by his people to be very brave, fought in the battle. His sister, Buffalo Calf Woman, had accompanied him to the Rosebud. She watched with great pride as her brother fought courageously at the forefront of the warriors. When a Shoshoni killed his horse under him, Buffalo Calf Woman raced across the battlefield on her horse, pulled Comes in Sight up behind her, and together they made good their escape. Her courageous deed rallied the Cheyenne warriors and they launched into Crook's force with renewed vigor. To this day the Northern Cheyenne remember Buffalo Calf Woman as a very brave woman.

Although the Lakota and Cheyenne believed they had scored a victory, any celebration had to wait because they had dead to mourn and wounded to care for. Now a death village, the women took down their tipis the next day and the camp moved away from Reno Creek deeper into the Greasy Grass valley. They left behind a single death lodge and in it a Sans Arc man killed in the Rosebud fight.

The village remained in its new location for six days. There was now time for celebration. Everyone danced and feasted and listened to the warriors endlessly describe their many feats and recite the coups they had counted in the Rosebud fight. They also welcomed droves of newcomers from the reservations. While basking in their success, no soldiers had fallen into their village so they knew that this was not the great fight predicted by Sitting Bull's Sun Dance vision. That was yet to come and, more unified and empowered than ever, the warriors were confident they could deliver the victory prophesied when it did. Newcomers arriving in those few days more than doubled the size of the camp, swelling the ranks of the warriors from eight hundred to eighteen hundred or even more. As their small parties converged on the Greasy Grass, they left behind trails etched deep in the ground by the travois that carried their possessions. And each trail led to straight to the village.

With resources in the immediate area depleted, the chiefs' council decided to move the village further up the Greasy Grass toward the Bighorn Mountains in search of buffalo but then their wolves discovered antelope herds to the north and west. Reversing direction, the Cheyenne led the way northward. On June 24 they established a new camp eight miles downstream. Its tribal circles stretched for nearly three miles along the west bank of the Greasy Grass. Beyond it to the west lay lush benchland upon which their thousands of ponies grazed. Bluffs of more than three hundred feet in height towered over them on the east bank of the river. It was a lovely, resource-rich, and tranquil spot. The Cheyenne camp circle was furthest downstream to the north; the Hunkpapa circle was furthest upstream to the south. Ranging between them from south to north were the Blackfoot (Lakota), Miniconjou, Brulé, Sans Arc, and Oglala camp circles. Scattered amongst them were a few Santee refugees from Minnesota, including the infamous uprising leader Inkpaduta, some Yanktonais and Black Kettles, and even a handful of Arapahoes.

That evening One Bull accompanied his uncle, Sitting Bull, across the river to a high bluff overlooking the Cheyenne camp circle. There, in the fading light, Sitting Bull conducted the *Hanble Ceyapi* ("Dreamy Cry") ceremony and made offerings to *Wakan Tanka*. After each offering— a buffalo robe, a pipe, tobacco, carved cherry sticks—he uttered a prayer, which the smoke from his pipe carried heavenward. Years later One Bull repeated his words to Robert P. Higheagle:[8] "Great Spirit, pity me; in the name of the tribe I offer you this peace-pipe. Wherever, the sun, the moon, the earth, the four (cardinal) points of the winds, there you are always. Father save the Tribe, I geg [*sic*] you. Pity me."

Later that night twenty or so young Lakota and Cheyenne warriors pledged to die in the next battle. The youngest of these "suicide boys" was just fifteen years old. Some wanted to avenge the deaths of loved ones killed by soldiers in the Rosebud fight; others sought the honor their own deaths in battle would surely bring. As they performed the Dying Dancing ceremony, seasoned warriors praised their courage and offered moral support while women trilled encouragement. Each of these young men knew that, if he successfully fulfilled his pledge, his tribe would sing praise songs to him and long remember his name. Throughout the long night of ritual and celebration the Kit Fox *akicita* policed the perimeter of the camp to prevent over-zealous warriors from sneaking out to attack the soldiers again. Despite their efforts, a few managed to slip away.

FROM THE YELLOWSTONE TO THE LITTLE BIGHORN

It was about noon on June 22 when company by company the roughly 830 officers and enlisted men of the 7th Cavalry and its large contingent of scouts, guides, interpreters, packers, and civilian employees passed in review before Custer, Terry, and Gibbon. Included were twenty-nine Arikara scouts and another six Crows on detached duty from Gibbon's column. Left behind were the infantry and the Gatling guns. The regiment buglers played a ragged but rousing rendition of *Garry Owen*, the 7th Cavalry's unofficial marching song, which added to the fanfare. The already troublesome mule train brought up the rear. It carried fifteen days of rations and forage for the command and a reserve of fifty rounds of carbine ammunition per soldier. Each trooper carried a Springfield single-shot carbine and a Colt revolver and had a hundred carbine cartridges and twenty-four pistol cartridges on his person or in his saddle bags.

Contrary to Hollywood depictions, none of the cavalrymen wore yellow cravats and there was but a single saber in the entire regiment, that for use in killing rattlesnakes. The troopers enjoyed wide leeway in how they dressed in the field. Most wore blue or gray shirts, regulation blue trousers (some with reinforced seats), and cavalry boots but many other combinations were in evidence and nearly everyone had replaced the army-issue hat with one more suitable for the conditions. Custer wore what he normally did on campaign: fringed buckskin coat and pants, scarlet cravat, knee-high boots, Civil War vintage wide-collared blue blouse, and a wide-brimmed hat. Despite the image of him created by Hollywood and the name given to him by some tribes, "Long Hair," he now had a receding hairline and had cut his hair short for the campaign (the Cheyenne called him "Son of Morning Star"). Several other officers also wore buckskins on the campaign.

As Custer led his troops away from the camp on the Yellowstone, Gibbon called after him "Now Custer, don't be greedy, but wait for us!" With his customary bravado, Custer retorted "No, I will not!" The orderly procession that trailed after him belied the tensions and animosities that divided the regiment. Some officers were staunchly loyal to Custer; others harbored long-standing resentments and a few were openly hostile. Several family members accompanied the expedition and they were predictably loyal to Custer. Brother Thomas was a captain in the 7th

Cavalry and commanded C Company. He was a veteran of the Civil War, where his daring service had twice earned him the Medal of Honor. Brother-in-law James Calhoun served at the rank of lieutenant and commanded L Company. Brother Boston was a civilian guide and nephew Harry Armstrong "Autie" Reed, Custer's namesake, was just along for a bit of adventure. Other loyalists included Captain Thomas B. Weir, D Company commander, and the regimental adjutant, Lieutenant William W. Cooke. The two most senior officers beneath Custer, Major Marcus A. Reno and Captain Frederick W. Benteen, were both Civil War veterans and ranked high among his foes. In the aftermath, both held Custer personally accountable for the debacle. Benteen commanded H Company.

Custer set a brisk pace. The first afternoon the regiment covered a dozen miles and on each of the subsequent two days it covered thirty miles or more. On the second day they struck the Indian trail Reno had found and began riding through abandoned campsites. According to John Burkman, Custer's personal orderly, the evidence at hand prompted an "unusually quiet and stern" Custer to comment "there's a lot of them, more than we figured." The following morning the regiment came upon the site of Sitting Bull's Sun Dance, where the scouts found unsettling evidence of powerful medicine. Pictographs scratched in the sandstone, drawings in the sand, a ritually positioned buffalo skull, carefully arranged piles of stones, and the remains of the Sun Dance lodge told them that this was sacred ground. More worryingly, they also indicated that the Lakotas who had only recently camped here were confident of an upcoming victory.

Just beyond the Deer Medicine Rocks, the 7th Cavalry encountered a tangle of fresh Indian trails. The scouts believed they pointed west and probably assumed that they had been made by reservation Indians heading out for the summer buffalo hunts. Custer feared that they pointed east and had been left by the non-treaty Indians dispersing, i.e. that his quarry was scattering. In reality, some had been left by the Lakota and Cheyenne as they moved on after Sitting Bull's Sun Dance and others by their reservation friends and relatives heading west to join them. The regiment halted for a long lunch break while the Crows, who were more familiar with the area than the Arikaras, scouted ahead. In the meantime, the Arikaras examined trails that branched off the main one. The Crows returned to report a fresh campsite twelve miles ahead where a creek dropped down from the divide and joined the Rosebud. The regiment continued up the Rosebud. Along the way it passed through several more abandoned campsites, some with their camp fires still smoldering. It was here that George Herendeen, who had been commissioned to scout Tullock's Creek and then ride through to Terry with a report, asked Custer for permission to depart. Contravening Terry's written orders, Custer ignored him.

The regiment finally bivouacked at about 7:45 p.m. A short time later the Crow scouts returned again to report that the Indian trail left the Rosebud and followed the adjoining stream—called Davis Creek today— up and over the divide then down into the Little Bighorn valley. It was now clear that no significant numbers of Lakotas or Cheyennes remained on the east side of the divide, making any further probe up the Rosebud a waste of time, despite Terry's orders. Moreover, Custer undoubtedly feared that to continue up the Rosebud would only give the Indians, now so tantalizingly close, a chance to slip away, a risk he was not willing to take. He reckoned that he would find his quarry on the lower Little Bighorn and modified his plan accordingly. The Crows described to him an elevation on the divide that they had long used as a lookout point when they went on raids. From what they called the Crow's Nest one could see into the valley without being detected. Custer ordered Lieutenant Charles A. Varnum, his chief of scouts, to make his way up to the Crow's Nest with several of the scouts and get into position to scan the valley at day break.

Custer assembled his officers and informed them that, rather than continue up the Rosebud, they would do a night march over the divide and rest in camp the next day while the scouts located the village. The plan was to attack at dawn the following day, June 26, by which time Gibbon should be in position to block the Indians' escape to the north. At midnight the troops mounted for the rough six-mile ride up to the divide. Two hours later they stopped just short of the summit. At dawn the scouts surveyed the vast stretch of land to west. The Crows could see smoke rising from a camp fifteen miles away and a wriggling black mass on the benchland beyond, which they took to be a huge pony herd. Varnum could see none of that but believed them. When he arrived a bit later, Custer couldn't make any of it out either but he, too, believed it was there; he just didn't believe the scouts' estimates of how big the village was.

But the scouts and interpreters knew—and some of the soldiers suspected—exactly what they were up against. Godfrey reports that Custer had heard Bloody Knife, his trusted Arikara-Lakota scout, talking to the others that morning.[9] An interpreter translated for him. "He says we'll find enough Sioux to keep up fighting two or three days." Custer dismissed the suggestion, saying "I guess we'll get through them in one day." Later on Bloody Knife predicted that a big and losing fight lay ahead of them and that he himself would not see the sun set. Up at the Crows Nest, much as he had done days earlier on the march from the Yellowstone, interpreter Mitch Boyer (French/Santee) also warned Custer that the village they were about to attack was huge. He estimated it was the biggest he had seen in his thirty years among the Indians. Even the soldiers had premonitions. Walking away from Custer's officer's call on the evening of June 22, Lieutenant George Wallace had commented to Godfrey "I believe General Custer is going to be killed." When Godfrey asked him why he thought that, he added "because I have never heard Custer talk in that way before." He was referring to Custer's subdued and conciliatory manner during what had been an unusually long and informative meeting.

Upon returning from the Crow's Nest, Custer received word that two Lakotas had been spotted nearby. The likelihood that they would raise the alarm fed his fears that the village would scatter before he could launch an attack. He decided then that he could wait no longer. It was a decision that would be forever debated and criticized, along with his earlier decision to break off his reconnaissance of the Rosebud and exhaust his already tired troops in a grueling night march. Custer gathered his officers and other key personnel and advised them of his plan. Herendeen again brought up the matter of Tullock's Creek. This time Custer rebuffed him more directly:

> Yes, but there are no Indians in that direction—they are all in our front. And besides, they have discovered us. It will be of no use to send you down Tullock's Creek. The only thing to do is to push ahead and attack the camp as soon as possible.[10]

Charlie Reynolds, a guide, and Mitch Boyer, an interpreter, both expressed concern over the size of the village, concerns Custer dismissed with disdain.

As the first ready to go, Benteen's H Company took the lead when the regiment moved out. Because he had overslept, Captain McDougall's B Company was the last to get ready and, consequently, Custer assigned it to escort the slow-moving pack train, much to the dismay of McDougall and his men. Shortly after noon the regiment crested the divide and halted while Lieutenant Cooke, as adjutant acting on Custer's orders, divided it into battalions, yet another decision that would prove controversial in years to come. Major Reno took command of the 131 or so men in companies A, G, and M plus another 35 scouts, guides, and interpreters. Captain Benteen assumed command of companies D, H (his own), and K, totaling approximately 113 men. Custer retained command of companies C, E, F, I, and L, which included about 215 men. All of the scouts except for four Crows went with Reno; Curley, Goes Ahead, Hairy Moccasin, and White Man Runs Him remained with Custer. The remaining company,

McDougall's B Company (about 120 men), was to bring up the rear with the pack train and its eleven civilian packers.

Presumably to confirm that there were no Indians to their rear and possibly in accordance with Terry's orders that they continually "feel to the left" to prevent any Indians escaping around the regiment's flank, Custer sent Benteen on a wide sweep over the ridges to the southeast, a maneuver Benteen later bitterly described as his "fool's mission." He also instructed Benteen to find a vantage point from which to get a good look into the Little Bighorn valley before rejoining the regiment. As Benteen's battalion veered away, Custer and Reno continued down what is now called Reno Creek toward the Little Bighorn, Reno on the left bank and Custer on the right.

RENO FIGHT

A ten-mile ride downstream brought Custer and Reno to within four miles of the Little Bighorn. Just after 2:00 p.m. they came upon a large, recently abandoned campsite. A lone tipi remained standing and in it they found the body of a dead warrior. Scouts counted coup on the tipi then set it on fire. A party of forty or so Lakota warriors suddenly appeared and went galloping off in the direction in which Custer presumed the village to lie. Interpreter Fred Gerard (or Girard), seeing the warriors, waved his hat to catch Custer's attention then shouted back to him: "Here are your Indians, running like devils!"[11] And that's exactly what it looked like they were doing. Custer couldn't see the village itself but a cloud of dust rising from beyond the bluffs in that general direction suggested to him that it was breaking up and scattering. Whether or not it was, he could be sure the warriors would soon alert its occupants to his presence.

Custer sprang into action. Three years later Reno described that moment to the Court of Inquiry convened to investigate his own conduct at the Little Bighorn. He reported that Adjutant Cooke rode up to him and told him that "the village was only two miles ahead and running away." Custer's orders were for him "to move forward at as rapid a gait as prudent and to charge afterwards" and "that the whole outfit would support me."[12] Accompanied by Varnum and the scouts, Reno led his battalion down the creek toward the Little Bighorn at a brisk trot. Order disintegrated into chaos at the river ford as their hot, tired, and thirsty horses stopped abruptly to drink. Once the orderly formation was restored on the opposite bank, the battalion continued out onto the valley floor. Ahead, through the rolling clouds of dust, the soldiers could just discern the vague forms of mounted Indians milling about. Varnum realized then that, contrary to

Custer's expectations, the Indians were getting ready to fight. He swung his horse around and hurried back up the trail to warn him. He soon overtook Adjutant Cooke and another officer, who had accompanied Reno to the river. After passing his message on to them, Varnum reversed course and rejoined Reno's command.

He was right. The camp was hastily preparing for battle, not fleeing. Although the Lakota and Cheyenne were expecting a fight at some point, they were not expecting it that day nor even in that location. Many of the men were off hunting and, according to Wooden Leg, most of the young warriors were splashing around in the river or lazing sleepily in the shade after celebrating with the newcomers until dawn. Few horses were picketed in the camp; most were grazing on the benchland to the west under watchful adolescent eyes. Because their camp circles were at the upper end of the village, the Hunkpapa and Blackfoot were first to realize the threat. Their warriors raced forward to meet Reno's battalion while the alarm went up in the other camp circles. As the news spread, pandemonium erupted. Young boys raced to the benchland for horses. Women gathered their children and fled northward. Warriors hastily, but nonetheless meticulously, painted their bodies and horses, dressed, and undertook personal rituals in preparation for battle. Older men wandered through the camps exhorting the warriors to be brave. Some women stayed behind to encourage their husbands, sons, and brothers with high-pitched trills. Sitting Bull escorted some of the women and children to safety then went to a high spot to pray and make medicine.

With his three companies riding side by side in standard columns of four, Reno trotted down the valley toward the Hunkpapa and Blackfoot camp circles. Midway between the ford and the village he stopped to place G Company in reserve at the rear. A short time later he stopped again and reverted to the original formation. A densely wooded bend in the river obscured his view ahead but he could see dust billowing up beyond it. Then, through the swirling cloud, he could make out the dim shapes of tipis and what appeared to be riders. He glanced around him; Custer's battalion was nowhere in sight. Reno dismounted his troops within sight of the village and every fourth trooper took the reins of his own and three other horses and moved to rear, as dictated by cavalry protocol. The rest of the command formed a widely spaced skirmish line that stretched part way across the valley floor. The right flank was anchored to the trees along the river but warriors were already dashing around the vulnerable left flank to the rear of the line. Soldiers aimed at whatever targets they made out through the thick clouds of dust kicked up by the warriors' ponies and the warriors returned fire with a variety of firearms and bows and arrows.

Less than fifteen minutes into the fight Reno realized that his position was untenable and ordered his troops to file into the trees by the river. The brush and rough ground offered cover but made it impossible for them to assume a coherent defensive formation. By now a great many warriors had joined the fight. Some stealthily worked their way through the trees and undergrowth toward the soldiers. Others fired into the trees from all sides. A half hour or so later, Reno decided that this position, too, was untenable. With Bloody Knife at his side, he ordered his men to mount. At that moment a bullet shattered Bloody Knife's skull, splattering warm brains and blood into Reno's face. It unnerved him. Reno ordered his men to dismount and then immediately ordered them to remount. Some dismounted and then remounted and some did not. Several never heard the commands at all and others misunderstood them. Confusion prevailed.

Those who did hear the order to withdraw tried to reassemble for a retreat back up the valley but as they came out of the trees an onslaught of warriors forced them toward the river and then across and up the bluffs on the opposite side. According to Varnum, some of the warriors were armed with Winchester repeating rifles. Gerard later reported that the "Indians picked off the troops at will." He described the scene as "a rout not a charge."[13] Time and again, Reno's detractors would repeat this depiction of the retreat as a rout, something that would haunt him for the rest of his life. In reality, the soldiers found themselves running a gauntlet as they struggled across the river and many never made it to the other side. Some were shot dead before they got to the water. Others were killed in the river or as they scrambled up the bluffs beyond. Many were shot but some were pulled from their horses and clubbed to death. In less than an hour, warriors killed forty of Reno's men and wounded thirteen more. Another seventeen got left behind in the brush. As the last of the soldiers reached the high ground, the warriors swung away to the north. Custer was still nowhere to be seen.

CUSTER FIGHT

As Reno's battalion rode down into the valley, Custer's command veered off to the right. From then on details of its movements become sketchier and sketchier. One can, however, arrive at a fairly accurate reconstruction of the general sequence of events that led up to its last fateful moments by piecing together information from a variety of sources. Particularly useful are native testimony, reports by the Crow scouts, accounts by the messengers Custer sent back to Benteen and the pack train, details noted by Gibbon's troops and the 7th Cavalry survivors when they surveyed the carnage, and archaeological evidence. More difficult to work with but nonetheless interesting is Peter Thompson's controversial account. Thompson and another trooper lagged behind Custer's battalion when their horses played out. They never managed to catch up and eventually joined the survivors on the hilltop. Thompson later claimed that he saw Custer at the river. Some of his comrades called him a liar and historians have found his story difficult to reconcile with other accounts. It is nonetheless worth considering. So, too, are Custer's known decision-making style and battlefield and command practices and the protocols that governed cavalry strategy and tactics.

From this information, it appears that after splitting from Reno, Custer continued down Reno Creek then crossed over to its north branch above the confluence. That is where Cooke caught up with him and relayed Varnum's message. If Custer did not already realize that the Indians were countering Reno's attack and not "skedaddling" as anticipated, he certainly did then. But rather than ride to Reno's relief with "the whole outfit," as promised, he swung up the slope toward the ridge. Leaving the rest of his battalion just below the crest, Custer, his trumpeter, and the four Crow scouts continued to the top. The scouts later reported that they could see Reno fighting in the valley below and the long string of camp circles. At last, Custer must have realized exactly what he was up against.

Returning to his command, Custer conferred with his senior officers then sent his brother Tom to find Sergeant Daniel Kanipe to dispatch with a message. Tom instructed Kanipe to ride back to the pack train. "Tell McDougall," he said, "to bring the pack train straight across to high ground—if packs get loose don't stop to fix them, cut them off. Come quick. Big Indian camp."[14] As the battalion started north again, a few skittish horses broke rank. The last thing Kanipe heard as he rode away was Custer shout: "Boys, hold your horses, there are plenty of them down there for us all!" Although the battalion appears to have moved along the back side of the ridge below the skyline, Varnum later claimed that he saw E Company, distinguishable by its gray horses, silhouetted against the sky as it passed overhead. Some of Reno's soldiers also reported seeing Custer on the bluffs waving his hat at them in encouragement. That was the last any of them saw of him.

Further on Custer led his troops down a long, narrow ravine that widens out at the bottom into what is now called Medicine Tail Coulee. On the way down he divided his battalion into two wings of roughly equal strength. He assigned command of the left wing, which consisted of E and F companies, to Captain George Yates. Captain Myles W. Keogh took command of the right wing, comprised of C, I, and L companies.

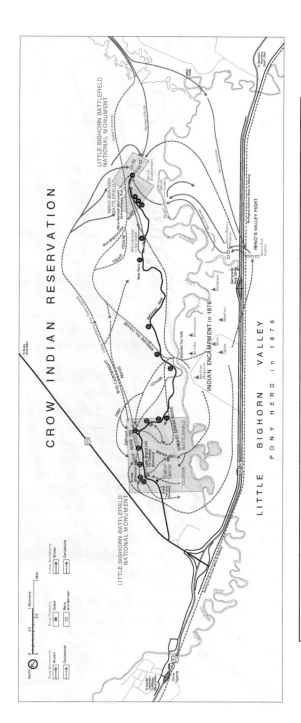

Figure 2.2 Greasy Grass/Little Bighorn Battlefield Map. Courtesy of the National Park Service.

It was about then that Custer dispatched his trumpeter, John Martin (formerly Giovanni Martini), with another message, this time for Benteen. Martin was an Italian immigrant. Perhaps doubtful of his command of English, Adjutant Cooke hastily scribbled the message on a page from his memorandum book and tore it out. It read: "Benteen. Come on. Big Village. Be Quick. Bring packs. W.W. Cooke. P. bring pacs [sic]." As Martin hurried up the backtrail, Custer continued down the ravine. The trumpeter later heard firing and glanced back. By then the battalion was out of sight and all he could see was Indians waving buffalo robes and shooting. As he rode south he met Boston Custer, who had abandoned his post with the pack train and was hurrying to join his brothers. Nephew Autie Reed would do the same. Martin had an eventful ride and, by the time he reached Benteen, his horse had taken a bullet to the flank. He did not rejoin Custer's battalion.

What happened after that is a matter of conjecture but archaeological research conducted in the mid 1980s has helped clarify troop positions and movements on the Custer battlefield. Notwithstanding this new evidence, much remains unknown and how best to interpret the archaeological data is a matter of continuing debate. However, it now appears that Captain George W. Yates led the left wing all the way down Medicine Tail Coulee to the river. Some soldiers may have entered the water before encountering a barrage of gunfire from warriors hiding in the brush on the far bank. Mounted warriors, some of them fresh from the Reno fight, soon reinforced those hiding in the bushes. Gall (Hunkpapa), enraged by the deaths of two of his wives and several children during the opening volleys of Reno's attack, led a fierce charge across the river. It pushed Yates' detachment back. Covering his retreat with dismounted skirmishers, Yates moved up Deep Coulee to the southernmost point of what is now called Battle Ridge. By then Custer had discharged the four Crows, who had been hired to scout not fight. At least three of them witnessed the action at the ford from a nearby hilltop, consequently, much of what is known about it derives from their reports. Sitting Bull also saw it, but from a different vantage point. In an interview published in the *New York Herald* on November 16, 1877, he said: "Our young men rained lead across the river and drove the white braves back."

Some theories have Custer accompanying Yates to the river and at least one warrior account describes a soldier in a buckskin coat falling wounded or dead in the water. Other officers also wore buckskin that day, so the man in question, if the incident actually happened, may or may not have been Custer. If it was, his men would have had to have retrieved his body and carried it to the hilltop where it was later found. In doing so, they would have put themselves at great risk. Lieutenant

Edward S. Godfrey, a 7th Cavalry survivor, visited the ford a couple of days after the battle. Testifying before the Reno Court of Inquiry three years later, he dismissed the notion that Custer was shot at the river, claiming that he saw no evidence of a fight there. However, the archaeological research in the 1980s confirmed action at the ford, as did Native testimony at the time.

If, as appears to be the case, the Yates wing (with or without Custer) tried to cross the river, why did it do so? Perhaps the objective was to relieve pressure on Reno's command by opening a second front. Or maybe it was to crush the Lakota and Cheyenne between the northern and southern battalions. Or it could have been to capture the fleeing women and children as Custer had done in the Washita battle. Or maybe it was a delaying tactic aimed at buying time until Benteen's troops and the pack train with its supply of ammunition arrived. Anything is possible; nothing is certain. Theories abound.

Such a thrust toward the camp was probably undertaken with Yates in command of E and F companies since it seems likely that Custer initially stayed with Keogh's command. While Yates was making his foray to the river, the right wing moved up the north slope of the coulee to what has since been named Nye-Cartwright Ridge, where they probably countered Gall's charge with heavy gunfire. They then shifted further north, where Lieutenant Calhoun's L Company took up position on what is now called Calhoun Hill and 2nd Lieutenant Harry Herrington's C Company (Tom Custer, its usual commander, was Custer's aide-de-camp at the time) appears to have formed a skirmish line. Keogh's own I Company may have been held back in reserve or it may have assumed a defensive position beyond L Company. Custer probably joined Yates' wing shortly after it reached the high ground and moved with it further north along the ridge. Some people theorize that Custer left F Company near what came to be known as Last Stand Hill and rode with E Company to the present-day National Cemetery. Warriors later reported seeing mounted soldiers in that area and some say they remained there for about twenty minutes. If that was the case, why? Was Custer waiting for reinforcements that would never arrive?

Most of the Indians fired at the troopers from a distance, concealing themselves in the many dips and gullies that punctuated the rugged terrain or behind sagebrush. They fought with bows and arrows, knives and clubs, their bare hands, and a wide variety of firearms, some of which they had captured during the Rosebud fight or earlier that afternoon in the Reno fight. The situation rapidly deteriorated for the soldiers. Even as Lakota and Cheyenne gunfire and arrows steadily picked away at them, Lame White Man (Northern Cheyenne) slammed into C Company at the head of a strong contingent of warriors. They inflicted heavy casualties and stampeded the cavalry horses, which still carried the spare ammunition. Lame White Man was killed by "friendly fire" during that maneuver. C Company survivors probably fell back to join L Company, which had also suffered badly in the charge. Meanwhile, hundreds of other warriors had followed Crazy Horse in a wide sweep around to the north. They now smashed through Keogh's wing from the rear. Many more soldiers fell dead or wounded. The few that survived withdrew to the low knoll where Custer was reassembling his command.

Two Moon (Northern Cheyenne) later described the final fighting to Hamlin Garland through an interpreter (see Documents). He said,

> the Sioux rode up the ridge on all sides, riding very fast. The Cheyennes went up the left way. Then the shooting was quick. Pop—pop—pop very fast. Some of the soldiers were down on their knees, some standing. Officers all in front. The smoke was like a great cloud, and everywhere the Sioux went the dust rose like smoke. We circled all around them—swirling like water round a stone. We shoot, we ride fast, we shoot again. Soldiers drop, and horses fall on them.[15]

As more and more warriors joined the fight and the "suicide boys" charged in, the situation became increasingly desperate for the tattered remnants of Custer's battalion. The soldiers killed their horses for breast-works and fought as best they could. At some point, a group of soldiers from E Company made a dash for Deep Ravine, where at least twenty-eight of them died. Maybe they were making a bid to escape or perhaps it was a failed charge aimed at driving the warriors back. Regardless of their objective, they all perished in a brief struggle that probably included close hand-to-hand combat. Hundreds of warriors were now converging on the remaining soldiers from all sides. Soon the fighting was over as the last of the 210 men under Custer's immediate command fell dead, forty or so of them clustered together on Last Stand Hill. The three Custer brothers and their nephew Autie died together there, along with Captain Yates, Adjutant Cooke, Lieutenant Algernon E. Smith and Lieutenant William Van W. Reily. Keogh and Calhoun fell with their men further south along the ridge. The bodies of three other officers and several enlisted men were never found.

This was the last stand of film and fiction. But archaeologist Richard Fox takes issue with the popular representation of the battle.[16] The archaeological evidence suggests two things to him. First, that the final fighting occurred at the top of Deep Ravine rather than on Last Stand Hill. And, second, that there was no last stand. By that point in the fighting, he argues, command structure had disintegrated and the battalion was in complete disarray. What most observers see as a tight group of courageous soldiers making a desperate and unified fight for their lives, Fox interprets as "bunching," a clear indication that command structure and battlefield discipline had collapsed. Despite his ability to marshal persuasive evidence from battlefield archaeology and Native testimony and to subject it to painstaking analysis derived from his own considerable knowledge of military strategy and tactics and combat psychology, Fox's analysis remains controversial, at least in certain quarters.

Regardless of whether they were making a "last stand" or not, as Custer and his men were fighting for their lives on the Little Bighorn, Libbie Custer and several other officer's wives were gathered in the sitting room of the Custer home at Fort Lincoln. Libbie describes the moment in *Boots and Saddles*:[17]

> We tried to find some slight surcease from trouble in the old hymns . . . I remember the grief with which one fair young wife threw herself on the carpet and pillowed her head in the lap of a tender friend. Another sat dejected at the piano, and struck soft chords that melted into the notes of the voices. All were absorbed in the same thoughts, and their eyes were filled with far-away visions and longings. Indescribable yearning for the absent, and untold terror for their safety, engrossed each heart. The words of the hymn, "E'en though a cross it be. Nearer, my God, to Thee," came forth with almost a sob from every throat. At that very hour the fears that our tortured minds had portrayed in imagination were realities, and the souls of those we thought upon were ascending to meet their Maker.

Throughout the fighting, Lakota and Cheyenne warriors scalped their victims if they had the time and opportunity to do so. After the fighting, their women moved amongst the dead stripping them of their belongings and clothes and, in many instances, mutilating their bodies. Although there was undoubtedly a great deal of anger vented in those actions, mutilation of the enemy dead was a long-standing tradition among many Plains tribes. It was believed to incapacitate them in the afterlife so they could pose no further threat. Some of the soldiers were mutilated beyond recognition. Tom Custer, for example, was identifiable only by the T.W.C. tattooed on his arm. Custer himself was neither scalped nor mutilated. The only marks on his body were from two bullet wounds, either of which could have been fatal. One was in his left temple and the other in his left side just below the heart.

Over the years, people have proposed various theories to account for why Custer's body wasn't mutilated. Some assume that the Indians did not scalp him because his hairline was receding and his hair cut short. Others suggest that the warriors recognized him as a great and courageous leader and left his body untouched out of respect. Early rumors that he had committed suicide, which were quickly discounted, led to another explanation: the Lakota do not scalp suicides. The most enduring explanation, although not necessarily the true one, involves two Southern Cheyenne women, who later recounted the incident to Kate Bighead. Apparently they came upon Custer's body on the battlefield and recognized him. Some Lakota men approached to cut his fingers off but the women stopped them. "The Cheyenne women, thinking of Me-o-tzi (i.e. Monasetah), made signs, 'He is a relative of ours,' but telling nothing more about him . . . The women then pushed the point of a sewing awl into each of his ears, into his head." "This was done," the women told Bighead, "to improve his hearing, as it seemed that he had not heard what our chiefs in the South said when he smoked the pipe with them. They told him then that if ever afterward he should break that peace promise and should fight the Cheyennes the Everywhere Spirit surely would cause him to be killed."[18]

There were many women at the Little Bighorn who did not run to safety with their children at the first sign of soldiers or simply mutilate and rob the dead after the fighting was over. Some followed the Lakota and Cheyenne warriors onto the battlefield and stood nearby singing brave heart songs to encourage their husbands, brothers, sons, nephews, uncles, and sweethearts. Kate Bighead (Northern Cheyenne) was one of them. She told Thomas B. Marquis about another Northern Cheyenne woman, Calf Tail Woman, who stuck close to her husband, Black Coyote, during the fight.[19] Calf Tail Woman had a pistol and ammunition. From time to time she would ride toward the soldiers and shoot at them. A week earlier she had ridden with the Cheyenne warriors to the Rosebud, where she fought Crook's soldiers. She was a very brave woman.

> A Hunkpapa Lakota woman named Moving Robe Woman (also known as Mary Crawler or She Walks With Her Shawl) fought in both the Reno and Custer fights at the Greasy Grass to avenge the killing of her brother, Deeds, by cavalrymen earlier that day.

HILLTOP SIEGE

While Lakota and Cheyenne warriors were closing in on Custer's battalion, Benteen was growing increasingly frustrated with his orders. After cresting several ridges, he abandoned his fruitless scout, or what later scholars described as his "left oblique," and turned back to rejoin the regiment. He intersected its trail just ahead of the pack train. Fifteen minutes later he stopped at a morass to water his horses and then moved on, passing through the abandoned campsite with its still burning lone tipi. A mile or so later Sergeant Kanipe galloped up. Before continuing on to the pack train, he repeated to Benteen Custer's message. A few minutes after that trumpeter Martin arrived with the note from Cooke. Now fully aware of the gravity of the situation, Benteen ordered his battalion into a trot. As he approached the Little Bighorn, he could see the last of Reno's men scrambling up the bluffs. He joined them on the hilltop, where an overwhelmed and rattled Reno begged him to halt his command and help because he had lost half his men. Despite Custer's orders, Benteen did just that (see Reno's and Benteen's official reports in Documents).

No one knew where Custer was but Lieutenant Winfield Edgerly later reported that when he first arrived on the hilltop with Benteen's command he "heard heavy firing and it continued for fifteen or twenty minutes. Then the heavy firing was all over."[20] That matches Two Moon's estimate that the final fighting lasted "about as long as it takes a hungry man to eat his dinner." When neither Reno or Benteen started toward the sound of the guns, as dictated by cavalry custom, Captain Thomas B. Weir, a Custer loyalist, took matters into his own hands. As he headed northward, Lieutenant Edgerly, his second in command, assuming he had received permission to move out, mustered D Company and followed. Other companies straggled along behind in confused disarray. A mile or so along the bluff tops Weir came to the high hill that now bears his name. He climbed it to get a better vantage point. He could see the valley filled with tipis but a cloud of dust obscured his view north along the ridge. Edgerly, it seems, was able to see a bit more. He later said they "could see quite a number of Indians galloping back and forth on the battlefield, where we afterwards found the bodies, and firing at objects on the ground, but we could not see what the objects were."[21] Regardless of what the detachment could or could not see from Weir Point, warriors soon converged on the hill from the north, forcing the troopers back to their original position, where Reno had remained with the wounded. Recognizing that the troops were very vulnerable, Godfrey stepped into the breach and dismounted his K Company into a skirmish line to cover the chaotic retreat.

Throughout the afternoon and into the evening, the Indians continually fired into the soldiers, making it impossible for them to dig in or fortify their positions. Some of the Lakota and Cheyenne proved uncomfortably good shots. Desperate troopers flattened themselves behind whatever mound of dirt or shred of cover they could find. Company by company, 350 or so men formed an outward-facing circle around a shallow hollow in which their last remaining doctor, Dr. Henry R. Porter, cared for the wounded as best he could in a makeshift field hospital. At nightfall the incoming fire eased. By then the warriors had killed or wounded eleven more soldiers. A few warriors remained through the night but most returned to their camp circles to take part in rituals and to mourn their dead. All night long, campfires blazed in the valley below. Those soldiers still fit to do so took advantage of the lull. Using anything they could find to dig with, they frantically scraped shallow trenches in the hard ground and arranged the dead horses and mules, saddles, and ammunition and ration boxes into breastworks.

At first light Trumpeter Martin sounded reveille. The Indians replied with a single rifle shot and then bullets and arrows rained down on the cavalrymen once more. Another day of fighting had begun and still no one had any inkling of Custer's whereabouts. Some of the men were beginning to suspect that he had withdrawn from the field, leaving them to their fates as he had done to Major Elliott's detachment at the Washita. A few reckoned that Lakota and Cheyenne warriors had him pinned down further along the valley. Others speculated that he had met up with Gibbon's forces and would soon return to relieve them. All morning the warriors maintained a steady fire and the soldiers took aim at any target they could see. Benteen strode around the circle urging the troops on, seemingly oblivious to the danger he faced. Once, seeing a group of warriors organizing to storm the defenses, he mustered his men for a charge, which succeeded in scattering the Indians. At another point he pressured a reluctant Reno into launching a general counter-attack, which again pushed the warriors back.

It was a sweltering hot day. As the sun rose higher in the sky the temperatures crept well into the nineties. With no shade to be had, the men, and especially the wounded, grew unbearably thirsty. Dr. Porter demanded water for his patients. Covered by four sharpshooters, a group of volunteers crept down the slope with whatever containers they could carry and managed to return with enough water to give the wounded some relief. Nineteen of the twenty-six Medals of Honor awarded for the Little Bighorn battle went to men in Reno's and Benteen's battalions, including fourteen to the water carriers and four to the sharpshooters who had risked their lives for their wounded comrades.

Mid-afternoon the villagers set fire to the dry valley grasses. In late afternoon the warriors began to mysteriously drift away. At about 7:00 p.m. a long procession of people, horses, dogs, and travois streamed out of the smoke and slowly moved across the bench toward the Big Horn Mountains. The few warriors that remained behind periodically fired into the circle of soldiers but even they slipped away after dark.

AFTERMATH

Throughout the long night of June 26 three questions must have weighed on the mind of every one left alive: Where is Custer? Why did the warriors abandon their siege and the village move off? And, will they return at dawn? Under cover of darkness the soldiers quenched their thirst, shifted closer to the river, and buried their dead. Those who had been stranded in the timber cautiously ventured out of the brush and crept up the bluffs, relieved to finally rejoin their comrades.

Morning dawned without hostile fire yet no one dared let down their guard. At about 9:30 a.m. a distant cloud of dust alerted the survivors to approaching horsemen. According to Lieutenant Godfrey, "assembly was sounded, the horses were placed in a protected situation, and camp kettles and canteens were filled with water."[22] Nervously, they watched a long column slowly wind its way up the valley. It appeared to be soldiers. Was it Custer? Was it Terry? Was it Crook? Or were the Lakota and Cheyenne returning? Accounts differ slightly regarding the sequence of events thereafter. According to Godfrey, a "white scout, Muggins Taylor, came up with a note from General Terry, addressed to General Custer, dated June 26, stating that two of our Crow scouts had given information that our column had been whipped and nearly all had been killed; that he did not believe their story, but was coming with medical assistance." A short while later Bradley arrived. The first question asked of him was: "Where is Custer?" "I don't know," he replied, "but I suppose he was killed, as we have counted 197 bodies. I don't suppose any escaped."[23] The survivors were stunned. Soon Terry arrived and repeated the news.

After Custer's command departed the Yellowstone on June 22, Gibbon's Montana column, accompanied by General Terry, backtracked to the mouth of the Big Horn, where the *Far West* ferried it across to the south bank of the Yellowstone. From there it made its way south across the rugged terrain east of the Big Horn River. The number of lodges the scouts counted in the abandoned campsites they passed through led Bradley, Gibbon's chief of scouts, to surmise that there were an awful lot of Lakotas ahead. "Should we come to blows," he wrote in his journal on June 23 "it will be one of the biggest Indian battles ever fought on this continent." The next night, while Custer was leading his regiment on its night march up Davis Creek to the divide, Gibbon and Terry were camped on Tullock's Creek. On June 24, while Custer's troops battled for their lives, Gibbon's column trudged up and over the divide into the Bighorn valley. Still well above the mouth of the Little Bighorn, they were a hard two-day march from Custer's position. On June 26 Gibbon's Crow scouts saw smoke rising in the distance. That seemed to confirm

Terry's suspicion that the Lakota and Cheyenne would be found on the Little Bighorn. Pushing ahead to get into position to block their escape, the column got bogged down in heavy rain. At about midnight the miserable and exhausted soldiers bivouacked on the banks of the Big Horn, which was still swollen with spring runoff from the mountains.

At daybreak Bradley and his Crows left camp to scout ahead. Later in the morning they spotted men on the opposite bank of the river. They were some of Custer's Crow scouts. After a bank-to-bank exchange between the two groups of Crows, Bradley's scouts returned visibly upset and with unsettling news. White Man Runs Him had just informed them that the Lakota and Cheyenne had completely wiped out Custer's command. Bradley rode back to the column with the news. After mulling it over for a moment or two, Terry and Gibbon both dismissed the Crows' report as exaggerated if not altogether bogus. They were willing to concede that there may have been a battle, and even that it might have gone badly for the 7th Cavalry, but they could not accept that everyone in Custer's command was dead. Nonetheless, Terry and Gibbon led their column up the valley with added haste. By afternoon they were seeing signs of Indians everywhere and soon small groups of warriors appeared to their front, on the opposite bank, and on the bluffs above them. That night the column rested uneasily on the west bank of the Little Bighorn just a few miles downstream from Custer's battlefield.

The next morning, with scouts fanned out ahead and skirmishers at the ready, the Montana column continued up the valley. Bradley was the first to discover Custer's fate. A dead horse caught his men's attention while they were scouting the bluffs on the east side of the river. When they went to investigate, they got gruesome confirmation of the previous day's news. While not entirely unexpected, they could hardly have been prepared for the scene that awaited them. Meanwhile, in the valley below, Terry and Gibbon had entered a very large and only recently abandoned campsite. Some tipis were still standing and in them they found dead warriors and, more worryingly, bloody cavalry uniforms. Shortly thereafter Bradley rode south in search of survivors, which he found.

On the morning of June 28, those 7th Cavalry survivors who were able to do so rode north to bury their comrades. Upon arrival they were confronted with a "scene of sickening ghastly horror," to borrow Godfrey's words. Godfrey described the scene as well as anyone.[24]

> The early morning was bright, and from the high bluffs we had a
> clear view of Custer's battlefield. We saw a large number of
> objects that looked like white boulders scattered over the field.
> Glasses were brought into requisition, and it was announced that

these objects were the dead bodies. Captain Weir exclaimed:
'Oh, how white they look!'

Nearly all of the dead had been stripped and scalped and a great many were mutilated. About forty bodies were found clustered together on Last Stand Hill, including those of the three Custer brothers, their nephew, and several other officers. Some of them remained largely untouched, except for their wounds; others were mutilated beyond recognition. Godfrey later recalled that Custer's "face and expression were natural; he had been shot in the temple and in the left side . . . *There were no powder marks or signs of mutilation*" (emphasis his).[25] Fred Gerard, who had seen Custer's body before anyone moved it, described its original position to Godfrey. He said he had

> found the naked bodies of two soldiers, one across the other and Custer's naked body in a sitting position between and leaning against them, his upper arm along and on the topmost body, his right forearm and hand supporting his head in an inclining posture like one resting or asleep.

Some soldiers' bodies were never found but it nonetheless appeared that Custer's entire command had been wiped out, 210 men in all. Among them was Mark Kellogg, the *New York Herald* reporter who had been sending regular reports to the *Bismarck Tribune* ever since the Dakota column left Fort Lincoln in May. Words from his final dispatch dated June 21 proved eerily prophetic: "We leave the Rosebud tomorrow and by the time this reaches you we will have met the red devils, with what results remain to be seen. I go with Custer and will be at the death." Another fifty-three soldiers and attached personnel were killed and sixty wounded in the Reno's valley fight or during the subsequent siege.

There were wounded to care for and transport back to the *Far West* and inadequate tools with which to dig proper graves but the 7th Cavalry survivors hastily buried their dead as best they could. For most, all they could manage was a shallow grave covered by a thin layer of loose soil and, perhaps, a bit of sage brush to top it off. They took slightly more care with the officers. On their graves they piled stones to keep out the scavengers and added markers to indicate which officer was buried where for future reference. All of the wounded horses were destroyed but one. Although badly injured, Major Keogh's horse, Comanche, was spared and transported back to the steamer with the other wounded. After several months of tender and attentive nursing, he fully recovered but was never again ridden. He spent the last fifteen years of his life as a pampered regiment mascot with free run of Fort Lincoln. On ceremonial occasions soldiers of the 7th Cavalry would saddle Comanche and place cavalry boots in the stirrups facing backwards. Even in death the horse lives on. Now stuffed, Comanche is on display in the Dyche Hall of the Natural History Museum on the University of Kansas campus.

After he had ferried Gibbon's troops across the Yellowstone, Captain Marsh had skillfully eased the *Far West* up the Big Horn River to the mouth of the Little Bighorn. On the morning of June 27 Curley, the youngest of Custer's Crow scouts, appeared on the bank near where it was moored. He was clearly distraught but, with no Crow speakers on board, the crew could not make out why. Eventually someone gave him a pencil and paper. Only after he drew a crude map did the cause of his distress become clear. His map consisted of two circles, a small one surrounded by a bigger one. Between the circles he made many dots while crying "Sioux! Sioux! Sioux!" Inside the smaller circle he made other dots and while crying "Absaroka! Absaroka! Absaroka!" which is how the Crow scouts sometimes referred to the soldiers. When he stood up and mimed getting shot dead, his message became clear. But, like Terry and Gibbon, the crew found it hard to believe. Captain Marsh tried to send him back to Custer with a message but Curley stubbornly refused to go. The next night scouts from Terry arrived and confirmed his story.

While they waited for Gibbon's troops to transport the wounded the fifteen miles downstream from the battlefield, the steamer's crew padded the deck with freshly cut grass. On June 30 Gibbon's troops loaded the fifty-two most seriously injured on board the *Far West*. Just as Marsh was about to cast-off, Terry called for him. Alone together, the very emotional general said to him:

> I wish to ask you that you use all the skill you possess, all the caution you command, to make the journey safely. Captain, you have on board the most precious cargo a boat ever carried. Every soldier here who is suffering with wounds is the victim of a terrible blunder; a sad and terrible blunder.[26]

With the wounded settled on the deck and Comanche in a makeshift stall between the rudders in the stern, Marsh carefully maneuvered the steamer back downstream to the Yellowstone, where he moored again. He waited there three more days to ferry the Montana column and the remnants of the Dakota column across the river. On July 3, the *Far West* finally set steam down the Yellowstone then the Missouri to Bismarck. Captain Marsh accomplished the 710-mile journey in fifty-four hours, a record time that has yet to be broken. Draped in black mourning cloth, flying her colors at half-mast, and with her whistle blaring, the steamer docked in Bismarck just before midnight on July 5.

As the crew moved through town with the news, Captain Marsh and Dr. Porter woke telegraph operator J.M. Carnahan and *Bismarck Tribune* editor Clement Lounsberry and accompanied them to the telegraph office. Once there Carnahan and Lounsberry set to work sorting through the suitcase of documents already generated on the battle. When the telegraph line became available in the morning, Carnahan sat down at the telegraph key. The first message he sent simply read: "Bismarck, D.T., July 5, 1876:–General Custer attacked the Indians June 25, and he, with every officer and man in five companies, were killed." He remained at the key until the end of the day. In all, he transmitted more than forty thousand words, including bits of the New Testament to keep the lines open while he waited for more battle-related copy. Lounsberry and his people cranked out a *Tribune Extra*, which they published on July 6. Not the first account of the battle to make it into print, it was the most detailed to date and the first to list the dead and wounded. Like all the others it was sensationalist.

The *Far West* weighed anchor and headed downstream to Fort Lincoln with its cargo of wounded three hours after it arrived in Bismarck. After depositing the wound in the post hospital, acting commander Captain William S. McCaskey gathered the post officers and enlisted their help in breaking the news to the widows and orphans. Accompanied by Lieutenant C.L. Gurley, Captain McCaskey began at 7:00 a.m. with Libbie Custer. Emma Reed, Autie Reed's sister, and Maggie Calhoun (Margaret Custer), Lieutenant Calhoun's wife, joined her in the parlor of the Custer's Fort Lincoln home. Gurley later described that heart-wrenching morning. It was one of the worst in his life. "Imagine the grief of these stricken women; their sobs; their flood of tears; the grief that knew no consolation . . . Men and women moved anxiously, nervously, straining their eyes for the expected messenger, listening as footsteps fell."[27] Nobly rising to the task ahead of her, Libbie took control of her emotions and accompanied the officers as they went from door to door breaking the news to twenty-six other new widows. "From that time the life went out of the hearts of the 'women who weep,' and God asked them to walk alone and in the shadow."[28] Only Mrs. Myles Moylan and Mrs. Edward Godfrey escaped the dreaded knock.

About noon on September 26 the battered remnants of the 7th Cavalry finally rode back into Fort Lincoln. No music or fanfare greeted them and they saw few familiar faces in the solemn crowd that met them. The widows and orphans had already left the fort and the windows and doors of the nearly vacant officers' quarters were painted black in mourning.

CHAPTER 3

Aftermath

LAKOTA AND CHEYENNE DISPERSE

Kate Bighead recalled that after the fighting ended, some of the Lakota and Cheyenne women rode up to the battlefield with travois to retrieve their dead and wounded loved ones. Others vented their grief and anger by wandering among the dead soldiers beating and slashing their corpses. As soon as the dead were brought into the camp, women in all the circles began taking down their tipis. By custom, the Lakota and Cheyenne moved their camp whenever a death occurred in it but this time they did not go far. The village just shifted back from the river and a bit downstream. The close proximity of the two locations may have given the impression that the village was even bigger than it was and thus contributed to the tendency for early reports to exaggerate its size. (Another possibility is that the inflation of enemy numbers made the catastrophe more palatable and comprehensible to the American public and thus served political ends.) Still unsure of what was to come, most of the women kept their tipi poles and hide covers packed so they could move quickly, if necessary. Some fashioned simple dome shelters out of willow branches for the night but most families slept out under the stars. Sheltered or not, few people got much sleep.

During the battle, throughout the night that followed, and into the next day, the women remained on high alert. At first they kept a close watch on the hills so they could flee if their warriors suffered defeat. Then they scanned the valley in both directions for more soldiers to appear. After their warriors had been away fighting for a long time, Bighead reports that women saw riders approaching.[1] As they drew near, the women could see that they wore blue soldier uniforms and rode big cavalry horses. "It appeared the Indian Warriors had all been killed," she said, "and these men were soldiers coming to kill the families. Women shrieked, some of them fainted. Mothers and children ran away into hiding." It was with great relief that they soon discovered the riders were their own warriors, wearing uniforms and riding horses taken from the dead soldiers. Black Elk (Oglala) recounts a similar incident, which he witnessed several days later at a camp further up the Greasy Grass.

Almost as soon as the fighting stopped, the Lakota and Cheyenne set to work burying their dead. Bighead told Thomas B. Marquis that six Cheyennes and twenty-four Lakotas were killed and another Cheyenne died later from wounds sustained in the battle. These are remarkably close to Wooden Leg's estimates—also recorded by Marquis—but both are probably on the low side.[2] The Cheyenne buried their dead in hillside caves away from the camp. Some Lakotas placed their dead on scaffolds. Others left them in tipis furnished as they would have been for everyday life. That night an outpouring of grief and mourning rituals replaced the joyous celebrations of the previous night. Two Moon recalled that "[w]e had no dance that night. We were very sorrowful . . . There were thirty-nine Sioux and seven Cheyennes killed, and about a hundred wounded."[3] According to Native testimony, some of those wounded eventually died from their injuries.

Late in the afternoon on June 26, the camp criers rode among the tipis announcing that more soldiers were coming. The chiefs, who felt too many warriors had already died, decided that the village should move on. Besides, game was getting scarce and the ponies had stripped the grazing land. By sunset the Lakota and Cheyenne were headed up the valley. They traveled through the night and into the next day. That night they camped near the mouth of a dry creek and celebrated their victory with a great feast. The next day they continued up the Greasy Grass valley to a stream at the base of the Bighorn Mountains. After that they crossed into the Rosebud valley and eventually moved east to the Tongue and then Powder rivers. They traveled fast. Although they spent only a single night at each campsite, they retained their original camp circle organization until the different tribes and bands went their separate ways at the Powder River in the Moon of Black Cherries (August). To thwart any pursuit, the Cheyenne and Lakota set fire to the vegetation behind them, thus destroying the grasses the soldiers would need to sustain their horses.

According to Kate Bighead, after the village split up the Cheyenne moved to the mouth of the Powder River, where they found a large cache of white people's food. For the rest of the summer their men hunted while the women tanned skins and prepared for winter. Black Elk reports that after the split, small groups of Lakotas quietly slipped back to their reservations, as some had been doing all along, while the main body continued eastward. In the Moon of the Black Calf (September), Sitting Bull and Gall turned north toward the upper end of the Little Missouri River and Grandmother's Land. Despite their stunning victory over the *wasichus*, it was destined to be the last summer of freedom for the Cheyenne and Lakota roamers and the end of their traditional ways of life.

APPORTIONING BLAME

Official confirmation of Custer's defeat and death did not reach Chicago until July 6. It was immediately forwarded on to General Sherman in Philadelphia. Thereafter the news spread quickly. According to Private William Nugent of A Company, Terry had struggled with the wording of his official report and that, not a need to ferry troops across the Yellowstone, is what had delayed the *Far West*'s departure for Bismarck. Regardless of the truth in that accusation, Terry did submit two reports (see Documents). The first, dated June 27 and intended for public circulation, did not apportion blame. It was followed by a confidential report to General Philip H. Sheridan dated July 2. The second, longer document was highly critical of Custer and outlined how he had breached Terry's orders. Circumstances conspired against Terry. The official report was delayed in a Bozeman telegraph office and arrived after receipt of the confidential report, which by then had fallen into the hands of a journalist and become public. From there it was a short and easy step to scapegoating Custer.

From the very moment the news broke, the press, the public, politicians, and the military establishment demanded: "How could this have happened?" It is a question people still ask. Robert M. Utley, former chief historian for the National Park Service and long-time student of the battle, offered one answer to that question in the official handbook he wrote for the Little Bighorn Battlefield National Monument.[4] "The Army lost because the Indians won. They were strong, united, well led, well armed, confident, and outraged by the Government's war aims. Rarely had the Army encountered such a powerful combination in an Indian adversary." The only problem with that answer, as Utley himself admits, is that it leaves no room for scapegoats. And scapegoats were exactly what the situation called for. Custer, Reno, Benteen, Terry, Crook, and Gibbon have each taken a turn or two in that role and neither Grant nor the Indian Bureau managed to escape criticism.

General Terry blamed Custer from the outset. His private July 2 communication to General Sheridan, which inadvertently went public, contained most of the criticisms other detractors would level against

Custer. He drove his men too hard day after day and then, on the morning after a particularly difficult night march, hurled them exhausted into battle against an enemy of vastly superior strength. He disobeyed Terry's orders by not examining Tullock's Creek, by not continuing up the Rosebud, and by not waiting until Gibbon was in position before he launched his attack. He acted on impulse with inadequate knowledge of the enemy and especially its location, strength, and disposition. He divided his command, which further weakened the already exhausted regiment and, as some people have noted, he did so not just once but twice. But then in conclusion, and somewhat disingenuously, Terry added,

> I do not tell you this to cast any reflection upon Custer. For whatever errors he may have committed he has paid the penalty and you cannot regret his loss more than I do, but I feel that our plan must have been successful had it been carried out, and I desire you to know the facts.

Frederic F. van de Water agreed with Terry. One of Custer's harshest critics, van de Water branded him a "glory hunter" and with some justification.[5] From the earliest days of the Civil War, the "Boy General" had shown himself adept at catching the eye of the press and skilled at buffing his public image to a high sheen. Many people have speculated that Custer hoped for a "big win" in the Sioux Campaign to redeem himself after the bruising he took in the Belknap affair. Others have argued that he sought a spectacular victory to advance his alleged presidential aspirations. To ensure that Custer got all the credit, according to the logic driving such arguments, his 7th Cavalry not only had to defeat Sitting Bull's warriors, it had to do so unaided. In support of their position, subscribers to such theories cite two pieces of evidence. First, en route back to Fort Lincoln from Washington, Custer had stopped off in St. Paul. While there, he ran into Captain Ludlow, Terry's chief engineer and an acquaintance from previous campaigns. Ludlow reports that Custer admitted to him that he planned to "cut loose" from Terry at the first opportunity. Second, before Custer left camp on the Yellowstone Terry had offered him four companies of the 2nd Cavalry and the three Gatling guns. Custer refused both, stating that the guns would slow him down and his own regiment could handle anything thrown at them. If accepted, those critical resources would have surely tilted the balance in his favor, or so goes the argument.

Other people have ridden to Custer's defense, if only metaphorically and long after the fact. While not an apologist for Custer, Robert M. Utley is one of them. He argues that Custer's legendary luck simply ran out. "Circumstance piled on circumstance to make him their victim."[6] Utley suggests that it was to Custer's misfortune that the Lakota and Cheyenne discovered his command before he was ready. That forced him to attack in the afternoon, when the village was bustling with activity, rather than at dawn when everyone would still be asleep in their robes, as had been his plan and was always his preference. Moreover, circumstances forced him to do battle on unfamiliar terrain and with inadequate knowledge of the location and strength of his foe. Finally, by the time he realized what he was up against, the battalions commanded by Reno and Benteen—about two-thirds of his regiment—were already out of reach.

Reno was (and still is) another popular scapegoat. Even before their relief arrived, some of his men were questioning his leadership. Over the years, a great many people have castigated Reno for not carrying the fight into the village. Others have been less concerned about that but have berated him for withdrawing up the bluffs rather than holding his position on the valley floor or in the timber. They suggest that, had he continued to engage the warriors at the upper end of the village, he would have taken enough pressure off Custer to have enabled him to attack its north end or capture the fleeing women and children. Either action, they argue, would have turned the tide in the soldiers' favor. Regardless of where they stand on the issue of Reno's valley floor performance, many people feel he mishandled the hilltop situation and exhibited cowardice under stress. He has been judged particularly harshly for preventing Benteen from continuing on to Custer, for not riding to the sound of the guns himself, and for what some perceive as his lack of leadership under fire. Reno has also frequently been accused of being indecisive, easily rattled, and even drunk.

Probably the most vociferous of Reno's early detractors was Frederick Whittaker, who recited most of these criticisms in his efforts to persuade the War Department to take action against Reno and, to a far lesser extent, Benteen. Failing to win over the War Department, Whittaker submitted a letter to Congress in which he reiterated his criticisms and requested an official investigation into Reno's conduct. He simultaneously forwarded copies of the letter to leading newspapers. Congress declined to act but the papers published Whittaker's letter on June 13, 1878.[7] Stung by this latest assault on his reputation, Reno appealed to the president for a Court of Inquiry "to investigate the affair, that the many rumors started by camp gossip may be set to rest and the truth may be fully known."[8]

Duly authorized by the president of the United States, the Reno Court of Inquiry convened at the Palmer House in Chicago on January 13, 1879. Its sole objective was to determine whether or not sufficient evidence existed to warrant court-martial proceedings against Major Reno. Various people, including Whittaker, submitted questions to be addressed by the court. Reporters from the Chicago papers were on hand to record in vivid detail the weeks of testimony taken under oath from twenty-three witnesses, including most of the surviving officers, some enlisted men, and civilians. The steady flow of newspaper copy they generated enabled the public to follow the daily twists and turns of the proceedings, which they did with almost voyeuristic interest. In the end, the tribunal did not call for a court-martial but its findings nonetheless fell short of completely exonerating Reno: "While subordinates in some instances, did more for the safety of the command by brilliant displays of courage than did Major Reno, there was nothing in his conduct which requires animadversion from this Court."[9]

After the tribunal delivered its decision, Reno detractors, among them members of the so-called Custer clique, accused the cavalry witnesses of closing ranks to protect themselves and the honor of the regiment. Some of the witnesses later claimed to have been coerced into tailoring their statements to reflect more positively on the major than they might otherwise have done. Individuals close to the proceedings dismissed

> In 1877, Reno was suspended from rank and pay for two years as a result of allegations of excessive drinking and making unwanted advances toward the wife of a fellow officer. Then in 1880 he faced a court-martial on unrelated charges originating once again in his excessive drinking as well as allegations of window peeping. This time he was convicted of conduct unbecoming an officer and dismissed from service.

the whole thing as a whitewash. Despite such attempts to undermine both the testimony given and the court's findings, military personnel, historians, and Custer buffs have found the hearing transcripts useful in their efforts to piece together exactly what happened on the Little Bighorn. The complete transcript and many of the exhibits presented in the case were finally published in 1933, having been meticulously transcribed under the direction of Colonel William A. Graham, the Military Affairs Sections Chief of the Judge Advocate General's Office. The resulting volume has since been digitized and is readily available online.

Accusations of incompetence bordering on criminal dogged Reno for the rest of his life and even beyond the grave. Decades later planning for the semi-centennial commemoration of the battle aroused renewed interest in the site of the Reno-Benteen siege, which was then still in private hands. After the National Custer Memorial Committee decided a commemorative marker at the site was long overdue, Godfrey, Mrs. Custer, and other Reno critics launched a strong campaign against any mention of Reno on the marker. When the memorial was finally erected in 1929, it listed the companies that had occupied the site but did not mention either Reno or Benteen.

Benteen, in turn, has been raked over the coals for dragging his feet on the backtrail and for not continuing on from Reno's position to Custer as ordered. His critics tend to ignore the fact that Reno was the ranking officer at the time and Benteen was thus required to comply with any orders he issued. Instead, they suggest that a vindictive Benteen was happy to comply with Reno's demands because he still harbored a grudge against Custer for abandoning Major Elliott's detachment during the Washita fight. There has also been speculation that he was seething with resentment over his "fool's mission" to the south, which he perceived as a snub by Custer. Countering such criticisms, many of the siege survivors commended Benteen for his cool head, leadership, and bravery during their ordeal.

Gibbon and Crook have come under fire for not sharing intelligence in a timely fashion and Terry for not making constructive use of the intelligence he received. Once again, Utley has weighed in on the side of the officers. He reminds his readers that hindsight brings things into much sharper focus than foresight. It is impossible to know the specific circumstances under which the officers made their decisions. Consequently, any decisions they made in the field should only be judged on the basis of what they knew at the time and not what we know now. Moreover, he argues, "to load so much blame on the military officers is to do disservice to the Indians. They fought well that day. Perhaps no strategy or tactics could have prevailed against Sitting Bull's powerful medicine."[10]

The Indian Bureau and President Grant—and in particular Grant's Peace (or Quaker) Policy—also took flak. An editorial published in the *New York Herald* on July 7, 1876 suggested that "It would hardly be too severe to say to President Grant, 'Behold your hands! They are red with the blood of Custer and his brave three hundred.'" A July 15 headline in the same paper demanded to know "Who Slew Custer?" Expressing sentiments rapidly growing among the general public, it claimed that the "celebrated Peace Policy of General Grant, which feeds, clothes and takes care of the noncombatant force while the men are killing our troops— that is what killed Custer." In a thinly veiled reference to the recent Belknap scandal, it also alleged that "That nest of thieves the Indian Bureau, with its thieving agents and favorites as Indian traders, and its mock humanity and pretense of piety—that is what killed Custer." In time, the army would place at least part of the blame for the debacle on inadequate and even inaccurate intelligence provided by crooked Indian agents who stood to profit from underestimating the spring exodus from their reservations and overestimating the number of people under their jurisdiction. More immediately the army took steps to prevent a similar exodus recurring in the future should hostilities erupt again.

RETALIATION AND SURRENDER

It did not take long for the army to begin exacting its revenge on the Lakota and Cheyenne roamers only its first victims had been nowhere near the Greasy Grass/Little Bighorn at the time of the battle nor, for that matter, had the soldiers who attacked them. Nonetheless, that initial clash, and it was really nothing more than that, would become the iconic fight of the post-Bighorn period, mainly owing to the showmanship of William Frederick "Buffalo Bill" Cody. As the momentum built in the Sioux Campaign of 1876, Cody had temporarily abandoned his stage career in the East to take part in the real life drama unfolding out on the Plains. A seasoned army scout and former buffalo hunter, he eventually signed on as chief of scouts for Colonel Wesley Merritt, commander of the 5th Cavalry. On July 14, Merritt got word that Dull Knife and about eight hundred other Cheyennes had left the Red Cloud Agency and were presumably headed west to join Sitting Bull and Crazy Horse. Merritt's command, already en route to Fort Laramie for supplies before continuing on to join Crook, intercepted them on July 17 at Warbonnet Creek, Nebraska. Cody and a small advance party exchanged gunfire with the Cheyenne wolves. The rest of the regiment soon caught up and joined in. During the exchange, the scout and a warrior named Yellow Hair faced off and simultaneously fired at one another. Yellow Hair missed; Cody did not. Seizing the moment, Buffalo Bill dramatically scalped the warrior. Then, brandishing Yellow Hair's bloody scalp and feathered warbonnet above his head, he declared it "the first scalp for Custer!"

Come fall Buffalo Bill recreated that feat nightly as part of a new show written for him by the popular novelist and playwright Prentiss Ingraham. *The Red Right Hand; Or Buffalo Bill's First Scalp for Custer* was an action-packed spectacle that thrilled audiences with dramatized scenes from the Sioux War. Theater critics were less impressed. What in reality was a long-distance exchange of gunfire had on stage become a manly duel between the hero of the show, Buffalo Bill, and his savage adversary, Yellow Hair. And it was thus that a western legend was born.

The Lakota and Cheyenne who had remained on their reservations all summer also suffered consequences. Within weeks of the Custer fight General Sheridan ordered them disarmed and unmounted. The General of the Army justified that move in the Secretary of War's report to Congress for 1876.[11]

> Deprived of their arms and their ponies it is reasonable to expect
> that on the next outbreak of hostilities the young warriors about
> the agencies will not at once start off to join the hostilities, and
> that the anomaly will not again be presented of the Government
> forces being met in summer by hostile Indians sheltered and
> cared for at Government expense during the previous winter.

The plan had the added advantage that "if the wild Indians can be compelled by lack of ammunition to submit, and can be concentrated on a few reservations and deprived of their instruments of mischief, it looks indeed as if the 'Indian Problem' was [sic] approaching a solution." By confiscating the guns and horses, the army and Indian Bureau may have silenced some of the most vocal critics of Grant's Peace Policy but they had also made it nearly impossible for the reservation Lakota and Cheyenne to supplement their meager rations by hunting. Faced with such harsh treatment and almost certain hunger when they got back to the agencies, some of those who had summered in the unceded territory reversed course and left the reservation again.

News of Custer's defeat and death finally reached General Crook at his base camp on Cloud Creek near the head of the Tongue River on July 10. He was stunned and perhaps more than a bit unnerved by the report and the magnitude of the death toll. Remembering the unprecedented attack those same warriors had launched against his own command little more than a week before Custer met his fate, Crook was reluctant to go after the Lakota and Cheyenne without reinforcements. General Terry likewise found the prospect of meeting them in battle daunting. As soon as he got word of Custer's catastrophic defeat, General Sheridan ordered more troops into the field but it took several weeks for them to get in place. It was early August before the reinforcements arrived and Terry and Crook were ready to get underway again. Terry left the Yellowstone on August 8 with about seventeen hundred infantry and cavalry and thirty-five days of rations and forage. What was now called the Yellowstone column followed Custer's route up the Rosebud, for lack of any better ideas. Terry was clueless as to the whereabouts of his quarry. The last news he had, and it was not recent, suggested they were headed toward the Bighorn Mountains. Reinforced to nearly twenty-three hundred men, Crook managed to get his Wyoming column back in the field a few days ahead of Terry. He started down the Tongue but soon struck the Indian trail and followed it west to Rosebud Creek. Even that trail was cold. The main camp had already moved far to the east and bands were beginning to scatter in all directions. Soon the combined village would split apart altogether. A few agency Indians had even returned to their reservations by then.

Unknowingly, the two columns were marching headlong into one another. When they met unexpectedly on the Tongue River on August 10, Crook and Terry joined forces and followed the month-old Indian trail east. Terry, as the senior officer, assumed overall command of the expedition. The weather was horrible, making for a miserable march. Day after day they slogged through cold rain and mud finding no fresh signs of the Lakota and Cheyenne. Morale slumped and illness and exhaustion took their toll on the troops. Having accomplished nothing, the combined forces hit the Yellowstone at the mouth of the Powder on August 17. Although they did not know it, by then the village they were searching for had split up. Sitting Bull and his Hunkpapas were headed northeast toward the Little Missouri River, Crazy Horse and the Oglalas and Minneconjous were moving south toward the Black Hills, and some of the Cheyennes still lingered along the Powder River.

The coordinated effort was not going at all well. Besides the foul weather and their failure to locate the Lakota and Cheyenne, the two generals disagreed on how best to proceed. Terry feared Sitting Bull was headed north and that he might even cross over the border into Canada. Consequently, he wanted the combined force to continue down the Yellowstone toward the Missouri. Crook thought the Indians might be heading south toward the Spotted Tail and Red Cloud agencies, which were in his Department of the Platte. He was also itching to get back to his own department, which had suffered a lack of military coverage during his prolonged absence campaigning in Terry's department. And, perhaps more than anything, he was simply fed up with being second in command to Terry.

Early in the morning on August 26 Crook marched his troops away from the Yellowstone without bothering to tell Terry he was leaving. Convinced he could catch up with the Lakota and Cheyenne within a few days if he moved quickly, he left his slow-moving supply wagons and Crow and Shoshoni support behind. That proved a grave mistake and the beginning of what came to be known as "Crook's Starvation March." The cold, wet weather continued and after just a couple of days Crook's already miserable men were on half rations. He nonetheless pushed on into the badlands around the Little Missouri River. On September 5 he finally swung south toward the Black Hills, where he knew he could resupply. His exhausted troops struggled on through the rain and mud. Their rations now depleted, they ate the meat from the horses and mules that dropped, as many did. Even that was inadequate. Out of desperation, Crook sent a mule train ahead to Deadwood to buy food on the open market. He assigned Captain Anson Mills and about 150 soldiers to escort it.

Mills, like everyone else, was preoccupied with the immediate problem of survival and no longer thinking about the Lakota and Cheyenne. On September 8 he stumbled upon American Horse's camp of about forty lodges near Slim Buttes. At daybreak his detachment attacked the sleeping Minneconjous. American Horse was fatally wounded and several women and children were killed but many people escaped. Some hid in caves while others made their way to Crazy Horse's nearby camp with word of the attack. Ransacking the tipis, the troops found the Minneconjous' winter stores and at last had food to eat. They also found 7th Cavalry paraphernalia, including a Company I guidon and a pair of gauntlets that had belonged to Captain Myles Keogh. Once again they were not thinking about the Indians.

Unbeknownst to the soldiers, American Horse's village was not alone. Several other Oglala, Sans Arc, Hunkpapa, and Minneconjou camps were scattered along nearby creeks. Later that afternoon Crazy Horse and two hundred warriors counter-attacked. Sitting Bull was among them. Even after Crook came up with the rest of the command, the warriors continued to fire at them from a distance. Throughout the night and into the next morning the warriors harassed the soldiers. With his men starving and exhausted and demoralized himself, Crook was no longer in the mood to fight. Rather than continue to exchange fire with the Indians or give chase he simply resumed his course to the Black Hills. The warriors followed and continued to shoot at the soldiers for a while longer and then moved off. Three days later the Wyoming column met up with a herd of cattle and a wagon train loaded with food. Crook's Starvation March was over and so was the summer campaign of 1876. The only small success to the army's credit was Captain Mills' accidental victory at Slim Buttes.

After Crook decamped, Terry made a few tentative and fruitless probes north and south of the Yellowstone round about the mouth of the Tongue. Failing to locate the Indians or any fresh sign of them, he ordered most of his troops back to their posts in the first week of September. As the 7th Cavalry worked its way east toward Fort Lincoln, it scouted the north bank of the Yellowstone then along the Missouri for sign of the Indians. When it reached Fort Buford, Reno handed command over to Captain Weir then joined his adjutant and the quartermaster on board a steamer headed downstream for Bismarck. The decimated regiment finally rode back into Fort Lincoln on September 26. Gibbon's troops arrived back at Fort Ellis in early October after more than six months in the field.

Not everyone got to return to their posts and some who did were soon back in the field. General Terry left Colonel Nelson A. Miles and the 5th Infantry along with several companies of the 22nd Infantry at a cantonment on the Yellowstone near the mouth of the Tongue. They remained at what was to became Fort Keogh through the winter and patrolled along the Yellowstone to prevent the Indians from escaping to the north. Based on the reputation he had earned campaigning on the central Plains, newspaper editors were already happily comparing the aggressive, ever resourceful, and energetic Miles to Custer and he did not disappoint them. He excelled at the task assigned him. Equipping his troops with winter gear and buffalo coats, and seemingly oblivious to the plunging temperatures and mounting snow drifts, he hounded the Lakotas all winter. By attacking when he could and keeping them constantly on the move the rest of the time, "Bear Coat," as they called him, managed to destroy most of their equipment and food supplies and prevent them from hunting.

During October Miles alternated between fighting Sitting Bull and talking with him. On October 11 and then again four days later, Lakota and Cheyenne warriors from Sitting Bull's camp attacked a supply wagon headed for Miles' cantonment. In each instance the infantry escort warded off the attackers. Afterwards Sitting Bull sent envoys to arrange a meeting with Miles. Miles agreed. The two leaders met at Cedar Creek on October 20, in what was essen-

In 1877, Miles chased and eventually intercepted Chief Joseph and his fleeing band of Nez Percé. In 1886, he replaced Crook in the campaign against Geronimo and the Chiricahuas. After they surrendered, Miles presided over their transfer to Dry Tortugas, Florida. By 1890 he was back on the Northern Plains, where his efforts to subdue a band of Lakota Ghost dancers resulted in the Wounded Knee massacre.

tially a face-off between the Lakota warriors and the infantry. Sitting Bull wanted to trade for ammunition so his men could hunt buffalo. He also promised that his warriors would leave the soldiers alone if the soldiers left them alone. Miles would have none of it. He merely repeated the government's demand that Sitting Bull and his people report to the agencies. With no agreement reached, the two leaders arranged to meet again the next day and returned to their respective camps.

Back in camp Sitting Bull discussed the matter with his followers. Some wanted to return to the reservations; others did not. Notwithstanding the mix of opinions they expressed, Sitting Bull remained intransigent on the issue: his people would not capitulate and report to the agencies. When he met with Miles again, he told the commander to take his soldiers and leave and to see to it that no more wagon trains passed through Lakota territory. Losing patience, Miles ordered the Lakotas to surrender immediately or be attacked. The talks broke down and the two sides exchanged gunfire.

The ensuing Battle of Cedar Creek was less of a battle than a relatively minor clash leading to a running fight. Over the next two days Miles' troops chased the Lakotas more than forty miles. During the pursuit, the village split up. Sitting Bull and the Hunkpapas turned north while White Bull's Minneconjous and the Sans Arcs continued toward the Yellowstone. All along the way the fleeing families lost or discarded tipi poles, dried meat, lame and exhausted ponies, and other possessions, things that may have slowed them down but which they desperately needed to survive the harsh Plains winter. Just a few days after the guns fell silent, about four hundred lodges of Minneconjous and Sans Arcs (an estimated two thousand people) surrendered to Miles and agreed to return to the reservations peacefully. To ensure that they did so without a military escort, Miles took a handful of hostages and sent the rest on their way to the Cheyenne River Agency in Dakota Territory. The first Sans Arcs and Minneconjous arrived at the agency on November 30. Meanwhile Sitting Bull's people continued north and in late November the first few bands crossed the border into Grandmother's Land. By late December over a hundred Lakota families were camped near a trading post in the Wood Mountains of what is now southern Saskatchewan.

Miles still did not rest. In early January he clashed with Lakota and Cheyenne followers of Crazy Horse and Two Moon, forcing them to abandon their combined winter camp and flee. His troops caught up with them again at Wolf Mountain on January 8 and this time engaged them in a more serious battle. Although the infantry considerably outnumbered the warriors and used artillery, the outcome could hardly be credited to the army as a victory. Nonetheless, the encounter accomplished two strategically useful things for the army. First, it resulted in the destruction of a significant proportion of the Indians' winter supplies and food stores. And, second, it served notice that not even in the dead of winter would they be safe from attack.

Miles was not the only commander in field. Crook soon resupplied and regrouped. In mid-November he headed north from Fort Fetterman toward the Powder River country with more than two thousand men. Oglalas from the Red Cloud Agency, who now served as his scouts, located a Cheyenne camp on the Red Fork of the Powder River near the base of the Bighorn Mountains. It was the village of Dull Knife and Little Wolf and it contained two hundred or so lodges. Colonel Ranald S. Mackenzie and eleven hundred soldiers attacked it at dawn on November 25, driving the Cheyenne out of their beds and out of the village. Thirty Cheyennes were killed and another twenty-six wounded but even more damaging was the loss of all their possessions: food, tipis, warm clothes, ponies, weapons, household implements. The attack left them destitute and on foot. After three weeks of trudging through the deep snow and temperatures so cold that babies froze to death in their mothers' arms, the refugees found Crazy Horse's village on the upper Tongue. Although critically short on supplies themselves, the Oglalas took them in and shared with them what little they had.

Between Crook and Miles, the off-reservation Lakota and Cheyenne were kept on the run all winter, losing many of their possessions and most of their food stores along the way. By the spring of 1877 bands of Lakotas and Cheyennes were trickling into the agencies to surrender. Among them was Dull Knife's band, which surrendered at Fort Robinson, Nebraska. On April 22, Two Moon (Cheyenne) and Hump (Minneconjou) and three hundred of their starving and demoralized followers surrendered to Colonel Miles. Then on May 6, Crazy Horse led more than eleven hundred Oglalas and other Lakotas into Fort Robinson to surrender. Lame Deer and Iron Shirt were not among them. The pair and three hundred or so of their Minneconjou followers had decided to hunt buffalo instead. The next day Miles attacked their camp, killing Lame Deer and at least thirteen other warriors. Some Minneconjous escaped into the hills but most put down their weapons and surrendered. Those who escaped soon had a change of heart and rejoined the others on the reservation. With that, nearly all of the Cheyennes and Lakotas had been returned to the reservations except Sitting Bull and his followers. On the very day that Miles attacked Lame Deer's camp, Sitting Bull led four hundred or so Hunkpapas across the border to Grandmother's Land.

After relinquishing their guns and horses, Crazy Horse and his followers were granted permission to settle at the Red Cloud Agency in Nebraska. Although his people still respected him and looked to him for guidance and leadership, Crazy Horse opted for a quiet life. He resisted getting drawn into reservation politics and declined invitations to visit Washington. All he wanted was a reservation of their own for his people and to be left alone. Despite his best efforts to keep out of the jockeying for power taking place on the reservation, tribal leaders like Red Cloud and Spotted Tail resented Crazy Horse. Rumors circulated, perhaps deliberately planted by his rivals, that Crazy Horse was about to return to the warpath and was plotting to kill General Crook. Such developments made the white authorities suspicious and very nervous.

Camp Robinson commander Colonel Luther Bradley finally issued orders to have Crazy Horse arrested and sent to Dry Tortugas, the island off Key West, Florida, where many troublesome Indians were imprisoned. On September 3, Red Cloud's men discovered Crazy Horse preparing to move his camp to the Spotted Tail Agency. After they confronted him and Spotted Tail and his men did the same, Crazy Horse agreed to go to

Fort Robinson to discuss his proposed moved with the authorities there. He left for the fort on September 5. Accompanying him were a large number of friends and supporters, a contingent of Spotted Tail's men, and Jesse M. Lee, the acting Indian Agent. Knowing what Crazy Horse did not—that he was about to be arrested—a crowd gathered at Fort Robinson. As soon as he arrived, Crazy Horse was taken into custody and then escorted to the guardhouse. As he stepped inside it must have dawned on him what was happening. He turned, drew a knife from under his clothes, and slashed his way out. In the scuffle that followed, a soldier bayoneted Crazy Horse through the back. Mortally wounded, he was carried not back into the guardhouse but to the post adjutant's office, where he died around midnight. The man who had always refused to have his picture taken and had come to yearn for a quiet life was placed on a burial scaffold by his grieving family.

Further turmoil followed as government plans to close the Red Cloud and Spotted Tail agencies became known. From that fall onward, the Indians who had been living near the Nebraska agencies were to draw their rations at locations on the Missouri River in Dakota Territory. People from the Red Cloud Agency were to be settled on was to become the Pine Ridge Reservation; people from the Spotted Tail Agency were to be settled on what was to become the Rosebud Reservation. The Lakotas did not want to relocate but had no say in the matter. In late October they were escorted north. Before they left Nebraska, Crazy Horse's family removed his body from its scaffold and placed it on a travois. Along the route north they reburied it at an undisclosed location, which to this day remains a secret. As the procession moved toward their new agencies, some of Crazy Horse's followers slipped away with their families and headed for Grandmother's Land. By spring around 240 lodges of the Crazy Horse band, as they came to be known, had joined Sitting Bull in Canada.

BLACK HILLS

In achieving their great victory over the 7th Cavalry and killing Custer and so many of his men, the Lakota and Cheyenne enraged not just the army but the American public, Washington politicians, and lawmakers. Each of those groups focused their wrath on the Lakota and zeroed in most particularly on Sitting Bull and his followers. To politicians and ordinary people alike, Sitting Bull symbolized all that was wrong with federal Indian policy of the day as well as the barrier the Plains Indians posed to the expansive American nation-building project.

Consequently, the threat they perceived was less to American *individuals* than to the *nation* itself.

After the Little Bighorn battle the army may have fielded an unprecedented number of troops to track down the non-treaty Indians and force them on to the reservations, and the Indian agents may have seized the guns and ponies of those Lakotas who had remained on their reservations, but it was Washington lawmakers who, at the urging of politicians, took steps that would forever change the Lakota way of life. Acting partly on their own initiative and partly in response to the clamoring of newspaper editors and the general public, Congress quickly set to work on plans to push the Lakotas down the road to civilization, regardless of whether or not they wanted to go there.

On August 15 Congress passed an appropriations bill that set in motion a two-pronged strategy to subdue, punish, and ultimately civilize the Lakotas. The subdue and punish prong involved coercing them into relinquishing the Black Hills, abandoning the unceded territory, and accepting a greatly diminished reservation. The other prong entailed undermining Lakota tribalism—or the Lakotas' sense of a shared identity— by breaking up the communal land base, eroding their cultural traditions, and eliminating their traditional political and economic structures. Congress and the Indian Bureau, like many politicians and reformers of the day, viewed individual property ownership as the keystone of a civilization program that would eventually result in the complete assimilation of Native Americans into mainstream society. Additional tactics for promoting that agenda included drawing the Indians ever more deeply into the market economy, taking control of their children's education, and encouraging the activities of Christian missionaries while discouraging customary religious practices. None of that was new, of course, but the attention now focused on and anger directed at the Lakota lent added urgency to their "civilization." Moreover, the politicians, Friends of the Indian groups, and general public all believed that the "civilizing mission" was in the best interests of the Lakota and Cheyenne.

Some people call the 1876 Indian Appropriations Act the "sell or starve" bill because it presented the Lakota with only three options: starve on the reservations, be attacked by the army and killed, or acquiesce to a list of government demands that included giving up their sacred *Pahá Sápa*. One must realize, however, that the option of *selling* the region was not actually on the table. Congress did not intend to pay for the land; it planned to take it. On August 24 Commissioner of Indian Affairs J.Q. Smith conveyed the wishes of Congress to former Commissioner of Indian Affairs George W. Manypenny, whom the president had appointed to head a commission charged with securing the Lakota signatures needed to legitimate the plan devised by Congress. Commissioner Smith instructed Manypenny to warn the Lakota that they would no longer receive the food and other goods and services promised to them by the 1868 Fort Laramie Treaty if they did not agree to the new terms and conditions set by Congress.[12] In that only a fraction of the Lakotas had actually engaged in the recent hostilities, those conditions constituted what would now be recognized as a form of collective punishment.

With those conditions, Congress implemented its strategy for subduing and punishing the Lakota. First, the Lakota were to relinquish all claims to the unceded territory. Second, they were to give up all of their lands west of the 103rd meridian, a strip that included *Pahá Sápa* (the Black Hills). Third, they were to grant the government right-of-way to build three roads across their reservation. Fourth, they were to agree to draw their rations anywhere in proximity to the Missouri River that the president deemed appropriate. And, finally, they were to cooperate with government-initiated programs designed to make them self-supporting. The most difficult conditions for the Lakota to accept were the cession of the Black Hills and abandonment of the unceded territory. Although unclear at the time, the language pertaining to drawing rations at locations on the Missouri also laid the groundwork for closing the Red Cloud and Spotted Tail agencies and relocating the Lakotas residing there to agencies further north, something they resented and resisted.

The government's goal of civilizing the Lakota and speeding their assimilation into mainstream society was to be realized largely through the inducements offered to get them to agree to the conditions just listed. During September and October the Manypenny Commission met with Indian leaders at various locations across the Great Sioux Reservation, starting at the Red Cloud Agency. With an already drafted agreement in hand, they made it clear to the Indians that there was no scope for negotiation. Their only choice was to sign it or not to sign it. In his report back to Commissioner of Indian Affairs Smith, Manypenny described how they had proceeded.

> We submitted to the Indians the conditions required by Congress, and stated that we had no authority to change them in any particular. We assured them that Congress and the President had given us full authority to devise a plan to save their people from death and lead them to civilization.

What he failed to mention to the Indians, but what they undoubtedly already knew, was that whichever option they chose—death or civilization —the outcome would be delivered by agents of the American government.

In his report, Manypenny summarized the inducements offered to the Lakota.[13] If they agreed to the conditions set by Congress, the government promised:

1. To provide ample rations for their subsistence until able to support themselves, such rations in all cases to be issued to the head of each separate family.

2. That when said Indians shall be located upon land suitable for cultivation, rations shall be issued only to those persons who labor, the sick, infirm, and aged excepted.

3. That whenever the Government shall establish schools, as provided by the treaty of 1868, no rations shall be issued to children between the ages of six and fourteen years, the sick and infirm excepted, unless said children shall regularly attend school.

4. That whenever any one of the Indians shall in good faith begin to cultivate the soil he shall have a title to his land and receive aid to build a house.

5. That they shall be subject to the laws of the United States, and select as many headmen from each band to maintain order as the President may deem necessary.

6. That all agents, traders, farmers, carpenters, blacksmiths, and other employees of the Government within their reservation shall be lawfully married and living with their families on the reservation.

7. That no person of white or mixed blood, whose fitness morally or otherwise is not, in the opinion of the Commissioner of Indian Affairs, conducive to the welfare of the Indians, shall receive any benefit from this agreement or former treaties, and may be expelled from the reservation.

Most of the promises contained in the agreement were aimed at reducing tribalism, undermining traditional forms of social and political organization, and promoting behaviors conducive to the eventual absorption of the Lakota into mainstream society. Note that rations were to be given directly to heads of families rather than to band or tribal leaders for subsequent redistribution and that individuals were to own and cultivate their own plots of land rather than communally held lands. They were also to be allowed to retain their band structure but the government rather than band members would determine how many leaders they should have. Moreover, the delivery of any goods and services would be contingent upon individual Lakotas actively working toward their eventual incorporation as productive members of the American body politic: only those adults able to work who were working and those children fit to go to school who were in school would benefit from the government largess.

Most of the Lakota leaders refused to sign the agreement. Those who did sign it felt they had no choice. Even the signers understood that by "touching the pen" they were legitimating the invasion of their sacred *Pahá Sápa* that was already an accomplished fact. Manypenny managed to persuade only a tenth of the adult male population to sign. Despite falling far short of the requisite three-quarters prescribed by the 1868 Fort Laramie Treaty, the agreement was considered a done deal and Congress confirmed it on February 28, 1877 (see Documents). In addition to agreeing to the cession of the Black Hills, each man who signed (and, once Congress ratified it, everyone else as well) agreed "to observe each and all of the stipulations therein contained, to select an allotment of land as soon as possible after their removal to their permanent home, and to use their best efforts to learn to cultivate the same." With ratification of the agreement, Congress achieved both of its objectives. The concessions made by the Indians satisfied government demands for the Black Hills and consolidated the tribe on a diminished reservation; the inducements offered promoted civilization of the Lakota.

President Grant used his 1876 State of the Union address to deflect blame for the crisis on the northern Plains from his own failed Peace Policy to unidentified greedy whites. He also used it to refashion the questionable outcome of the Manypenny Commission into a great achievement.

> A policy has been adopted toward the Indian tribes inhabiting a large portion of the territory of the United States which has been humane and has substantially ended Indian hostilities in the whole land except in a portion of Nebraska, and Dakota, Wyoming, and Montana Territories—the Black Hills region and approaches thereto. Hostilities there have grown out of the avarice of the white man, who has violated our treaty stipulations in his search for gold. The question might be asked why the Government has not enforced obedience to the terms of the treaty prohibiting the occupation of the Black Hills region by whites. The answer is simple: the first immigrants to the Black Hills were removed by troops, but rumors of rich discoveries of gold took into that region increased numbers. Gold has actually been found in paying quantity, and an effort to remove the miners would only result in the desertion of the bulk of the troops that might be sent there to remove them. All difficulty in this matter

> has, however, been removed—subject to the approval of
> Congress—by a treaty ceding the Black Hills and approaches to
> settlement by citizens.

But by no means had all difficulty in the matter been removed. From the outset the Sioux, and most particularly the Lakota, claimed that the government took *Pahá Sápa* illegally. However, until Congress passed a special jurisdiction act in 1920, there was no legal mechanism whereby they could pursue that claim. The 1920 legislation enabled the Sioux to file suit in the U.S. Court of Claims, which they did. In that suit, they alleged that the government had taken *Pahá Sápa* without their consent and without paying just compensation, which was a violation of the Fifth Amendment of the U.S. Constitution. The Court of Claims dismissed the case in 1942, arguing that the 1920 act did not give the court the authority to rule on compensation. After Congress established the Indian Claims Commission to deal with tribal land issues in 1946, the Sioux resubmitted their claim. The Claims Commission eventually determined that the Sioux were entitled to just compensation for the Black Hills. The Court of Claims once again considered the case and upheld the Indian Claims Commission decision. It ruled that the Sioux were entitled to at least $17.5 million in compensation but were not entitled to interest. The Sioux appealed. After years of legal wrangling between the Indian Claims Commission and the Court of Claims, which was theoretically the court of appeal in the case, Congress ordered the Court of Claims to consider the merits of the tribe's claim. In 1979 the Court of Claims ruled that the Sioux Tribe was entitled to interest on a principle sum of $17.5 million at an annual rate of 5 percent dating from 1877, the year Congress ratified the agreement.

The Supreme Court also agreed to consider the case and delivered its decision in *United States v. Sioux Nation of Indians* on June 30, 1980. The issue at stake in the case was whether the United States government owed the Sioux compensation with interest for taking the Black Hills in violation of the three-fourths consent clause of the 1868 Fort Laramie Treaty. As a religious site, the region was deemed of special interest to the Sioux, which added to the merits of the case. In its decision, the Court supported the earlier Court of Claims decision. It ruled that

> the 1877 Act effected a taking of tribal property, property which
> had been set aside for the exclusive occupation of the Sioux by
> the Fort Laramie Treaty of 1868. That taking implied an obligation
> on the part of the Government to make just compensation to the
> Sioux Nation, and that obligation, including an award of interest,
> must now, at last, be paid.

Based on the Court of Claims calculation, the Sioux were to be awarded $106 million for the taking of the Black Hills. Despite the decades of legal wrangling, the Sioux refused to accept the money. Arguing that *Pahá Sápa* is sacred to them and that the transfer had been concluded without the consent of three-quarters of the adult males of the tribe, they continue to demand that *Pahá Sápa* be returned. The issue has yet to be resolved.

CHEYENNE BREAK OUT

The Indian Bureau had something different in mind for at least some of the Northern Cheyenne. After soldiers under Colonel McKenzie destroyed Dull Knife's village in late November of 1876, most of the surviving members of his band struggled through the cold and snow to Crazy Horse's camp. Dull Knife's starving and demoralized band surrendered at Fort Robinson the following spring. Two Moon and his followers spent the winter running from and fighting the soldiers then finally surrendered to Colonel Miles at Fort Keogh. Soon some of Two Moon's warriors were scouting for the army. Other Northern Cheyennes held out a bit longer or sought refuge with the Southern Cheyennes in Indian Territory.

Those Cheyennes who had surrendered at Fort Robinson wished to settle nearby but were denied permission to do so. Instead the army escorted them to the Southern Cheyenne-Arapaho Reservation on the Arkansas River in Indian Territory, where they arrived on August 5, 1877. For more than a year they languished there with nothing to do, little to eat, and no game to hunt. They soon fell ill with fevers and dysentery and began to die. Under cover of darkness in the very early hours of September 10, 1878. Dull Knife and Little Wolf slipped away with 85 men and about 250 women and children. The Cheyennes alternated between fighting and fleeing and somehow managed to elude the thousands of troops sent to stop them. Regardless of what the government planned to do with them, they were determined to return to their northern homeland or die trying.

After six weeks of constant running and fighting some of the Cheyennes were ready to give up but others were committed to continuing north. After they crossed the North Platte, they split into two groups. One group, led by Little Wolf, wintered in the Sand Hills of Nebraska then moved into the Powder River country and surrendered to Lieutenant W.P. Clark. Soon after, Little Wolf and his warriors joined warriors from the Two Moon band in scouting for the army out of Fort Keogh. The other group, about 150 people led by Dull Knife, continued north to surrender at Fort Robinson, where they assumed they would now be allowed to stay. On October 23, just two days out from the fort, they were surrounded and disarmed by soldiers. Before they handed over their weapons, they picked out the very best, broke them apart, and hid them among the folds of the women's clothing. They then completed their journey to Fort Robinson under military escort. At first the Dull Knife band was treated well but the situation deteriorated after they asked to be permitted to move to the Red Cloud Agency. The government refused their request and on January 3, 1879, ordered them to return to the Southern Arapaho-Cheyenne Reservation. When the Cheyennes refused to go, they were locked in a barrack without food, water, or fuel for heating. They broke out through a window on a cold night a week later. This time the soldiers were there to stop them and gunned down nearly half as they fled. By morning about sixty-five Cheyennes had been returned to the fort, a couple of dozen of them with wounds. Thirty-eight had made good their escape, most of them traveling together in a group with the army in hot pursuit. Nearly all of those were killed. Soldiers found another six hiding in the rocks nearby and returned them to the fort. In the end, the government relented and allowed most of the survivors to settle at Pine Ridge with the Lakota. Some voluntarily returned south and a few had to stand trial for depredations committed during their flight north from Indian Territory. In 1884 Dull Knife's band rejoined the Little Wolf and Two Moon bands on a reservation of their own on the Tongue River in Montana.

The 444,157-acre Northern Cheyenne Reservation (formerly the Tongue River Reservation) is bordered on the west at the 107th meridian by the Crow Reservation. It sits on lands defined as Crow Territory by the unratified 1851 Fort Laramie Treaty and ceded by the Crow tribe in the 1868 Fort Laramie Treaty.

SITTING BULL: SURRENDER TO WOUNDED KNEE

Throughout the winter of 1876–1877 Sitting Bull outmaneuvered the troops that pursued him. Finally, on May 7, the day after Crazy Horse surrendered, he and his band of about four hundred Hunkpapas crossed over the border into Grandmother's Land. Shortly after they arrived in Canada, Major James M. Walsh of the Northwest Mounted Police met with Sitting Bull. Of the opinion that the Lakota had been treated unfairly, he told Sitting Bull that his people would be allowed to stay in Canada for the time being but only if they obeyed its laws and caused no trouble.

Walsh warned him, however, that they could not expect to receive land, food, or supplies.

In an attempt to resolve what had now become an international crisis, General Terry arrived in Canada five months later with a message for Sitting Bull from the president of the United States. The president, he said, desired peace and was willing to pardon Sitting Bull and his people if they handed over their guns and horses and agreed to return south and settle on a designated reservation. Finding little reason to trust the U.S. government, Sitting Bull stubbornly refused to go. Besides, the buffalo were still plentiful and his people had enough to eat, at least so long as they had guns and horses with which to hunt.

Sitting Bull remained in Canada for more than four years. To feed themselves, the Lakotas continued to hunt, which depleted the game in their immediate vicinity. That created friction with the neighboring Blackfoot (not to be confused with the Blackfoot Lakota), Cree, and Assiniboine tribes, which viewed the Lakotas as foreign trespassers who ought to go back to where they came from. But Sitting Bull did not consider himself a foreigner at all. Because the Lakota had always ranged across the northern Plains at will and had sided with the British against the Americans in the War of 1812, he reasoned, he was entitled to hunt and live on either side of the border . . . and he did. Lakota hunters frequently followed the shrinking buffalo herds across the border into Montana. When they did, they sometimes committed depredations against settler communities or stirred up the agency Indians, both of which were unacceptable to the American authorities.

In the spring of 1879 Miles moved his troops north from Fort Keogh to patrol along the border in an attempt to stem the Lakota cross-border forays. On July 17 his forces clashed with Sitting Bull and a party of Lakota hunters and forced them back to Canada. Thereafter the continual presence of soldiers made it difficult and dangerous for the Lakotas to hunt south of the border. To disrupt the buffalo migration patterns and thereby ratchet up the pressure on the Lakotas, Miles had his soldiers set fire to the prairie at strategic intervals. As the buffalo became scarcer and scarcer and the Lakotas' hunger increased, the unity of the refugee bands disintegrated. Gall crossed back over the border with his followers in the fall of 1880 and set up camp near the Poplar River Agency. A group of Sans Arcs soon joined them there. In the winter of 1881, after a series of failed negotiations with Gall and Crow King, the army forcibly relocated the Poplar River Lakotas to Fort Buford and then onward to Fort Yates on the Standing Rock Reservation.

Sitting Bull held out a bit longer, but things became even more desperate for his people after the army stepped up its patrols along the border in early 1881. By then Major Walsh had been given an extended leave of absence and the Canadian authorities had installed the far less sympathetic L.N.F. Crozier as superintendent at Fort Qu'Appelle. Destitute, facing starvation, and no longer supported by the Canadian authorities, Sitting Bull and forty-three families finally rode into Fort Buford on July 19, 1881, where he presented himself to Major David H. Brotherton, the post commander. The formal surrender occurred the next morning at a specially convened council. After Crow Foot handed his father's rifle over to the major, Sitting Bull made a brief speech in which he stated:

> I surrender this rifle to you through my young son, whom I now desire to teach in this manner that he has become a friend of the Americans. I wish him to learn the habits of the whites and to be educated as their sons are educated. I wish it to be remembered that I was the last man of my tribe to surrender my rifle. This boy has given it to you, and now he wants to know how he is going to make a living.[14]

Never again would Sitting Bull fight.

For the duration of their stay at Fort Buford, Sitting Bull and his people were kept apart from the other Lakotas to ensure that they did not incite trouble. By the end of the month most of them were on their way downstream to the Standing Rock Reservation. Sitting Bull was taken further down the Missouri to Fort Randall, where he was held as a prisoner of war for twenty months. Upon his release, he was returned to Standing Rock, where he arrived on May 10, 1883. He settled there near his birthplace.

Life at Standing Rock failed to live up to Sitting Bull's expectations. To his dismay and humiliation, Major James McLaughlin, the Indian agent, refused to acknowledge him as a Hunkpapa leader. When Sitting Bull asked to be allowed to distribute the annuities to his band himself in keeping with Lakota tradition, McLaughlin not only denied his request but bluntly informed him that, just like everyone else, he would receive only his own allotted portion. Agent McLaughlin exhibited little respect for Sitting Bull, dismissing him as neither a "hereditary chief, nor even a chief by election or choice." Apart from that, he found Sitting Bull's stature among the Lakotas rather puzzling. Reflecting on it later, he wrote:

> Crafty, avaricious, mendacious, and ambitious, Sitting Bull possessed all of the faults of an Indian and none of the nobler attributes which have gone far to redeem some of his people

from their deeds of guilt. He had no single quality that would
serve to draw his people to him, yet he was by far the most
influential man of his nation for many years.[15]

Now a celebrity of sorts, Sitting Bull did not stay on the reservation
long. In September 1883 he traveled with McLaughlin to Bismarck,
where he attended a ceremony for the laying of the cornerstone of the
new territorial capitol building and rubbed shoulders with dignitaries. The
next spring he and one of his wives accompanied the agent to St. Paul.
He returned to Standing Rock much impressed with what he had
seen and experienced. That fall a St. Paul hotelier and showman toured
Sitting Bull and several other Lakotas around eastern cities, where they
demonstrated aspects of Plains Indian life on stage before large paying
audiences. Then, in June 1885, Sitting Bull signed on to tour with Buffalo
Bill. Rather than reenact his role in the Custer fight, Sitting Bull rode in
parades and charmed visitors to his tipi. In between those longer trips
he visited neighboring agencies. In 1886 he traveled with a group of
Custer fight veterans to Crow Agency, where they spent two weeks near
the Greasy Grass battlefield feasting and reminiscing with the Crow.
During that time the Crows and Lakotas shared mutual concerns over
federal Indian policy and particularly over the proposed allotment of
reservation lands.

By now McLaughlin had come to view Sitting Bull as the leader of
the non-progressive faction on the reservation and, hence, as a
troublemaker. Whether or not McLaughlin was jealous of the influence
he exerted over his people, as Sitting Bull often alleged, it is clear that
there were those among the Lakota who were jealous of him. Sitting Bull
once compared the politicking he encountered on the reservation to the
"whipping tops" game Lakota boys played. The object of that game was
to whip contending tops out of the way and be the first top into a small
willow-twig "corral." To Sitting Bull, it seemed like all the Lakotas were
playing an adult version of the game.

The corral is the agent's office. Everybody wants to get inside
and become a favorite. But no sooner does he do this than all the
rest combine against him, and knock him, and try to drive him
out. So a good many have failed in their attempt, though a few
have managed to get ahead and are now spinning happily inside.

As for himself, he believed he had "no chance whatever of getting into
that corral. But so long as I know I am not betraying my people, I shall
be content to remain outside."[16] Regardless of whether or not he made

it into the corral, Sitting Bull could not avoid getting knocked around in the power vacuum that existed on the reservation.

More land losses, ration cuts, broken promises, failed crops, disease, and curtailed dreams and aspirations drove the Lakotas to despair in the 1880s. Congress passed the 1887 General Allotment Act (also known as the Dawes Act) to provide for the allotment of tribal lands to individual Indians, usually in 160-acre parcels. It was a key strategy in their civilization program. With cunning verging on chicanery, and despite nearly universal opposition to the initial plan, special government negotiators eventually won the consent of the requisite number of Lakotas to transfer the remaining, or "surplus" lands, into the public domain. Once there, the government opened the lands to settlement under the homestead laws. The allotted lands were to be held by the federal government in trust for the Indians for twenty-five years, after which time individuals would receive a fee patent for their land and along with it citizenship. With the issuance of fee patents, the lands became liable to property taxes and the owners able to dispose of them as they saw fit. Unable to afford the taxes, many people lost their lands through tax forfeiture.

Most tribes with reservation lands were subject to the Allotment Act but there was another step in the process for the Lakotas. The 1888 and 1889 Sioux acts carved six separate reservations out of the Great Sioux Reservation: Pine Ridge, Rosebud, Cheyenne River, Standing Rock, Crow Creek, Lower Brulé. The remaining nine million acres reverted to the public domain and were immediately opened to settlement by non-Indians. Those individuals living outside the borders of the newly demarcated reservations had to relocate. Lands on the new reservations were then allotted to tribal members. Sitting Bull opposed this two-fisted land grab. Although the so-called progressives didn't like the loss of half of their land base any more than Sitting Bull did, they eventually hashed out an agreement they could live with and consented. Not surprisingly, many of the terms they agreed to did not make it into the final bill passed by Congress.

By 1889 the Lakota were primed for the new religion that swept across the Plains. The Ghost Dance originated in Nevada, the home of its prophet, a Paiute Indian named Wovoka. It blended traditional Native American religious beliefs and practices with Christianity and offered great hope for a future free of deprivation and suffering. Wovoka prophesied that, if the Indians joined together and correctly performed the Ghost Dance, the world would be transformed. After an apocalypse in the form of a cataclysmic earthquake all of the white people would be gone, the Native peoples who had died and the buffalo and the antelope would return, and the natural order of things would be restored. Although Wovoka urged his followers to remain at peace with the whites, to live tranquil lives, to reject alcohol and other vices, and to embrace high moral standards, the movement's millenarian elements and promise of a world free of *wasichus* alarmed non-Indians and government authorities. Government officials soon banned the Ghost Dance and threatened its practitioners with imprisonment.

Ghost Dance

The Ghost Dance originated in a vision Jack Wilson, a Paiute religious leader from the Carson Valley of Nevada, had in early 1889, perhaps around the time of a solar eclipse. First adopted by the Paiute in Nevada, the dance spread quickly throughout the region, into California and Oklahoma, and then across the northern Great Plains. The Ghost Dance was a millenarian religious movement that incorporated widely shared traditional elements, like the round or circle dance, and expressed and addressed aspirations and frustrations widespread among the beleaguered Native American peoples of the West. Its teachings, which predicted a peaceful end to white domination, the return of the ancestors and the buffalo and other game, and the restoration of good health and the traditional way of life, had great appeal. Badly misunderstood by non-Indians, and especially by government officials who misread its millenarian message as a call to arms, it advocated a life of abstinence and hard work, honesty, and cross-cultural cooperation and forbade its practitioners from engaging in warfare or self-mutilation during mourning. The different groups that took up the dance modified it to meet their own particular needs and to fit their cultures but generally adhered to its prescriptions and proscriptions. Consequently, while the Ghost Dance changed their cultures they, in turn, changed the ritual.

Throughout the short-lived popularity of the Ghost Dance, Jack Wilson, who most people knew as Wovoka, remained its leading figure and prophet. Many tribes sent envoys to the Prophet to learn about this new religion. He taught them that the several day long ritual, if practiced correctly and undertaken at regular intervals, would transform their worlds. In 1890, a Lakota named Kicking Bear, who had traveled west to learn about the new religion first-hand, returned home and introduced the Ghost Dance to his people. The Lakota elaborated it to fit their culture and worldview and to address their particular circumstances. Unlike Wovoka, who emphasized peaceful coexistence with the whites, they believed that if they danced long enough and with enough sincerity an apocalypse would occur that would remove the whites from their world, return the ancestors and the buffalo, and restore their traditional way of life. They also adopted Ghost Dance shirts, which were specially decorated shirts believed to be imbued with spiritual powers that would protect their wearers from bullets.

The Ghost Dance was introduced to the Lakotas living on the Standing Rock Reservation at a time of great stress. Earlier that year, government officials had broken the 1868 Fort Laramie treaty by splitting the Great Sioux Reservation into six much smaller reservations. The new reservation lands were then allotted in parcels to individual Lakotas, who were expected to farm and raise livestock on them, while the remaining lands were opened up to homesteading. Due to high temperatures, low rainfall, and the lands being generally unsuited to cultivation, the first year's yields were abysmal. That coincided with cuts in government rations and thus placed the Lakotas at great risk of starvation. As a result, the promise of a better world to come offered by the Ghost Dance proved attractive to many people and they joined the new movement. But rather than bring about a new world, the dance resulted in the death of Sitting Bull and the massacre of hundreds of Lakota children, women, and men at Wounded Knee. Having failed them, the Lakotas threw off their Ghost Dance shirts and abandoned the dance.

Sitting Bull took up the Ghost Dance religion and gave his first Ghost Dance sermon at Pine Ridge on October 31, 1889. The ever-suspicious McLaughlin doubted Sitting Bull's commitment to the movement.[17] He suspected that the weakened former leader was trying to use it to kick-start his moribund political career.

> I am convinced that the new religion was managed from the beginning, so far as the Standing Rock Sioux were concerned, by Sitting Bull, who had heard of the new faith that was making some headway in the southern reservations, and who, having lost his former influence over the Sioux, planned to import and use it to reestablish himself in the leadership of the people, whom he might then lead in safety in any desperate enterprise which he might direct.

On November 20, 1890, President Harrison ordered the military to take action to curtail the Ghost Dance movement. Fearing Sitting Bull's growing influence in the movement and its millenarian message, Nelson A. Miles, now a general, ordered him arrested. In the early morning of December 15, 1890, Indian police officers surrounded Sitting Bull's cabin on the Grand River. A few forced their way inside to arrest him. A fight broke out and Sitting Bull, his son Crow Foot, and several of his supporters were killed.

Fearing further arrests and reprisals, many of the Standing Rock Ghost dancers fled south to Big Foot's camp of Minneconjous on the Cheyenne River Reservation. Big Foot had also been ordered arrested, so under cover of darkness on December 23 about 350 people slipped out of his camp and headed south toward the Pine Ridge Reservation. The reconstituted

7th Cavalry, now headed by Major Samuel M. Whitside, surrounded them on December 28 and forced them on to Wounded Knee Creek where they were disarmed. Colonel James Forsyth arrived that night with reinforcements and took over command of the operation. The next morning the five hundred or so soldiers, reacting to a single accidental gunshot, let loose on the largely unarmed Lakotas with all their fire power, including two Hotchkiss guns. By the end of that cold afternoon in the Moon of the Popping Trees scores and scores of Lakota men, women, and children were dead. The army later buried 150 bodies in a mass grave at the site but the Lakota estimate that they lost as many as 300 of their people that day. Twenty-nine soldiers also died, most of them victims of friendly cross-fire. Twenty-three cavalrymen later received the Congressional Medal of Honor for their role in the slaughter. Robert Utley has called it the last stand of the Sioux Nation.[18] Other people point to the incident as the 7th Cavalry's moment of revenge.

CHAPTER 4

Reverberations

CONTEMPORARY BATTLEFIELD

Although the dust has long since settled, the Greasy Grass/Little Bighorn battle remains a captivating and defining moment in the American past. But more importantly, it has continually been a defining moment in the ever unfolding American present. National Park Service historian Robert M. Utley once described the battle as a "bellwether of changing popular attitudes" and he was right.[1] The battle story and the battlefield have not just reflected changing attitudes, diverse stakeholders have strategically used them to instigate change, shape public sensibilities, and define how the world is and how it should be.

Part of the Greasy Grass/Little Bighorn battlefield is now a national monument under the jurisdiction of the National Park Service (NPS). It receives more than three hundred thousand visitors in an average year, many of them over the late June battle anniversary. The historic battlefield and Indian village site stretches for five miles along the river and covers more than fourteen square miles in all but the Park Service controls only a fraction of that. At just over 765 acres, the Little Bighorn Battlefield National Monument is one of smallest units in the national park system. For a time it was also one of the most controversial. The monument is currently composed of two non-contiguous parcels connected by a tour road: the Custer Battlefield at the north end and the Reno–Benteen Battlefield about four miles to the south. Nestled within the Custer Battlefield is the Custer National Cemetery, where dead from the frontier wars and more recent conflicts are buried but very few from the battle itself. Most of those are interred in a mass grave at the base of the 7th Cavalry obelisk on Last Stand Hill.

The rest of the land over which the fighting ranged and the village stretched is owned by the Crow Tribe, private individuals, or a group dedicated to preserving the historic site. Some of the private landowners are Crows whose lands are still held in trust by the federal government. Others are Crow or non-Indian ranchers and entrepreneurs. In the late 1980s a former battlefield superintendent spearheaded an effort to protect the historic resource by purchasing additional battlefield lands for eventual inclusion in the national monument. Faced with resistance from the Crow Tribe and legal complications stemming from the battlefield's location within the borders of the Crow Reservation, the monument boundaries have not yet been extended but work continues toward that objective.

One of most challenging responsibilities facing Park Service staff is how best to interpret the historic site and thereby narrate the battle story. Although the NPS represents the story it tells as authentic and definitive, and the visiting public imagines it to be so, battlefield historians and interpreters inevitably craft it out of a blend of fact, conjecture, and conflicting evidence. More than simply recount the Greasy Grass/Little Bighorn fight, the story they tell reflects decades of conflict and contention. In addition, how they and others narrate the story and what they emphasize, ignore, and downplay has always changed in response to new evidence, altered circumstances, evolving sensibilities, and shifting objectives. At any point in time the story and the place can mean different things to different people because, as Utley told those gathered at the monument for the 1976 centennial observance, "history, like life, is complex, contradictory, and ambiguous."[2] History is not just a thing of the past. It is an assemblage of facts, theories, and assumptions about past events re-articulated according to current sensibilities and oftentimes in service of future objectives.

For nearly a century the meanings the battle and battlefield held for white Americans were privileged above all others. That is attributable at least in part to a long-held assumption that indigenous peoples like the Cheyenne and Lakota would be, and indeed should be, stirred into the great American "melting pot." But views on how best to accomplish that were a matter of debate and changed considerably over the years. Sometimes federal Indian policy and public opinion stressed assimilation, or the complete absorption of Native Americans into mainstream society. If carried to its logical conclusion, assimilation would erase the cultural distinctiveness of Native American peoples and render them indistinguishable from other Americans. At other times policy and public opinion promoted acculturation, or the gradual adoption of the language, values, customs, and practices of the American mainstream. Advocates of acculturation accepted that Native Americans might retain cultural practices and beliefs that would distinguish them from their non-Indian neighbors but believed that such traits would be superficial and not impede their ability to function as full-fledged citizens. Under both scenarios Native Americans were the ones expected to do the changing not dominant society. These shifts in policy and public opinion and the social, political, and economic conditions that gave rise to them have always been evident in the changing battle story.

ASSIMILATION AND THE CUSTER FIGHT

Grant's Peace Policy was based on the premise that there was still time and geographical space for Native Americans to gradually acculturate. However, the series of events that climaxed in the Greasy Grass/Little Bighorn battle made it clear to most people that time had now expired and the space was gone. Besides, Congress was finding it increasingly difficult to absorb the high cost of maintaining the reservation system and was looking for ways to streamline the management of Indian affairs and thereby reduce the fiscal burden. During the 1870s, a number of crises involving Native American peoples, including the Greasy Grass/Little Bighorn debacle, coupled with budgetary concerns, precipitated a shift from acculturation to assimilation as the federal policy objective. Business leaders and settlers who coveted Indian lands and resources strongly supported the change in emphasis. By the early 1880s, hastening the Indians' assimilation by undermining their tribal ties had become a federal policy priority. Policy-makers sought to accomplish that by eroding the tribal land base, providing the right sort of education for Indian children, and promoting citizenship. That furthered an ongoing, federally-backed campaign to "Christianize" the Indians, suppress their traditional religious practices and forms of marriage, and undermine their political and economic institutions. All of that was reflected in how people remembered the battle and recounted the story.

The nation initially memorialized the Custer battlefield as a cemetery for the cavalrymen killed there. Its care fell to soldiers from Fort Custer, which the army built near the confluence of the Bighorn and Little Bighorn rivers in 1877. That same year, the 7th Cavalry's newly reconstituted I Company returned to the battlefield to retrieve the remains of two civilians and the officers, including Custer, for reburial back east. At Libbie's request, Custer was reinterred at West Point. Two years later the battlefield gained official recognition as a national cemetery of the fourth class. That summer, soldiers from the nearby fort erected a log memorial to their fallen comrades on Custer Hill and marked the cavalry graves with wooden stakes. In 1881, they replaced the log memorial with the present granite

Custer's Views on the Indians[3]

"If I were an Indian, I often think that I would greatly prefer to cast my lot among those of my people who adhered to the free open plains, rather than submit to the confined limits of a reservation, there to be the recipient of the blessed benefits of civilization, with its vices thrown in without stint or measure. The Indian can never be permitted to view the question in this deliberate way. He is neither a luxury nor necessary of life. He can hunt, roam, and camp when and wheresoever he pleases, provided always that in so doing he does not run contrary to the requirements of civilization in its advancing tread. When the soil which he has claimed and hunted over for so long a time is demanded by this to him insatiable monster, there is no appeal; he must yield, or, like the car of Juggernaut, it will roll mercilessly over him, destroying as it advances. Destiny seems to have so willed it, and the world looks on and nods its approval. At best the history of our Indian tribes, no matter from what standpoint it is regarded, affords a melancholy picture of loss of life. Two hundred years ago it required millions to express in numbers the Indian population, while at the present time less than half the number of thousands will suffice for the purpose. Where and why have they gone? Ask the Saxon race, since whose introduction into and occupation of the country these vast changes have been effected."

shaft and moved the troopers' remains to a mass grave at its base. In 1886, President Cleveland signed an Executive Order that defined the boundary of the National Cemetery of the Custer's Battlefield Reservation. That boundary now marks the Custer Battlefield portion of the national monument. The present white marble headstones replaced the wooden stakes in 1890. Three years later the first superintendent arrived to oversee the cemetery and for the next several decades a succession of retired soldiers cared for the battlefield and, when they felt like it, interpreted the site for visitors. Some of those early guardians were veterans of the 1876 campaign. Predictably, the information shared by these former and still serving soldiers emphasized the army side of the story.

Some Crows called the early battlefield caretakers Ghost Herders because they thought their role was to prevent the ghosts of the dead from wandering away from the cemetery. They assumed that the morning flag-raising called the spirits of the dead soldiers back to their graves.

As the development of memorialization at the battlefield just outlined would suggest, for several decades after the battle official acts of commemoration at the site paid little attention to the Lakota and Cheyenne side of the story: their casualties, their reasons for fighting, and the consequences the battle held for them were ignored. They were, after all, the "uncivilized" enemy that was supposed to be "vanishing," either through assimilation into the American mainstream or into the metaphorical sunset. But that did not stop the Lakota and Cheyenne from taking their own steps to memorialize their fallen friends and relatives and to remember the battle. Immediately after the fight they raised stone cairns to mark spots where their warriors were killed. The next day Lakota and Cheyenne leaders returned to the Custer battlefield to count the dead soldiers using tally sticks. Later, when it was safe to do so, they visited it again to reflect upon what had taken place there. Cheyenne warriors were probably the first to do so. Some returned just a few days after the fight to look around and catch stray horses. Others visited that fall. They shared their experiences with one another and scoured the site for ammunition. The next year Pretty Shield toured the battlefield with two of Custer's Crow scouts, Half Yellow Face and her husband Goes Ahead. As was their custom, all Native American groups touched by the Greasy Grass battle memorialized it and those who fought and died there in honor songs and oral tradition. The Lakota, Cheyenne, Crow, and Arikara still sing those songs and recount those stories today. The Crow even have an honor song for Custer.

Non-Indian Americans also engaged in unofficial acts of remembrance in the immediate aftermath of the battle. Within days of learning of Custer's defeat, a group of easterners formed the Custer Monumental Association to ensure that the cavalry dead were suitably remembered and within six months Frederick Whittaker had cranked out his overblown but hugely popular *A Complete Life of Gen. George A. Custer.*[4] Some people had always addressed Custer according to his Civil War rank but after his death it became commonplace, almost obligatory, to call him "General" rather than "Lieutenant Colonel." Compiled from Custer's own publications and letters, newspaper articles and official documents, information gathered from Libbie and other family members, and reports by battle survivors and former comrades, Whittaker's volume was a heroic celebration of Custer's life. It also laid the foundation upon which the Custer myth would be constructed. Whittaker roundly condemned Reno and Benteen. Not only did he blame them for what happened, he demanded an official inquiry into the matter and especially into Reno's battlefield conduct. Full of inaccuracies and sensationalist in tone, the book provided fodder for a wide array of popular treatments of the subject. Poets, painters, playwrights, and authors of juvenile and dime novels turned to it for material on the best-selling subject of the day—Custer's Last Stand. Some of their output was good, most of it was mediocre at best, and nearly all of it extolled the sacrificial valor displayed by General Custer and his heroic band of cavalrymen when vastly outnumbered by a "screaming horde of savages" (see Documents for Lakota and Cheyenne versions of the story).

Inspired by the Little Bighorn story as depicted in the press, artists and poets immediately elevated the cavalry and Indian dead to the personification of a clash between civilization and savagery and the last stand to the archetype of heroism and valor. In Custer himself they found a welcome model of manly sacrifice for God and country. Poets may have captured (or created) the poignancy of the battle but it was the artists who visually defined the "mythic moment" for posterity.[5] Although not necessarily the ranking artistic geniuses of their era, it is largely thanks to the early efforts of such painters as William M. Cary, A.R. Waud, Feodor Fuchs, and H. Steinegger and the works of men like John Mulvany, E.S. Paxson, and Cassilly Adams a decade later that the American public came to visualize the battle as a dusty hilltop scene in which a tightly clustered group of soldiers heroically fought for their lives amidst a swarming mass of Indians. But it was F. Otto Becker who inadvertently brought the last stand to life for ordinary people and especially those perched on bar-stools across the country. Cassilly Adams' massive *Custer's Last Fight* (1886) ended up hanging on the wall of a St. Louis saloon. It features a long-haired Custer as the last soldier standing. With saber in one hand, pistol in the other, and fallen comrades heaped at his feet, Custer courageously and defiantly meets his fate blazing and slashing away at the circling Indians. After the Anheuser-Busch company acquired the Adams' painting in a claims settlement, it commissioned Becker to repaint it and then make a lithograph from it. After he completed the work in 1895, the brewing company distributed the lithograph in a Budweiser beer promotion. Eventually more than 200,000 copies were in circulation. Like the Adams original, most of them ended up on bar-room walls.

Over the years battle reconstructions and reenactments have also helped shape and promulgate the Custer myth. While undoubtedly the first to do so, Cheyennes, Lakotas, and Crows were not the only ones to visit the battlefield in the aftermath of the fight. Army personnel also arrived on the scene soon afterwards. Some tended the cavalry graves and others tried to piece together what happened. Before long Indians and whites visited together. The army instigated the first joint visits to learn more about how the battle had unfolded, with General Nelson A. Miles leading two such trips in 1878. In 1886, cavalry and Native American battle veterans met on the battlefield to mark the tenth anniversary of the fight. Among them were Major Benteen, Captain Godfrey, and Gall (the Hunkpapa war leader). Photographer David F. Barry was on hand to document it all. He and a handful of others accompanied Gall on a battlefield walk to learn what he saw and did during the battle (see Gall's story in Documents). Later that day troopers fired a tribute to Custer and simulated Gall's account of the fight. No one asked the Lakota and Cheyenne veterans to reenact their parts in the battle. Another small ceremony occurred on the twentieth anniversary. A few troopers and some Lakota veterans visiting in the area attended the poorly publicized event.

Other reenactments were more readily accessed by the general public. Within just a few months of taking the "first scalp for Custer" Buffalo Bill Cody, for example, was on stage recreating his fight with the Cheyenne warrior Yellow Hair before large audiences. By the time his Wild West show toured England a decade later "*The Battle of the Little Bighorn, Showing with Historical Accuracy the scene of CUSTER'S LAST CHARGE!*" was a headline act. The sequence of events it depicted would recur in each of the many battle reenactments to follow. The opening scene was a log fort, where Custer first learned the whereabouts of the Sioux from his scouts. Upon receiving the news, he instantly mustered his troops and led them out of the fort and straight into the Indian camp in the next scene. The fight was on and the heroic band of soldiers quickly succumbed to their fates. An 1889 promotional brochure described Buffalo Bill's rendition of the battle with melodramatic flourish: "Actual death and carnage could alone add a single touch to the vivid truthfulness of the stupendous, animate, indescribable reflex of surprise, savage onslaught, desperate defense, murderous combat and annihilation."[6] Although obviously over-stated, this could be a description of the action-packed climax of just about any of the reenactments that followed: a loud, dusty final fight that inevitably results in a battlefield littered with dead but heroic soldiers who presumably "sold their lives dearly."

The Crow were the first to reenact the Custer fight in the immediate battlefield vicinity. They did so in 1891 as part of their Fourth of July celebration. Crows played all of the roles while non-Indians watched peacefully from the sidelines. In a 1902 reenactment staged in Sheridan, Wyoming, Crows again played the Cheyenne and Lakota while a National Guard unit stepped in to play the troopers. In that its last stand scene disintegrated into a full-fledged slug-out after a "warrior" audaciously captured the "cavalry" colors, it was the most realistic reenactment to date. The Crow reenacted the battle again during the 1909 Crow Fair. This was a much calmer production in which Crows once more assumed all the Indian roles and a Montana National Guard unit played the 7th Cavalry.

That September a different sort of reenactment took place on the Greasy Grass/Little Bighorn valley floor. Promoted as the Last Great Indian Council, it climaxed an expedition sponsored by wealthy East Coast businessman and self-styled "friend of the Indian" Rodman Wanamaker. The council itself was organized by photographer Joseph K. Dixon, who later published a description of what transpired at the gathering and liberally illustrated it with his own photographs. Not only does the title he chose for the volume, *The Vanishing Race*,[7] accurately signal the assumptions and motivations that lay behind the Wanamaker venture, it and Dixon's illustrations reflect the assimilationist sensibilities of the day. The Last Great Indian Council was the first of three expeditions sponsored by Wanamaker, each of which he envisioned to serve a dual purpose: to record tribal lifeways before they vanished and to help re-make American Indians into American citizens and thus save them from extinction.

While billed as a gathering of great Indian "chiefs" from tribes across the country, most of those who attended the Last Great Indian Council were from northern Plains groups and a significant number of them had participated in the Greasy Grass/Little Bighorn battle. Consequently, much of the discussion and activity focused on the Custer fight. In his book, Dixon visually and textually depicted the battle as the last futile victory in a war the Indians had already lost to preserve their traditional ways of life, a theme upcoming anniversary observances would develop more fully. The second expedition took place shortly after the council adjourned and included the filming of a Little Bighorn battle reenactment. Wanamaker's 1913 Expedition of Citizenship was the final excursion in the series. It drove home his assimilationist agenda by carrying the American flag from tribe to tribe and asking tribal members to pledge their allegiance to the United States.

As transportation improved after the turn of the century, more and more people visited the Greasy Grass/Little Bighorn battlefield. Soon area entrepreneurs began staging public events to coincide with the anniversary. In 1916 as many as eight thousand people attended a fortieth battle anniversary observance on the battlefield. Once again the assumption that the Lakota, Cheyenne, and Crow would soon be assimilated into mainstream society was readily apparent in the proceedings. That year's April issue of *The Teepee Book* promoted the event as one last chance "to see and become acquainted with real Indian war chiefs, standing upon the ground which is made dear to them by the blood of their comrades."[8] The June issue declared the upcoming event unique in the history of the country:

> Never before, the [sic] probably never again, will representatives of two races who took prominent parts in the last great battle of the wars between them, meet for the purpose of grasping in friendship hands extended over the graves of their dead, and for paying a fitting tribute to the memory of those who died there defending the principles which each upheld.[9]

By now it was obvious that, for assimilation to work, there first had to be reconciliation.

In honor of the occasion, General Godfrey retraced Custer's route from the Yellowstone to the Little Bighorn. In the ceremony that followed, he represented the cavalry and White Man Runs Him (Crow) and Two Moon (Northern Cheyenne) represented the scouts and warriors, respectively. Joining them were a handful of battle veterans from both sides. Godfrey and Colonel Henry Hall, a self-proclaimed expert on both Native Americans and the battle, addressed the gathering. The two men paid tribute to the cavalry dead as gallant and heroic soldiers sacrificed to open the West for settlement. With the United States' entry into World War I seemingly inevitable, Godfrey also called upon listeners to defend the country for which his comrades had sacrificed themselves.

Hall, in particular, stressed the great strides made in civilizing the Indians and voiced what were to become two enduring themes. First, that the Little Bighorn battle was a "last stand" for the Indians as well as the soldiers. And, second, that the Indians may have won the battle but they had lost the war to preserve their traditional ways of life. He told his audience that

> those 40 years span the gulf between barbarism and civilization, paganism and Christianity, ignorance and knowledge, the tepee of the nomad and the hearth of the homebuilder . . . Whether by fate or design, it was here that the American Indian made his last stand. Here, he turned his face from the setting to the rising sun. With his back to the west, towards which he had marched for a century, he again faced the east and his foes . . . Here the last remnant of a heritage "rich beyond the dreams of avarice" was the stake, and here the doom of a brave and proud people was knelled—for this last victory was their sorest defeat.[10]

The words Hall spoke could have been written by Dixon himself and that they resonated with his audience can be inferred from the fact that an area newspaper printed his speech verbatim.

UNITY, PATRIOTISM, AND THE GREASY GRASS/LITTLE BIGHORN BATTLE

Before World War I the Lakota and Cheyenne side of the battle story received scant attention and the heroism of the warriors was ignored. Most people agreed with Colonel Hall. They assumed that the die had been cast and it was just a matter of time before the Indians would be completely assimilated into mainstream society, either by choice or by force. Many Native Americans—Cheyennes, Lakotas, and Crows included—had voluntarily served in the American armed forces during the war and some had died. Afterwards those who survived were rewarded with citizenship. Then in 1924 the Indian Citizenship Act extended citizenship to all Native Americans, a step deemed essential to their complete assimilation. Meanwhile the wave of unity and patriotism that had rippled across the nation during the war years lingered on. Although policy-makers and the general public were now more willing to accept acculturation as an alternative to assimilation and to allow the tribes a greater degree of self-determination than at any time since the end of the Indian wars, the focus was nonetheless on a nation united, on *e pluribus unum* ("out of many one").

Such sentiments were evident in the 1926 semi-centennial battle anniversary observance, which remains the most elaborate event ever held on the battlefield. The railroads and the State of Montana joined with area communities to promote it—and themselves—as widely as possible. The Burlington Route produced a brochure that described the event as a reunion of cavalry survivors and their Indian foes to "revere the memory of fighting men, both red and white, who fell in battle here."[11] These former adversaries, it said, would "smoke the ancient peace pipe and renew the pact of esteem and friendship." It also promised that the event would bring the Crow and Sioux, who were hereditary enemies, together as friends for the first time.

The State of Montana used the occasion to promote its tourism and agricultural industries. Notions of manifest destiny echoed across the pages of its brochure, which declared the battle "the beginning of a new era in Montana."[12] Custer and his troopers had not died in vain, it said. Their sacrifice had "roused the nation to action and a determination to clear this section once and for all of the hostiles." In 1876 there were only 851 farms in Montana. Once the army quelled the Indian threat, the state flourished. By 1926 it had forty-seven thousand farms, the lowest land prices and second lowest property taxes in the country, above average yields per acre, and advanced real estate laws. For those not wanting to relocate, the state offered spectacular places to visit. Just as Custer had called for Benteen to "come on" in 1876, so the state called for tourists and investors to "come on" in 1926. And they did.

Between forty thousand and fifty thousand people gathered to mark the semi-centennial battle anniversary, among them celebrities, dignitaries, reporters, film-makers, and Custer's grand-niece. The 7th Cavalry, now commanded by Colonel Fitzhugh Lee, came up from Fort Bliss, Texas, to participate. Many of the warriors who fought Custer still feared reprisals but a few joined the aging army veterans to mark the battle semi-centennial. Friends, relatives, and other members of their tribes accompanied them. Their tipis covered the valley floor just as the Lakota and Cheyenne tipis had done half a century earlier. A carnival atmosphere prevailed but there were also many solemn and deeply symbolic moments.

On June 25, as the cavalry band played a funeral dirge, soldiers and warriors met on Last Stand Hill. With Godfrey and White Man Runs Him at their head, the troopers approached the 7th Cavalry memorial from the south. A contingent of Lakota and Cheyenne warriors dressed in war regalia and headed by White Bull approached from the north. When the two groups drew near, White Man Runs Him and White Bull rode forward. The former scout lifted a peace pipe to the sky then offered it to White Bull. White Bull raised his hand in a gesture of peace and Godfrey responded by returning his saber to its scabbard. Grasping hands, the former enemies confirmed their reconciliation with an exchange of gifts: Godfrey gave White Bull an American flag and White Bull reciprocated with a Hudson Bay blanket. Afterwards Godfrey and the other cavalry survivors laid floral wreaths at the base of the memorial and, as a trumpeter played Taps, the 7th Cavalry fired a volley over the mass grave. Troopers and warriors then paired off and left the battlefield together in yet another symbolic gesture of friendship.

The activities on June 26 revolved around the reburial of the recently discovered remains of a trooper presumably killed in the battle. Once again the emphasis was on peace and reconciliation. The ceremony began with a brief service led by the regimental chaplain. After the rendering of military honors, troopers escorted the flag-draped coffin up the valley to a special crypt, where the chaplain delivered a eulogy, an honor guard fired a volley, and a bugler played Taps. Godfrey solemnly received the flag from the coffin of the Unknown Soldier. Afterwards, he addressed the crowd. It was then that he introduced the "burying the hatchet" metaphor. "Time out of mind," he said, "the Hatchet [sic] has been with the Red Race, the symbol of war. We now unite in the ceremony of burying the Hatchet [sic], holding it a covenant of our common citizenship and everlasting peace. We pray (to) the God of our Fathers, the Great Spirit, to assure this covenant to all future generations."[13] This blend of unity, patriotism, and Christian devotion was by now standard fare at such events.

With Red Tomahawk representing the Lakota and Colonel Partello, a veteran of the 1876 campaign, representing the army, Indians and whites symbolically buried the hatchet. (While there is nothing to suggest that it influenced his selection to represent the Lakota, it is noteworthy that Red Tomahawk was one of the Indian police who killed Sitting Bull.) Partello later described the moment of reconciliation:

> with each of us on either side of the sarcophagus, the Indian held
> one end of the tomahawk, myself the other end, then both
> reached down, and plucked a small bunch of native grasses, and
> sprinkled it in the crypt, shook hands across the opening and
> thus symbolized by the burying of the hatchet, the end of all wars
> between the two races.[14]

Afterwards, the cavalry veterans retraced Reno's retreat across the river and up the bluffs to place a marker at the siege site.

At a gathering later in the day, Red Tomahawk spoke of Native American patriotism during the recent world war and confirmed that his people now wanted to live in peace with their former enemies. Godfrey acknowledged that wrongs had been committed against Native Americans but reiterated that the battle had been a last stand for their way of life. He and James Marquisee, chair of the Custer Memorial Association's executive committee, both emphasized the triumph of civilization over savagery and stressed the common citizenship of Indians and whites along with the rights and duties that citizenship entails. The governor of Montana repeated those themes but also celebrated the promise for the future unleashed by the cavalry's sacrifice.

Back in 1916 General Godfrey had initiated plans to preserve what he called the hilltop fight site. He was forced to abandon them when the United States entered World War I. Ten years later Congress authorized acquisition of the site from the Crow Tribe and the army finally took control of it in 1930. Maps now label the spot the Reno-Benteen Battlefield but it was originally designated the Sioux Indian Battle Monument Site. Despite that name, neither Godfrey nor Congress intended it as a memorial to the warriors nor did anyone see it that way. They were merely avoiding use of the clouded Reno and Benteen names. Any official memorialization of the battle's Indian participants was still in the distant future.

By the late 1930s the world was in chaos. With war once again seemingly imminent, it was perhaps inevitable that the Warner Brothers' film *They Died With Their Boots On* (1941) would be a smash hit. With the dashing and debonair Errol Flynn cast as Custer, accuracy beside the point, and a last stand scene straight out of the Becker lithograph, it was just what a nation facing the specter of war needed. Night after night Errol Flynn's Custer courageously held his ground in the face of overwhelming odds, providing the young men of the country with a suitable role model for how to meet death with valor and dignity while fighting for American ideals in foreign lands. It also served to remind everyone of the renown that awaits those who sacrifice themselves for the good of the nation.

Moreover, as Edward Linenthal has suggested,[15] the last stand offered the American public a template for how to transform defeats like those soon to be suffered at Wake Island, Bataan, and Corregidor into moral victories.

In 1940, responsibility for the battlefield shifted from the War Department to the Department of the Interior, where it came under the auspices of the National Park Service. Edward S. Luce, who had once served in the 7th Cavalry, became the first NPS superintendent at the battlefield. His avid interest in the subject and the site shaped battlefield interpretation and had a lasting effect. In 1946, Congress changed the site name from the Custer Battlefield National Cemetery to the Custer Battlefield National Monument to reflect a shift in emphasis from active cemetery to American historic site in need of preservation and interpretation. The new name, however, did not result in added attention to the Lakota and Cheyenne side of the story.

When the Park Service took over at the battlefield it limited the scale of the events it allowed in order to protect the historic resource. Consequently, the program was purely commemorative when seven thousand people gathered on Battle Ridge in 1951 to mark the battle's seventy-fifth anniversary. A 7th Cavalry representative, several army officers, Colonel Brice C.W. Custer, and one cavalry and two Native American battle veterans were among those who attended. The program began with the placement of a wreath on the cavalry mass grave. Various speeches then rehearsed the paired themes of peace and patriotism. General Wedermeyer was the keynote speaker that day. He referred to the battlefield as "a tribute not to war but to the spiritual strength that motivated sacrifice."[16] According to one witness, the Native American speakers, in turn, conveyed their regrets for past misunderstandings and reiterated their desire to live in peace. They also "expressed pride in and allegiance to the great nation which has evolved from their cherished 'hunting grounds' through the efforts of the once spurned white man."[17]

When Libbie Custer died in 1933, she left her husband's belongings to the government with the attached condition that they be housed in a museum at the battlefield. A few years later Congress authorized acceptance of the collection and construction of a museum but did not fund it. That had to wait until after World War II. The NPS officially opened the new museum on June 25, 1952, the seventy-sixth anniversary of the battle. Reflecting sentiments widespread in the Cold War era, the dedication ceremony emphasized patriotism and valor in a manner that included both Indians and whites. Among those present were General Jonathan M. Wainwright and Colonel W.A. Harris. One newspaper reporter described the officers as the "hero of the 'death march' of Bataan" and the "liberator of Seoul, Korea," respectively.[18] But more relevant to the day, she suggested, were Wainwright's childhood years spent at Fort Custer and Harris' command of the 7th Cavalry in Korea.

The new inclusiveness acknowledged Native Americans' outstanding military service. It was also consistent with a federal Indian policy agenda that since the end of World War II had been aggressively promoting the assimilation, or complete absorption, of Native Americans into mainstream society. To that end, and just as the semi-centennial observance had done, the museum dedication ceremony celebrated a unified America.

The museum did not ignore the battle's Native American participants but from the outset it favored the army side of the story. The label for the first exhibit visitors encountered as they entered read: "These men and 250 of their comrades were killed here in battle June 25 and 26, 1876." It made no mention of the warriors and non-combatants killed. Other exhibits focused on the Custer end of the fight and especially on those officers who died there. A diorama of the final stages of the battle as seen from Last Stand Hill reinforced that orientation. According to Harry B. Robinson,[19] who designed the Exhibit Plan, those displays that pertained to the Lakota and Cheyenne sought "to tell who the Indians were that participated in the Custer Battle; to emphasize the characteristics of the Indian warrior—his war motives, practices, and honors; and to stress the importance of magic in the Indian's life." Those factors influenced how the warriors fought and, as such, mattered a great deal to the soldiers they met in battle. In that sense, the museum portrayed the Lakota and Cheyenne battle participants from the troopers' point of view rather than from that of their own people.

BATTLE FOR THE GREASY GRASS/ LITTLE BIGHORN

For nearly a century the public viewed the battle almost exclusively through the eyes of the soldiers. During that time nearly everyone assumed that Native Americans were on the brink of vanishing into the great American melting pot. As distinct peoples they were thus as peripheral to contemporary American social, political, and economic life as the Lakota, Cheyenne, and Crow were to the battle itself: all were relegated to minor supporting roles in an unfolding drama of European American destiny. While anthropologists scrambled to record—or "salvage"—what they could of Native American cultures before they were forever beyond intellectual scrutiny, policy-makers and so-called Friends of the Indian groups debated how fast assimilation was occurring and how best to speed it up. But contrary to all their expectations, Native Americans refused to dive into the melting pot. Not only that, in the 1960s they reclaimed the Greasy Grass battle story, which to them epitomized all that was and is wrong with federal Indian policy and Indian–white relations.

By then the meanings the battle held for some non-Indian Americans had also changed dramatically. To anti-war and civil rights activists, in particular, the battle had come to signify what in their view were the genocidal wars the United States had been waging in pursuit of its global dominance, with the ongoing war in Vietnam only the most recent, and hence most salient, of many possible examples. Popular culture treatments of the Greasy Grass/Little Bighorn battle shifted accordingly. Arthur Penn's *Little Big Man* (1970), the box office hit starring Dustin Hoffman in the title role, reflected such sentiments. It refashioned the Little Bighorn story into a genocidal saga and reconstituted Custer, now played by Richard Mulligan, as a raving villain. Many people saw the madness of Mulligan's Custer as a metonym for—or symbol of—the insane colonial practices that had nearly driven Native Americans to extinction and were now threatening to do the same to the peoples of Indochina.

By the 1960s Native Americans were organizing to fight the draconian assimilationist policies of the Cold War era and to defend their rights, sovereignty, lands, and tribal identities. Partly empowered by the Civil Rights movement and other forms of political activism sweeping the country and certainly strengthened by newly formed inter-tribal alliances, they began to demand an accurate and equitable telling of the nation's, and hence their own, history. That inevitably led them to the Greasy Grass. The Trail of Broken Treaties Caravan made a well-publicized stop at the battlefield en route to Washington, DC, in 1972, as did the Trail of Self-Determination Caravan four years later. Each group used their visit to highlight historical and contemporary injustices and inequities inflicted upon Native Americans by whites. In doing so, they drew attention to the lack of balance in the story told at the monument and to the absence of a memorial to the Lakota and Cheyenne battle participants. Those visits constituted the opening volleys in a battle for control of the Greasy Grass/ Little Bighorn story.

Coinciding with the nation's bicentennial and just three years after the long and violent stand-off between the American Indian Movement (AIM) and heavily armed federal agents at Wounded Knee, the battle centennial came at a particularly poignant juncture in modern Indian and white relations. In the early months of 1976 rumors that Native American activists were planning violence and massive protests over the anniversary period kept the NPS and local officials on edge. The Crow Tribe and the nearby community of Hardin canceled most of their plans for the battle centennial and American bicentennial and the Park Service scaled back its commemorative program to a low-key observance. It also brought it forward by a day in an attempt to avoid the widely anticipated disturbance.

Over the anniversary period around two hundred Lakota activists joined a group of Cheyennes at the Austin Two Moon ranch on the Northern Cheyenne Reservation, where they held a three-day victory celebration in honor of their battle dead. A respected spiritual leader, Austin Two Moon was the great-grandson of Two Moon, the famous Cheyenne leader who had fought in the battle. Some of the activists drove over to the battlefield to protest on June 24, taking the monument administration by surprise. Superintendent Richard T. Hart diplomatically granted Russell Means, then a high-profile member of AIM, time at the microphone during the official observance. Means mounted the platform carrying the American flag upside down. He did this, he explained to the audience, not out of disrespect for the flag but to signal that American Indians were in distress. He then briefly addressed issues of current concern to Native American peoples. When he finished, he and the rest of the protesters moved up to Last Stand Hill, where they danced around the 7th Cavalry memorial singing "Custer Died for Your Sins," a phrase popularized by Vine Deloria's scathing indictment of white interference in Native American lives.[20]

Meanwhile the Park Service got on with its commemorative program. In his opening comments, Superintendent Hart urged the audience to "honor all who died in the Battle of the Little Bighorn—civilian, soldier, and warrior." While some may question whether those were the words he initially intended to speak or a response to the situation at hand, it is worth noting that for at least five years staff had been discussing the possibility of renaming the Custer Battlefield National Monument to better reflect all sides of the story. In his keynote address, Robert M. Utley, then Assistant Director for Cultural Resources at the NPS, argued that the battle can only be understood within the context of its day. He asked his listeners to consider "the forces that caused essentially decent people to do what they did" and reminded them that the "injustices of the past did not necessarily spring from evil motives but rather from a set of values and assumptions that were entirely plausible in their time and place."[21] With those words, Utley skillfully dodged accusations of being an apologist for either side yet called on both to strive for a balanced and historically contextualized understanding of the site and, presumably, each other.

The commemorative programming continued the next day, which was the actual battle anniversary. This time Russell Means had a seat on the official platform. He used his turn to speak to address the unfair exploitation of Native American mineral resources and the exclusion of Native Americans from the world economy, issues he linked to the same colonial impulse that had led to the battle in the first place. Hal Stearns, director of the Montana branch of the American Revolution Bicentennial Administration, was the keynote speaker that day. He avoided language that celebrated civilization of the Indians. His words—some of which were lifted from Lincoln's Gettysburg Address—nonetheless echoed sentiments from the semi-centennial observance and the museum dedication and were tinged with patriotism.[22] "We are here to re-dedicate this sacred site as a Shrine for those who died here," he said.

> We cannot consecrate, we cannot hallow this ground. The brave ones who struggled here hallowed it far above our poor power to add or detract . . . It is for the living of 1976, 5 score years after this conflict to resolve that these dead, red and white, shall not have died in vain, that the nation will in its next 200 years have a new birth of freedom, as we citizens resolve to learn from the admitted mistakes of our forbears [sic], so that government, by and for the people of all races and creeds, shall not perish from the earth.

Listening to Stearns, one could be forgiven for assuming that acculturation and assimilation were no longer on the agenda and that unity had at last been achieved. But that was not the case, at least not yet at the battlefield with two names.

Several unofficial ceremonies took place on the anniversary. At sunrise, Frank Fools Crow, a Lakota spiritual leader, conducted a prayer on Battle Ridge in remembrance of the Lakota and Cheyenne who died in the fight. Later that morning he blessed a sign recently mounted on the outside wall of the visitor center. Its words, "KNOW THE POWER THAT IS PEACE," derived from a vision Black Elk, an Oglala holy man, had as a boy. In that vision a being came to him and said

> give them now the flowering stick that they may flourish, and the sacred pipe that they may know the power that is peace, and the wing of the white giant that they may have endurance and face all winds with courage.[23]

That afternoon, acting on behalf of the Custer family and not under the aegis of the Park Service, Lieutenant Colonel (U.S. Army, retired) George Custer III laid a wreath at the base of the 7th Cavalry memorial. Two other Custer descendants, George Armstrong Custer IV and Dr. Lawrence Frost, accompanied him along with Robert Utley.

Although peaceful, the events of June 1976 challenged what Linenthal calls the "patriotic orthodoxy" and spawned a struggle for control of the

Greasy Grass/Little Bighorn story that continued beyond the end of the century.[24] Some people, including a few exceptionally vocal Custer buffs, were unhappy with how the Park Service handled the battle centennial and particularly the protests. These "guardians of the patriotic faith," to invoked Linenthal again,[25] accused the monument administration of caving in to threats by Native American radicals in order to avoid a confrontation and the bad press it would engender. Some interpreted the failure to invite Lieutenant Colonel Custer to participate in the observance as a snub of the Custer family driven by political correctness. In a complaint sent to the NPS, John Carroll, a well known Custer buff, contrasted the treatment accorded the protesters with that received by Custer's grand-nephew. "It is a sad state of affairs," he wrote, "when the parties responsible for the wanton destruction at Wounded Knee are provided a platform, and a man who served his country in its armed forces is ignored and insulted."[26] Besides expressing views shared by some Custer buffs, his words reflected tensions prevalent in American society throughout the Cold War era and especially during the Vietnam years.

The Black Elk quotation was another point of contention. When it first went up in the centennial summer people referred to it as "the Sioux memorial" and the local paper described it as a "tribute to the Sioux and Northern Cheyenne who fought, died and won in the Battle of the Little Big Horn."[27] Most people were moved by its message of peace but a few Custer buffs found it deeply offensive and inappropriate since Black Elk, then a young warrior, was in the village at the time of the battle. What most of them failed to mention was that he also had the misfortune of being at Wounded Knee in 1890. Those who objected to the sign believed it not only disparaged the soldiers who "gave their lives" in the battle but reflected a creeping bias toward the Native American viewpoint in battlefield interpretation. Carroll felt the sign "should be removed as it is a disgrace to the memory of the men who wore the uniform of their country and lost their lives performing their duty." He argued that to have "a quote by an 'enemy' . . . placed on a sacred ground decreed by Federal Law to memorialize General Custer and his men of the 7th U.S. Cavalry" contributed to "the continuing erosion of the pride and honor of the U.S. Army."[28] If the sign was to remain, he demanded that it be counterbalanced with a quotation from Custer and suggested the following line from a letter he wrote while a West Point cadet: "If it is to be my lot to fall in the service of my country and my country's rights, I will have no regrets."[29] The Park Service ignored the suggestion.

Superintendent James Court defended the sign's message of peace.[30] He noted that the Lakota and Cheyenne had merely acted in defense of their right to live where and how they wanted within their own territories.

Besides, they didn't start the war, the government did. Another Custer buff weighed in on the matter.[31] She felt the real issue was "the fact that the men of the 7th Cavalry are being denied fair and equal representation at the one place they paid for that right with their lifeblood." She added that

> too many of us are tired of seeing the U.S. Cavalry cast in the role of unwavering aggressor in the Indian Wars to allow this type of thought and [the] one sidedness of the Black Elk quote to go unchallenged. We are cautioned that to neglect the Indian side of the story is to do injustice to everyone concerned. It should be recognized that an equal injustice is done by neglecting and misrepresenting the cavalry's side of the story.

As seen here, a small group of Native American activists used the centennial observance as a vehicle to challenge conventional views of the battle and of Indian and white relations, and they did so with unprecedented success. Some Custer buffs and other battlefield visitors recognized that for what it was—an attempt to subvert and thereby reclaim the battle story—and fought back. Both sides were able to effectively cite the issue of balance in arguing their case.

A dozen years later Native American activists led by Russell Means once again seized the symbolic initiative at the national monument on the battle anniversary and underscored the need for a more balanced telling of the story. The group started the day with a sunrise prayer ceremony at the Austin Two Moon ranch. From there they moved to the battlefield, where around 150 people gathered not far from the 7th Cavalry memorial to pray for world peace. After the prayer, about forty activists moved along the ridge to the memorial, among them a group of Lakota riders and Russell Means. As they approached Last Stand Hill, the riders charged ahead. Whooping, they circled the obelisk and struck it, counting coup. Then, after a speech by Means, the group set a large steel plaque in cement near the base of obelisk. A simple memorial to the battle's Native American participants, it read:

> In Honor of our Indian Patriots who fought and defeated the U.S. Calvary [sic] in order to save our women and children from mass murder. In doing so preserving our rights to our Homeland, Treaties and Sovereignty. 6/25/88 G. Magpie, Cheyenne.

In that its wording emphasized Native American resistance to colonial domination and referred to atrocities committed by the army, the plaque offered a point of view not readily available elsewhere at the monument.

Although the protesters apparently lacked permission for the gathering, and despite having had enough warning to bolster security, the Park Service did not intervene. Several buffs commented on the coup counting in print but what really irked them at the time was the plaque and how the NPS handled the matter. From their point of view, the Park Service had let the protesters "desecrate the mass grave" with a "crude 'plaque' defaming the dead" rather than risk the media attention a confrontation would bring.[32] Intermingled with their objections, however, were calls for an officially sanctioned, sensitively rendered, and appropriately located memorial to the Indians.

Richard Real Bird (then Crow tribal chairman) and other Crows were among those who installed the plaque but not all tribal members initially supported the idea of an Indian memorial, at least not without reservations. Mardell Plainfeather—at the time a historian at the battlefield—was one of them. She expressed her views on the matter in a paper on battlefield interpretation she delivered at a history conference that fall.[33]

> If it's a monument only to the Sioux, Cheyenne, and Arapaho victors, where does that leave the Crow and Arikara allies? Their involvement in the battle story is relevant to proper interpretation and must be considered in the design and dedication of a monument if it is to be for ALL the Indians involved in the battle story. If it is a monument for the victors only . . . we will have yet another dilemma to deal with soon.

Other Crows shared her concerns over the relevance of any memorial to their ancestors who were in the fight and, hence, to modern Crows.

The 1989 appointment of Barbara Sutteer Booher (Cherokee/Ute) as superintendent at the national monument did little to stem the controversies that plagued the battlefield. In addition to being the first woman and the first Native American to hold the top post, she made her commitment to more even-handed interpretation clear by hiring more Native Americans and by actively pursuing a site name change and a memorial to the battle's Indian participants. She was not the first person to propose those changes but they became reality on her watch; consequently she got credited or blamed for making them happen. Calls for a name change had been floating around for some time, even within the Park Service. The preliminary draft of the Custer Battlefield National Monument master plan issued in 1972 noted that many Native Americans and Custer critics took issue with the Custer emphasis implied by the name. It further acknowledged that the name must change in order for the NPS to tell an impartial and objective story at the site.[34]

The move to commemorate the battle's Native American participants similarly predated any steps Booher took as well as the demands made by activists. Several of the rock cairns the Lakota and Cheyenne built at the spots where their warriors died remained into the 1990s yet nothing had been done to officially mark their locations. The first known request that the battlefield caretakers do so came in 1924, when a Cheyenne woman wrote to the superintendent to ask that the place where Lakota warriors mistakenly killed her father, Lame White Man, be marked. Her request was not honored. John Stands in Timber, the grandson of Lame White Man, located the exact spot for a battlefield historian in 1956. Two years later monument staff finally placed a simple wooden marker there. However, the NPS still did not indicate its location on the battlefield maps. The rest of the cairns remained unmarked for several more decades.

By the 1990s, the movement for an Indian memorial and a battle-field name change was gaining momentum. The NPS, most Montana politicians, and Native American activists from around the country strongly supported both moves. Suzan Shown Harjo (Cheyenne/Hodulgee Muscogee), a prominent Native American leader, explained the deep meaning the battle holds for Native peoples in her statement to the House subcommittee hearings on the matter. She wrote that it is

> because of the valor and sacrifice of the past generations of all Indian nations in defense of treaty, sovereign and human rights that there are any Indian people alive today. The heroism of our relatives at the Battle of the Little Bighorn has become the symbol for Indian people generally of the just and provident actions of all our ancestors to protect family and home.[35]

Other people—including some non-Indian battlefield area entrepreneurs and a few Custer buffs—condemned the proposed changes as an "Indian-ization" of the battlefield and complained of "reverse discrimination" and "revisionist history."[36] Some even argued that the Custer Battlefield name should be retained as a historic artifact.

The Indian memorial enjoyed much wider support throughout the legislative process than the name change. The first bill to authorize a memorial was introduced in 1990 but died in committee after language was added to authorize a name change. Senator Ben Nighthorse Campbell (R–Colorado, Northern Cheyenne) re-introduced the name change and memorial bills separately the next year. When he was confident he had enough support in committee to secure passage, he attached the name change as a rider to the memorial bill. Campbell argued that the bill, if passed, would give equal stature to both sides and both, he observed, had been fighting for what they believed was right. He also suggested that the name change (and, presumably, the Indian memorial) would serve as an important symbol to Native American peoples and thereby give them a sense of cohesiveness and spirit, something particularly important, he thought, for those children torn between two cultures.

With the support of the entire Montana delegation, and despite continuing opposition from certain quarters, the bill passed both houses and President George Bush signed it into law on December 10, 1991. In that it reflects the location of the battle rather than the loser, many people felt the new name—the Little Bighorn Battlefield National Monument—is more objective and adheres more closely to battlefield naming conventions than its predecessor. The bill also retained the Custer name for the national cemetery and authorized a memorial to the battle's Indian participants to be built on the ridge near the 7th Cavalry memorial. For many Native Americans, the memorial was by far the most important part of the bill.

A ceremony held at the battlefield on Veteran's Day 1992 marked the name change. Lionel Bordeaux (*Sicangu* or Brulé Lakota), president of Sinte Gleska University on the Rosebud Sioux Reservation in South Dakota, gave the keynote speech. Reflecting on how the Lakota use names to honor individuals and their deeds, characteristics, and spiritual power, he depicted the name change as a major step forward in the process of healing and reconciliation. He also noted that the memorial and name change would commemorate two victories for Native Americans: their short-lived 1876 military victory and their modern victory in the fight for recognition.

STRUGGLING FOR PEACE THROUGH UNITY

The battlefield name change and congressional authorization of an Indian memorial at the monument were major steps forward but the struggle for meaning at the site was not yet over and Congress had not appropriated any funds for the memorial. During the last few decades of the twentieth century people gradually stopped bandying about terms like "assimilation" and "acculturation" and the question of how best to deal with the so-called Indian problem lost salience. Nonetheless serious concerns remained to be addressed at the battlefield and, once again, they mirrored issues elsewhere in society. What it came down to were three interrelated questions: (1) Whose national monument is it? (2) Whose story should be told there? and (3) Who gets to decide? Implicit in those questions was an assumption that the United States is composed of diverse stakeholders who attach different and inevitably irreconcilable meanings to the site. Those questions were debated in very public and often dramatic ways on the battlefield itself and reflected the widespread tension in society between the "*pluribus*" ("many") and the "*unum*" ("one") in the American national motto. The significance of such questions cannot be exaggerated because together they raised an issue of overriding importance: who gets to author history? Because the answer to those questions had profound implications for other historic sites as well as for the American people's self-concept, the struggle for meaning at the monument attracted a great deal of attention.

The Crow Tribe, National Park Service, and North Shield Ventures (a private enterprise) signed a Memorandum of Understanding in 1992. It outlined the conditions for a feasibility study of a joint venture between the three parties that would lead to shared administrative responsibility and the creation of a "living history experience" at the battlefield. The proposal proved highly controversial and the NPS withdrew from the negotiations two years later.

The twin campaigns for a name change and an Indian memorial were a clear attempt to move Native Americans from the margins to the very heart of the story told at the national monument. They also sought to undermine the answers traditionally given to those all-important questions and thereby open up the Greasy Grass/Little Bighorn battle story to other readings. Both campaigns were successful and together they set in motion a process that would continue for years to come and ultimately diversify and complicate the story told at the Little Bighorn Battlefield National Monument.

The Indian Memorial Advisory Committee and the NPS announced the design competition for the new memorial on the 1996 battle anniversary. The theme they chose was "Peace Through Unity." According to the competition booklet produced by the committee, the prayers for world peace Austin Two Moon (Northern Cheyenne) had been conducting on the battlefield embodied the peace element. The following words from Enos Poor Bear (Oglala Lakota) expressed the unity element:[37]

> During the time of our elders, things were better for our Indians than they are today. The way that our elders made things better was through unity. Unity of purpose; unity of dedication; and unity of effort. When we look back over the pages of time, we observe that all major accomplishments of Indian people were brought about when unity was present. The major victory which our people enjoyed here at this very battlefield was the result of a unified effort among Indian people.

> Major progress among Indian people will come about only when there is unity of effort. The failures that we Indian people have experienced have come about when we were not united, and when divisiveness was the order of the day.
>
> If this Indian Memorial is to serve its total purpose, it must not only be a tribute to the dead; it must contain a message for the living. I earnestly suggest to you that power through unity would serve us well as an interpretive theme for this Memorial.

Two non-Indians, John R. Collins and Alison J. Towers of Philadelphia, PA, submitted the winning design. A summer of 1996 battlefield museum exhibit described it in detail:

> From a distance the memorial appears to be an elemental land form, recalling the ancient earthworks found throughout the continent. An integral relationship is established with the 7th Cavalry monument via an axis which connects the center of each element. Where this axis bisects the earthen enclosure, a weeping wound or cut exists to signify the conflict of the two worlds. Two large adorned wooden posts straddle this gap and form a "spirit gate" (not for passage of visitors) to welcome the cavalry dead and to signify the mutual understanding of the infinite all the dead possess. This gate also serves as a visible landmark and counterpoint to the 7th Cavalry obelisk.

While recognizing the pain of the "clash of cultures" memorialized at the battlefield, the memorial design visually symbolized the healing power of unity and did so in a way that had potential relevance for all parties concerned, including the Crow. According to the design plan, once construction was completed the enclosure would house a combination of permanent and rotating exhibits comprised of textual material, petroglyphs, pictographs, and artifacts. These would immerse visitors in Native American culture and convey the "Peace Through Unity" message in an always-current manner.

Most people praised the design but not everyone was overjoyed with it. Wayne Sarf was probably its most vocal opponent but he was not alone. He used his regular *Custer/Little Bighorn Battlefield Advocate* column to raise a question others were asking: "should the annihilation and mutilation of over 200 U.S. soldiers be celebrated a mere 67 yards from the mass grave where so many of them lie, with the shadow of a 'victory' pole falling over that grave?"[38] He argued that it is sacrilegious to position the memorial so close to the troopers' grave. He also highlighted what he felt were serious

Figure 4.1 Indian Memorial. Courtesy of the National Park Service.

conceptual flaws in its symbolism. Besides pointing out that the Lakota and Cheyenne did not use earth mounds of that sort in 1876, he questioned the relevance of the design to all "Indian nations." Some Indians, he observed, fought on the side of the army: "if one is a Crow or Arikara, is one supposed to celebrate this victory over one's ancestors?" He also worried that the memorial might serve "a *de facto* role as handy jumping-off point for the grave desecrations that are now NPS policy. First, gather at the Indian monument, then up the hill for some coup-counting and monument-kicking!"

Not everyone agreed with Sarf. Tom Pream, the Custer Battlefield Historical & Museum Association president, found the design "beautiful and meaningful." He suggested that the Indian memorial might give Native American activists a new focal point at the monument and "start a healing process that will begin to close the gap that has formed between two peoples who care deeply about the Battlefield and the events that happened there."[39]

Gerard Baker (Mandan/Hidatsa) replaced Barbara Sutteer (formerly Booher) as superintendent the year after the site was officially renamed the Little Bighorn Battlefield National Monument. Long-time critics of the battlefield administration initially took a wait-and-see approach to his appointment but the honeymoon proved short-lived as he quickly picked up where Sutteer left off. He continued to hire Native Americans to work at the site, slowly but steadily revamped the interpretive program to be more balanced, and took concrete steps to make the battlefield more welcoming to Native Americans. Like Sutteer, Baker proposed answers to those fundamental interpretive questions—Whose monument is it? Whose story should it tell? Who gets to decide?—that some people found unpalatable. Before long the critics forgot all about his strong qualifications for the post and began to suggest that his had been a politically correct appointment, i.e. that he got the job because he was Native American. They wanted him out.

Throughout the 1990s events staged to coincide with the battle anniversary offered the most personal and often controversial views available at the monument, just as they always had. Despite the lapse of time, the battle still held deep meaning for a wide variety of people and most especially for those who connected with it on a personal level: Lakota, Cheyenne, Crow, Arikara, and Arapaho tribal members, descendants of soldiers who fought in the battle, and more recent 7th Cavalry veterans. Baker invited all of them to the monument to tell their stories and mark the battle anniversaries in their own ways. From 1994 onward many of them gathered at the battlefield to do just that. Some of the means they used were highly emotive and very personal. Three types of activities typically occurred over the anniversary period: those coordinated by the Park Service, those coordinated by the Custer groups, and those undertaken by Native Americans. Inevitably, some of them and the perspectives they reflected clashed.

June 25–26, 1995, marked the one-hundred-and-nineteenth anniversary of the battle and for the first time since 1876 representatives from all the groups involved reconvened on the battlefield. The Cheyenne, Lakota, Arapaho, 7th Cavalry, and Crow and Arikara scouts each had their own honor day. They were free to mark it however they wished so long as it was non-violent, open to everyone, and welcoming. The five-day period began with a flag raising followed by a pipe ceremony conducted by a Crow religious leader who called for peace and respect. Over the next several days the tribes conducted prayer and honor ceremonies, made special presentations, and held dance demonstrations. Speakers addressed those gathered on a variety of topics. The last day was the 7th Cavalry Day. It focused more exclusively on the battle than did the others and attracted many Custer buffs who were in the area for their annual gathering.

Custer buffs tend to take a keen interest in all things Indian and especially those that pertain to warfare. Most, however, did not appreciate the counting coup ceremony activists conducted in 1988 and the Lakota repeated as part of their 1995 and 1996 Attack at Dawn ceremonies. Writing in 1997, one woman suggested that the NPS tolerated the coup counting because the troopers had "fought in a Politically Incorrect war."[40] She also questioned the function and authenticity of the practice, noting that:

> Whacking an unarmed stone with sticks may be therapeutic, but it does not promote harmony . . . By inventing a ceremony that never existed, today's activist Amerindians rewrite their history and insult the **real** (emphasis hers) Indian warriors who fought here. Dancing on a grave, hitting a stone with a stick and calling it "counting coup" is not only a mockery of their own ancestors, it is an act of pathetic desperation.

The writer of these words may be guilty of essentializing history, undoubtedly failed to grasp the significance of the practice of counting coup in Plains Indian culture, and clearly misunderstood the role of ritual in society but, in doing so, she inadvertently articulated a major issue in a publicly accessible way: history is always in the process of being rewritten.

After the 1996 battle anniversary, a group of Custer buffs mounted stiff opposition to the counting coup ceremony. Although the Lakota did not perform that part of their Attack at Dawn ceremony in 1997, it was obvious that they wanted to. Just in case they tried, a contingent of determined buffs posted themselves around the 7th Cavalry memorial to make a stand against the feared "grave desecration." Some of the men wore 1876 cavalry uniforms and one or two of the women wore period style dresses. All were particularly vigilant during the Attack at Dawn ceremony and while Lakota and Cheyenne spiritual leaders conducted prayers at the nearby Indian memorial site and blessed it. Equally vigilant were Indian activists, who posted themselves around the periphery of the 7th Cavalry memorial. As always, the NPS had pulled in additional security personnel over the anniversary period; they kept a close eye on both sets of watchers. Despite being welcome at the ceremonies under way further along the ridge, most non–Indian visitors bunched nervously on Last Stand Hill. Other than heightened tension and a rather loud debate between a Custer buff and an Indian memorial committee member over who *really* owns the battlefield, both ceremonies were concluded peacefully and with respect. Immediately afterwards the watchers dispersed.

Figure 4.2 7th Cavalry Memorial. Photo taken on the battlefield during the 1886 tenth
anniversary observance. Courtesy of the Denver Public Library, Western
History Collection, David F. Barry, B-245.

A few years earlier the following words from the statement of purpose
for the *Custer/Little Bighorn Battlefield Advocate* summarized the feelings
many buffs still shared about what was happening at the battlefield, albeit
with more inflammatory prose than most would have chosen.[41]

> For many years, the National Park Service has cringed and
> kowtowed in obeisance to the forces of "political correctness",

even when these forces seem to consist of tiny groups of irresponsible lawbreakers . . . While indulging thugs and terrorists, the NPS has gone out of its way to alienate serious scholars and those truly interested in the preservation of the battlefield.

As one can see here, although assimilation and acculturation, as terms at least, were off the political agenda, and the name change and Indian memorial had been approved, "peace and reconciliation" had yet to be achieved and unity remained a distant dream at the battlefield with two names. But change was in the air.

Gerard Baker was transferred to another site in 1997 and replaced as superintendent by Neil C. Mangum, a former battlefield historian. Although they had previously waged war with him over the books he approved for sale in the Visitor Center, the Custer buffs welcomed Mangum back with open arms. Like his most recent predecessors, he committed himself to promoting more balanced interpretation at the battlefield. It was during his tenure that the NPS began to mark with red granite tablets the spots where Lakota and Cheyenne warriors were killed. They placed the first markers on Memorial Day 1999 for the Cheyenne warriors Lame White Man and Noisy Walking. Two years later a marker was installed near the Reno-Benteen Battlefield for the Lakota warrior Long Road. After the Indian memorial was dedicated on the 2003 anniversary, a marker was dedicated to the Unknown Warrior. The next day a headstone was added for the Lakota warrior Dog's Back Bone. Although not complete, headway towards more balanced memorialization and interpretation was at last well under way at the battlefield.

The plaque Native American activists installed on Last Stand Hill in 1988 to highlight the lack of an Indian memorial at the monument was moved into the battlefield museum that fall. It remained there until 2003, when it was brought out to stand near the open microphone during the Indian memorial dedication. Afterwards, it was not returned to the museum. It can now be seen at the Fire Lightning Visitor Center at Wounded Knee, South Dakota.

Darrell J. Cook replaced Mangum in 2002. He remained in the lead position until he retired six years later. Eventually the Park Service selected Kate Hammond as his successor. With the distance from the controversies of the previous decades underscored by the successive change of leadership, the rancor slowly subsided at the monument. Progress toward more balanced battlefield interpretation nonetheless continued at a steady pace.

Although it had not yet secured funding to build the Indian memorial, in 1997 the Park Service contracted a Denver architectural firm to develop construction documents from the design. On Veterans Day 1999 the Indian Memorial Advisory Committee, representatives from all the tribes concerned, NPS officials, and veterans from several wars assembled on the battlefield for a ground-breaking ceremony for the memorial.[42] The event also launched a major drive to raise the estimated $2 million needed to complete the project. Despite the push, donations were slow to trickle in. When Congress initially authorized the memorial the expectation was that it would be financed out of tribal coffers and through private donations. The tribes, however, had always believed that the memorial should be federally funded just as the original installation and subsequent maintenance of the 7th Cavalry memorial had been. Eventually Mangum persuaded the Montana delegation to argue the funding case in Washington. They were successful and in October 2001 $2.3 million for the project was added to the Department of Interior's 2002 appropriation.

Once again shifts in emphasis in battle interpretation were to reflect shifts elsewhere in American society. It is noteworthy that funding for the Indian memorial was finally authorized only a few weeks after the September 11, 2001 attacks on the World Trade Center and the Pentagon. That is not to suggest that the attacks prompted the funding decision but rather that the American public and their elected officials reacted to the attacks with a renewed sense of unity. That, in turn, may have impacted how Washington viewed the request. What once had been a movement for recognition by Native Americans was now an acknowledgment and celebration of the diversity within national unity. The national motto—"e pluribus unum"—once again resonated with the American people . . . this time with all the American peoples.

CHAPTER 5

The Battle in Memory
and History

WHY THE GREASY GRASS/LITTLE
BIGHORN BATTLE?

W hat sets one event apart as a critical moment in history while another
features as a side-bar to a larger story and a third is relegated to the
footnotes? Timing factors in important ways and so do the personalities
involved, but there is much more to it than that. Certain events effect
profound changes and thus become critical moments. Sometimes those
changes are immediately apparent but more often they become manifest
over the longer term. Furthermore, what was originally a seemingly insig-
nificant moment can gain added or new importance in light of subsequent
developments. Other events are of such a scale or are so unprecedented
that they cannot but attain historical stature. Still others resonate with
ordinary people in ways that transcend time and place or that render them
a metaphor for their age. Yet other events are so ambiguous in their
meanings and significance as to be "multivocal." Open to diverse and even
contradictory "readings" or interpretations, they speak to different people
in remarkably different ways and can thus be deployed in support of a
wide variety of political, economic, and social agendas.

The battle of the Greasy Grass/Little Bighorn shares characteristics
with some of the other types of events just mentioned but it is an archetype
of the latter sort. It is and always has been multivocal. Because their
ambiguities are unresolved and quite often unresolvable, the meanings of
such events tend to be fluid and are thus capable of shifting in step with
changing circumstances and sensibilities. This enables different people to
read meanings into them to suit their own purposes or that are seemingly
evident to them at a given point in time. In other words, the meanings
conveyed by and significance of events like the Greasy Grass/Little Bighorn

battle are situated: they are contingent upon not only the context in which the event initially occurred but, more importantly, on the specific context of any subsequent retelling of the story and the sociocultural positioning, past experience, and current aims and sensibilities of both the storytellers and their nearly always heterogeneous audiences.

Compared to the carnage of Antietam and other major Civil War battles, which was still a recent and painful memory in 1876, the Greasy Grass/Little Bighorn battle was a relatively minor military engagement that could easily have slipped out of memory with the sands of time. But it did not. Why is that? The ironic timing of the Greasy Grass/Little Bighorn battle and the fact that it struck a chord with the American public in the summer of 1876 and has resonated with people ever since have factored in its enduring salience. So, too, have public perceptions of Custer and Sitting Bull and the clash between the two men. Nonetheless, the lion's share of the battle's significance can be traced to its multivocality, which derives mainly from the mystery that shrouds the Custer end of the fight. Despite Lakota, Cheyenne, and Crow eyewitness accounts, observations recorded by military personnel who visited the site two or three days after the battle, and the archaeological evidence, much of what happened at the north end of the battlefield, and especially the reasoning that led the soldiers in Custer's command to do whatever they did, is not only unknown but ultimately unknowable. Those question marks—those ambiguities—are what give the battle the versatility and malleability that enable it to speak to diverse audiences and to serve varied ends. And it is mainly that which has made the Greasy Grass/Little Bighorn battle a critical and enticing moment in American history.

Newspaper reporters and popular writers of the late 1870s certainly played a major role in securing the battle's place in history but one must not overestimate their contribution. Distracted by the actions and personalities of Custer—whom they construed as an endearing, almost recklessly courageous, and youthful icon of blossoming civilization—and Sitting Bull—whom they construed as Custer's polar opposite and a stereotypically stoic and menacing symbol of the untamed wilderness and "savage" past—they generally promoted a Great Man reading of the Greasy Grass/Little Bighorn battle and the events that preceded it. But what happened cannot be reduced to an outcome of decisions and actions taken by a few "great" men and women nor can its continuing resonance be explained by this simple polarization. Context was and still is everything: the battle itself and the challenges it posed to American sensibilities were very much a product of their time, as were the decisions made by Sitting Bull and Custer. The symbolic contrast between these two colorful and powerful antagonists and the detailed focus on their actions and motivations have always fired the imaginations of ordinary people by adding drama and dimension to the historic moment. Nonetheless, social, cultural, political, and economic factors that originated in the particular context in which the battle occurred and the many contexts in which it has since been recounted, coupled with its multivocality, have been more crucial to securing its enduring salience than any clash of personalities.

Many other factors have undoubtedly contributed to the battle's status as a critical, if discursively unstable, moment in the American past but two are particularly noteworthy. The first is the overarching but generally unspoken objective of the military campaign against the off-reservation Lakota and Cheyenne. The second is the painful irony of the battle's centennial year timing.

Although ostensibly a major victory for the Lakota and Cheyenne and a catastrophic defeat for the cavalry, Custer's Last Stand or the Little Bighorn battle was less a military engagement than a calculated maneuver in the American nation-building project, albeit one that appeared at first to have gone badly wrong. Access to land and natural resources and the safety of the settlers and other security issues ranked high among the army's officially stated objectives in its campaign against the Lakota and Cheyenne roaming off the reservation. Nonetheless, it was a less tangible objective that arguably did most initially to install the battle as a critical moment in the American past. The nature of that objective is intimated by the alternate names for the army's campaign popularized by writers in later years: the Sioux War and the Centennial Campaign. Together these two designators invoke the hopes and fears of the American people in the centennial year: optimism for a future at the vanguard of progress tinged with unease over the militant independence of the non-treaty Indians still wreaking havoc out on the northern Plains. The unspoken but widely recognized objective of the 1876 campaign was to enhance and consolidate the integrity of the nation by subduing the unruled and unruly northern Plains tribes and sequestering them on reservations until they either died off or were ready for incorporation into the American body politic. It was an assimilationist objective that dovetailed neatly with post-Civil War efforts to cobble unity out of diversity within the newly reunited nation's borders, which now stretched from coast to coast. It also conveniently promised to open badly needed lands to white settlers and economic exploitation.

Those, however, were objectives of the politicians and some elements of the American mainstream. The Lakota and Cheyenne and even the Crow and Arikara had their own goals and aspirations, which are what brought them to the Greasy Grass and shaped their actions there. Each of those peoples was desperately trying to maintain their traditional independent way of life, safeguard their rapidly diminishing resources, and retain control over territories they had long claimed as homelands. This disjuncture between the seemingly irreconcilable goals and aspirations of the Native American and non-Indian battle participants has echoed down through the decades and helped open the Greasy Grass/Little Bighorn battle story to diverse and sometimes contentious readings.

The ironic coincidence of the battle with the American centennial probably influenced how the public reacted to it more than the defeat itself. That reaction was expressed in and shaped by popular culture and the mainstream media of the day. Brian Dippie,[1] a long-time student of the battle in popular culture, argues that the reaction to Custer's defeat must be viewed within the context of a forward-looking nation nostalgic for its youthful past. He believes that

> precisely because it was a deviation from the relentless pace of Western conquest, because it was a temporary impediment in the path of that "resistless restless race" of pioneers, Custer's Last Stand was elevated into a realm apart. Custer, a horseback hero in an increasingly mechanized world. The Little Big Horn, an improbable name evocative of wide open spaces in an era of urbanization. Custer on that ridge above the Little Big Horn, both a distillation and a culmination of one phase of the American experience . . . on the eve of the nation's Centennial, with America's horizons diminished, its geographical immensity contained, its wilderness tamed, and its youth irrevocably lost, there was Custer, perpetual Boy General, making a Last Stand for all of yesterday.

The alienation fostered by the rapid pace of industrialization and cultural change that Dippie describes may have played a part in shaping how people initially understood and reacted to the battle but there is more to it than that. Disenchantment with the American nation-building project fomented by the bloody Civil War and the unanswered questions the battle itself raised must also be taken into consideration. In that the clash out on the distant Plains underscored residual disunity within the country's borders and thereby challenged the citizenry's fragile sense of national identity and wholeness, such disenchantment probably factored more than any degree of wistful nostalgia, regardless of how widespread it was in society.

These two factors—the objectives sought and the timing of the battle—were each enmeshed in their own tangle of politics, economics, memory and aspiration, and sociocultural patterns and processes. Those tangles were neither isomorphic nor stable but were specific and fluid. To be fully understood, the unofficial and official objectives of the military campaign and the impact of the timing of the 7th Cavalry's defeat, like the battle itself and any subsequent instantiation of it, must be situated within their specific contexts. The word "situated" is key to making sense of that sequence of events variously remembered as the Battle of the Little Bighorn, the Battle of the Greasy Grass, and Custer's Last Stand because its meanings have always and inevitably hinged upon the context of the moment. And it is those meanings and contexts that have determined what label people apply to the battle in any particular instance. Moreover, different stakeholders have always brought distinct configurations of memory, history, and culture to bear in making sense of and strategically using the battle.

The ambiguities that continually swirl about the battle have given it a versatility that has allowed differently positioned stakeholders to strategically exploit the story to their own advantage. Since the beginning of the twentieth century some people have recognized that there is money to be made from Greasy Grass/Little Bighorn tourism but more often the ends pursued have been primarily ideological. Almost since the dust settled people have used the battle to negotiate, contest, and assert various forms of collective identity; to define how the world is and how it ought to be; to address specific questions of meaning, identity, and cherished ideals and values; and to secure overtly political objectives. It is because of its continuing resonance, fluidity, and utility that the Greasy Grass/Little Bighorn battle could never be a mere side-bar to the larger story of American westward expansion or disappear into the footnotes of history. It was—and remains—a multivocal event that continually speaks to a wide range of people but not with a singular voice. Different stakeholders and stakeholder groups have always read different meanings into the battle but what those meanings are have shifted with the changing times. An indication of the battle's semiotic versatility and utility can be readily seen in how different groups in the immediate battlefield area deployed the same set of relatively uncontroversial facts about the battle to very different ends within the context of tourism during the 1990s.

WHO HAS THE RIGHT TO AUTHOR THE BATTLE STORY?

One last and relatively recent example should make clear at least some of the ways in which individuals and groups have used the battle story to pursue self-interested objectives. It also conveniently recaps what is thought to have happened in the battle on the river with two names and once again raises but does not answer the question of who has the right to author the story. Chapter 4 briefly considered battle reenactments staged by the Crow tribe in the late nineteenth and early twentieth centuries. Many other reenactments have taken place since then but a pair held near the battlefield throughout the 1990s illustrate several points, particularly when juxtaposed to the story then told by the National Park Service at the monument. First, a comparison of the two pageants shows how differently positioned stakeholders use battle stories constructed from more or less the same set of "historical facts" and assumptions to convey remarkably different meanings. Second, although things have changed considerably since 2001, the versions marketed to area visitors in the 1990s demonstrate that such stories can be made to serve diverse and even conflicting ends. Finally, the reenactments illustrate how different renderings of the story reflect the controversies and sensibilities of their day.

Nearly everyone has always assumed that the story told at the Little Bighorn Battlefield National Monument is the "official" and, therefore, most accurate and unbiased account available. First-time visitors inevitably tour the battlefield before doing anything else. Consequently, if they attend a reenactment, they arrive armed with a basic understanding of what happened, strongly influenced, if not actually shaped, by the Park Service's battlefield interpretation. During the 1990s two competing reenactments responded to and built upon that version of the story. The Custer's Last Stand Reenactment echoed it and therefore reinforced its meanings. The Battle of the Little Bighorn Reenactment fleshed out both accounts, highlighted alleged inaccuracies in them, and challenged their meanings. To fully understand the reenactments, one must view them in relation to one another and against the backdrop of the national monument yet within the context of local, regional, and national social relations and politics.[2] This brief example focuses mainly on what went on at the local level.

Every visitor to the national monument receives an interpretive folder that outlines the army's 1876 campaign and maps out the action (Figure 2.2 reproduces the battlefield map from the NPS interpretive folder distributed during the 2011 tourist season). The version in use throughout the 1990s firmly established the battle as the outcome of a "clash of cultures." It told a cautious story constructed from facts known with a reasonable degree of certainty. The folder's opening paragraph explained that the "Little Bighorn Battlefield National Monument memorializes one of the last armed efforts of the Northern Plains Indians to preserve their ancestral way of life." A few lines later it stated what by then was certainly an adage: "Although the Indians won the battle, they subsequently lost the war against the white man's efforts to end their independent nomadic way of life." One can trace this now conventional framing of the battle back to at least the fortieth and fiftieth anniversary observances. Detectable within it is an assumption that the inexorable erosion of Native American cultures was accompanied by the steady assimilation of Indian peoples into mainstream society and was thereby solving the so-called Indian Problem.

> Regularly scheduled "ranger talks," museum exhibits, story boards positioned at key points on the battlefield, films, a battlefield handbook available for purchase, special events, and guided tours provided by Apsaalooke Tours, a training program run out of the nearby Little Bighorn College, flesh out the story told at the national monument.

Expanding on this introduction, the folder described the battle as an episode in a conflict that began when Europeans arrived in North America. After the Civil War, settlers once again surged west. Ignorant of the peoples and cultures they encountered, they violated Native American hunting grounds and disregarded the treaties. The Indians resented their encroachment and resisted. Violent clashes between the two groups occurred with increasing frequency. In an attempt to stem the conflict, the government forged a treaty with most of the northern Plains tribes in 1868. Based on the assumption that it was "cheaper to feed than fight" them, the Fort Laramie treaty created a large reservation for the Sioux and promised them protection against "depredations by people of the United States."

After gold was discovered in the Black Hills in 1874, prospectors flooded onto the new reservation. When the army's efforts to keep them out failed, the government tried to buy the hills but the Indians refused to sell them. Defiant Sioux and Cheyenne resumed their attacks on white settlements and travelers. In December 1875, the Commissioner of Indian Affairs ordered them to return to their reservations by the end of January 1876 or be "deemed hostile." When they failed to do so, the Commissioner handed the matter over to the army. The army devised a plan that called for three columns to converge on the Sioux and Cheyenne bands roaming in eastern Montana: the Wyoming column headed by General Crook, the Montana column under Colonel Gibbon, and General Terry's Dakota column, which included Custer and the 7th Cavalry.

Crook's column retreated in mid-June after a large party of Sioux and Cheyenne warriors attacked it on the Rosebud. Afterwards, more confident than ever, the Sioux and Cheyenne moved farther west toward the Little Bighorn. By then Terry and Gibbon had rendezvoused on the Yellowstone near the mouth of the Rosebud. Just a few days later, hoping to catch the Indians in the Little Bighorn valley, Terry sent the 7th Cavalry, now led by Custer, up the Rosebud to approach from the south. Terry accompanied Gibbon's troops up the Yellowstone to approach from the north.

The 7th Cavalry located the Indian camp at dawn on June 25. Underestimating the Indians' fighting power, Custer split his regiment. He retained command of five companies, assigned three each to Major Reno and Captain Benteen, and left one to guard the pack train. After dispatching Benteen to scout the hills to the south, he and Reno rode on toward the Little Bighorn. As they approached the river, Custer ordered Reno to attack the village from the south while he led his own command north toward the lower end of the village. When a mass of warriors confronted Reno, he formed his troopers into a skirmish line and tried to make a stand. Outnumbered, they made a chaotic retreat across the river to the bluff tops. Responding to written orders from Custer to hurry forward with the packs, Benteen soon joined them there.

Neither Reno nor Benteen knew where Custer was but the sound of heavy gunfire to the north indicated he was under attack. After resupplying, their troops followed an advance party led by Captain Weir to a high hill a mile in that direction. From there they could see the Custer battlefield in the distance but by then the gunfire had stopped and Custer's troops were nowhere to be seen. The soldiers came under renewed attack at Weir Point and soon retreated to their original position above the river, where they entrenched and fended off the warriors for the rest of that day and most of the next. The siege ended when Terry's and Gibbon's column approached and the Indians withdrew. The folder's narrative concluded by reporting the number of Indian and army dead and wounded and noting that before long most of the Sioux and Cheyenne returned to their reservations and surrendered.

In this bare-bones outline of the sequence of events, and despite its disproportionate emphasis on the army side of the equation, the folder offered a fairly conventional view of the battle that few non-Indians quibbled with. What it did not do was highlight the unknowns, ambiguities, and controversies that still engulf it. Other interpretive media at the monument introduced a degree of uncertainty into the story but it was controversies provoked by Indian and non-Indian visitors to the site (see Chapter 4) and the questions raised by the Battle of the Little Bighorn Reenactment that most destabilized the narrative.[3]

Throughout the 1990s a committee supported by the local Chamber of Commerce and a Crow family and their friends staged concurrent battle reenactments over the late June anniversary period. This is when visitation peaks at the national monument and the Park Service supplements its interpretive schedule with special programs. Although the story each reenactment told closely resembled that told at the national monument,

Figure 5.1 Crow Scouts on the Greasy Grass/Little Bighorn Battlefield. Photo taken
between 1908 and 1913, probably in conjunction with The Last Great Indian
Council sponsored by Rodman Wanamaker. Courtesy of the Denver Public
Library, Western History Collection, Joseph Kosseth Dixon, Z-3204.

the meanings they conveyed and politics they actuated differed in
noteworthy ways. That was particularly true with regard to the way in
which each harnessed their story to long-standing grievances and current
political and economic objectives, some of which reflected local concerns
and issues while others had regional or national salience. By contrasting
and comparing these three renderings, one can readily see how ambiguities
inherent in the story open it up to diverse readings and give it the
versatility and malleability that make it semiotically useful to diverse
stakeholders.

The Crow Tribe inaugurated the Custer's Last Stand Reenactment
for Montana's 1964 Territorial Centennial. Conceived and written by Joe
Medicine Crow, their historian, it purported to tell the story from the
Indian point of view, or "from the west side of the river looking east."
The next year a bi-cultural local group took it over. They staged the show
annually from then through 1973, when financial problems and dwindling
interest brought it to an end. By that time, whites controlled the production

and the script paid added attention to the cavalry side of the story. Plans to stage a reenactment over the 1976 battle centennial were abandoned owing to security concerns. In a bid to lure more tourists to the area, the Chamber of Commerce finally resurrected the show in 1990 after first winning Medicine Crow's enthusiastic support by agreeing to tell the story from the Indian point of view using his original script.

> Joe Medicine Crow, an anthropologist by training and the Crow Tribe's historian, is the last person to have counted all four types of coup recognized by the Crow. In combat against the Germans in World War II, he touched a live enemy, captured an enemy gun, stole enemy horses, and led a successful war party. By doing so he became a war chief.

The Crow Real Bird family launched its own pageant in 1991, a move most local people interpreted as an act of defiance. It competed with the Last Stand for performers and audience and, like the Last Stand, relied on a bicultural cast and claimed to tell the story from the Indian point of view. Area residents distinguished between the two pageants on racial or cultural grounds. The Custer's Last Stand Reenactment was the white, Chamber, or Hardin show, they said, and the "other one"—variously dubbed the Real Birds' or Medicine Tail Coulee reenactment but officially titled the Battle of the Little Bighorn Reenactment—was the Indian or Crow show. Despite similarities in content, the two shows differed noticeably in their tone, tenor, and aims.

The producers of the Last Stand Reenactment used their show to promote the area as a tourist destination, a strategy the predominantly white business community, its most obvious beneficiary, supported. Throughout the 1990s their reenactment celebrated freedom, democracy, and a shared national identity rooted in patriotism and ignored themes and issues that might suggest ongoing discord. It did not deny that Indians had suffered injustices during American westward expansion but bracketed them off as a matter of historical interest rather than ongoing concern. Moreover, the question posed in the prologue to the action—"Did the Red Man triumph in victory? Or was this a last defiant but futile gesture against a fate from which there would be no escape?"—implied that the triumph of civilization was preordained. Combined with the marketing of their show as a laudable product of cross-cultural cooperation, such tactics allowed community leaders to draw a bold line under what was clearly a divisive legacy.

A committee operating under the aegis of the Hardin Area Chamber of Commerce staged the Custer's Last Stand Reenactment at a site several miles from the battlefield. The show unfolded in a series of episodes framed by the prologue referred to above and an epilogue that honored the dead and united the living. The initial episode featured Lewis and Clark and Sacajawea, the Shoshoni woman who aided them, while the next two briefly touched on aspects of Plains Indian life. The following five set the stage for the battle. One described missionary activity and treaty negotiations. Another reenacted the 1868 Fort Laramie treaty council, which ended Red Cloud's war and created the Great Sioux Reservation. The next depicted rising tension as whites encroached upon Indian lands. Two more episodes focused on the village on the Little Bighorn and Sitting Bull's Sun Dance vision. The final episode was the dusty and chaotic battle scene. Securing the desired impression that harmony prevails in the present, the pageant ended with the following words, which further partitioned off past differences: "History cannot be changed, but as fellow Americans of the 20th century, we, Red Man and White Man, live in a united fortress of democracy . . . the United States of America!" That assimilation had been achieved and unity forged out of diversity, was confirmed by the audience and cast joining together to sing the American national anthem. Notwithstanding the well-intended thrust of this epilogue, unity was more a matter of wishful thinking than an achieved fact. Deep divisions remained between Indians and non-Indians, a point the Real Birds underscored in their reenactment.

Local people believed that the Real Birds staged their show in deliberate opposition to the Last Stand Reenactment and the national monument. The Real Birds themselves saw it as a way to reclaim their history and to tell their own story. Unlike the Last Stand Reenactment's display of unity, their show asserted a Native American identity crafted within and against the white American mainstream and a Crow identity crafted, first, within and against the non-Indian mainstream and, then, within and against the currents of Crow tribal politics. Moreover, their show did not come to a tidy end on Last Stand Hill but continued on to illustrate how past events impact present lives. It was a multi-layered tale of the subjugation and disenfranchisement of Indians by whites, Indian resistance and resilience, and political jockeying within the tribal sphere. As such, it had local, regional, and national referents and resonance.

Although their story line paralleled that of the Last Stand and the national monument, the Real Birds strategically developed the historical, social, and cultural context of the battle to foreground what they believed to be critical issues and to advance their own political agenda. There were three main strands to that agenda. One addressed tribal politics. Another addressed Indian and non-Indian relations in the immediate area. And the last addressed Indian and white relations—past and present—across the region and nationwide. Not all of those strands were readily apparent in the reenactment itself, at least not to those outsiders in attendance.

The local and regional ramifications were most clearly reflected in the talk around town, which revealed a widespread understanding of the politics at play in telling the battle story.[4] Crows and non-Indians alike recognized most of the Crows who took part in the Last Stand Reenactment as supporters of the then-current Clara Nomee tribal administration. They identified those who took part in the Medicine Tail Coulee pageant as supporters of the previous Richard Real Bird tribal administration. Most people described the Real Birds' Crow cast and crew as "Traditionals" and those of the Hardin show as "Progressives." Many people substantiated those labels by noting that Traditionals tended to own land, to be "Northsiders," and to participate in traditional religious practices like the Sun Dance and Native American Church. The Progressives, in contrast, tended not to own land, to be "Southsiders," and to practice evangelical forms of Christianity. Finally, everyone assumed that the Real Birds and many of their supporters were political activists with links to militant Red Power groups like the American Indian Movement. Many people cited specific incidents in which one or another of the brothers allegedly participated as proof of their activism. Such actions accentuated and sought to correct imbalances in Indian–white relations in much the same way the Real Birds were trying to do with their show.

Although the entire extended family pitched in, the most visible faces behind the Real Bird's reenactment were three brothers, Richard, Hank (or Henry), and Kennard. Richard is a former tribal chairman, Kennard is a well-known western artist, and Hank is a former Montana Poet Laureate. In one way or another, all three are educators and political activists.

The Real Birds staged their pageant from their family lands on the banks of the Little Bighorn River at Medicine Tail Coulee. This is where many people believe Custer tried to ford the river to attack the village and where some think he died. Their pageant tended to vary more from show to show and to ramble on longer than the Hardin production. It related aspects of Plains Indian life, worldview, and ritual to warfare and described in relative detail the Vision Quest and Sun Dance, as well as the practice of counting coup, leadership styles, and the role of the horse and buffalo in Plains Indian life. In addition to the material covered in the Last Stand Reenactment and at the national monument, the Real Birds included the Washita massacre, Custer's alleged liaison with Monasetah, and other controversial topics. They also described injustices whites, and in particular the U.S. government, had committed and continue to commit against Native American peoples. In most shows their narrators reported that Custer was shot at the river but the performances nonetheless climaxed in a wild hilltop fight. Rather than the national anthem, the shows ended in a victory dance.

The Real Birds worked with the same key facts and most of the same assumptions as the NPS and the producers of the Custer's Last Stand Reenactment. Consequently, all three told similar stories. The Real Birds, however, imbued their story with very different meanings and used it to make social and political points. They aimed some of those points at their political adversaries but most of them at non-Indian visitors, who they sought to re-educate about this particular slice of the American past as well as the realities of past and contemporary Native American life. In addition to entertaining and educating the traveling public, the Real Birds were making statements about how they perceived the world to be and how they thought it should be. For example, unlike the Last Stand Reenactment and battlefield interpretation at the national monument, their story assumed the persistence of Native American cultures rather than the assimilation of Native American peoples into mainstream American society. They also used their show to highlight the injustices Native Americans suffered and continue to suffer on a daily basis and to stress that social relations in the area and across the country are still marked by disunity and discrimination.

GREASY GRASS/LITTLE BIGHORN HISTORIOGRAPHY: EVIDENCE AND CONTROVERSY

Just as popular interest in the battle has never waned so too have scholarly and pseudo-scholarly interest in the subject remained high. The secondary literature on the Greasy Grass/Little Bighorn battle is massive and still growing. Most of the primary documents it relies upon—Native testimony, accounts by 7th Cavalry survivors and other army personnel, government documents, official reports, archaeological evidence, journals, letters, telegrams, transcripts from the Reno Court of Inquiry, early photographs, etc.—are readily available online, in major libraries and archives, or reprinted in edited volumes. Consequently, students of the battle have an overwhelming, although generally accessible, body of evidence and analysis to plow through. But to do so requires an ability to read critically because, while some of the research and writing on the battle is of very high caliber, much of it borders on fiction and a little of what passes for scholarship really is fiction. Besides, even the very best of that work is riddled with ambiguities and unknowns and nearly all of it is contradicted or challenged by other equally credible scholarship.

Battlefield Archaeology

In August 1983 a wildfire blazed across the Greasy Grass/Little Bighorn battlefield and reduced the tall prairie grasses, sage brush, and other vegetation to cinder and ash. Archaeologists from the Midwest Archaeological Center, a unit within the National Park Service, took the opportunity to conduct an extensive archaeological investigation on the newly exposed site. During six summers of field research conducted between 1984 and 1996 they recovered more than five thousand artifacts, which after painstaking analysis led to new insights into how the battle had unfolded. Their findings tended to support Indian eyewitness accounts previously discredited or ignored, altered the way the National Park Service interprets the battlefield for visitors, and provoked debate among amateur and professional historians and other students of the battle.[5] Richard A. Fox's subsequent reanalysis of the data—which suggested a breakdown in discipline and a collapse of the command structure and called into question the very idea of a "last stand"—provoked much more heated debate.[6]

The most innovative technique the archaeologists employed was to treat the battlefield much like a crime scene. Arming a crew of committed volunteers with metal detectors, they systematically swept the Custer battle site. After marking and mapping the precise location, or provenance, of all items found, or what archaeologists call artifacts, they carefully removed them to an archaeological laboratory for further analysis. Included among those artifacts were a great many bullets and cartridge cases. By studying the firing pin marks on the cartridge cases and the rifling marks, or scratch patterns, on the bullets, forensic techniques more commonly employed in crime labs, the archaeologists were able to link the bullets and cartridges to the exact gun from which they were fired. Combining that information with other sorts of data, including that pertaining to spatial patterning, they could then trace the movement of specific guns across the battlefield. This enabled them to verify cavalry positions, identify previously unknown warrior locations, and trace the movements of specific individuals.

Excavations were also undertaken around some of the white marble markers that had been placed where individual soldiers fell. Because they were positioned fourteen years after the battle and nine years after the soldiers' remains were moved to the mass grave at base of the 7th Cavalry Memorial, there was some question regarding the accuracy of their positioning. Additional doubts were raised by the simple fact that there are 252 markers on the battlefield but only 210 men died there. The archaeologists found a strong correlation between the markers and human bones and fragments of guns and clothing but it quickly became evident to them that some single graves had two markers associated with them.

Physical anthropologists were called in to study the bone fragments and teeth recovered at the site. Their findings provided tangible evidence of just how difficult the life of a cavalryman was. In examining the teeth, for example, they discovered that the troopers suffered many dental problems. Staining on the teeth further suggested that most of the men drank coffee and used tobacco. In analysing the bones and bone fragments, they detected a great many healed fractures and widespread back problems. They were also able to do a facial reconstruction on one of the skulls recovered but have not as yet been able to put a name to the face.

Then, of course, there is the steady stream of fiction itself to contend with as well as the poetry, films, paintings, reenactments, essays, cartoons, and so forth. Each of these genres engages the battle in important ways and thus warrants serious study. While this body of creative work is far too large to deal with here, solid overviews and analyses by Dippie,[7] Hutton,[8] and Langellier[9] serve as useful guides for those just beginning to delve into popular culture treatments of the battle.

Most people automatically assume that research and writing by academic and amateur historians and similarly inclined students of the battle is rooted in fact and therefore almost certainly more accurate than popular culture treatments of the subject. One must not, however, underestimate the interpretive, persuasive, emotive, and even political power of popular culture nor its ability to respond to and shape public sensibilities. Similarly, one must not overestimate the accuracy and authenticity of scholarly renderings of the Greasy Grass/Little Bighorn battle story. Whether they posture as creative or scholarly endeavors, all battle accounts are best approached as constructed or manufactured. However, that is not to say that they are necessarily artificial or false. Rather, it is merely to acknowledge that no matter how well established the facts are upon which such accounts are based, writers pick and choose among them and those facts never speak for themselves. Facts don't speak at all: they attain their significance and derive their meanings only in relation to other facts and through interpretation. Consequently, while a core of facts exists that are known with a reasonable degree of certainty, those facts can be (and have been) assembled and reassembled into a variety of different and often contradictory configurations. In reality, much of what passes for knowledge about the battle is a matter of theory, guess-work, poetic license, wishful thinking, self-interested obfuscation, or a by-product of the literary conventions of narrative and plot development.

Given its uncanny centennial summer timing and the many questions that remain unanswered, the Greasy Grass/Little Bighorn battle story has always lent itself to embellishment and melodramatic and heroic re-tellings. Poets, newspaper and magazine writers, and political essayists all beat Frederick Whittaker to the punch in reworking the battle story for a popular audience and the writers of dime and juvenile novels followed closely on their heels but Whittaker exceeded all of their efforts in scale, if not in accuracy, emotional force, or literary finesse. Published in 1876, his *A Complete Life of Gen. George A. Custer* strongly influenced how people of his day and later told the story and thereby contributed significantly to the image of Custer that lingers on in the popular imagination. For a long time Whittaker's volume served as a handbook of sorts for others writing on the topic, which led to the widespread promulgation of its many inaccuracies.

Libbie Custer supported Whittaker in his efforts, but within just a few years she began to make her own contributions to the rapidly accumulating literature on the battle and her husband. In all, she published three best-selling volumes on their life together, none of which addressed the battle itself and all of which burnished Custer's heroic image to a high sheen. Because it covers the period leading up to the battle, *Boots and Saddles*, published in 1885, is the most significant of her books for those interested in the Greasy Grass/Little Bighorn story. It focuses on the couple's years in Dakota Territory and describes the 7th Cavalry's departure from Fort Lincoln and then the moment the officers' wives received the terrible news. A related and equally important volume is a compilation of the letters that passed between the couple during their long separations while Custer was on campaign.[10] Not only do the letters illuminate Custer's Black Hills, Yellowstone, and other campaigns, they shed light on the man himself and cavalry life on the frontier.

Seemingly more credible information on the battle, how it unfolded, and its immediate aftermath than that offered by Whittaker and the other popular writers was soon forthcoming. Among the earliest of the contributions by soldiers who had taken part in the campaign were two long articles by Colonel John Gibbon published in 1877. The first focused on his role in the 1876 campaign and the second on his part in the subsequent hunt for Sitting Bull.[11] John G. Bourke, an aid to General Crook, included his recollections of the Wyoming column's movements and actions in *On the Border with Crook*.[12] The narrative of Peter Thompson, the lucky trooper who was forced to drop out of Custer's battalion when his horse went lame and thus became the last survivor to see him alive, is also invaluable.[13] Scouts, other enlisted men, and Native American participants and observers also recounted their experiences. Many of those stories have been reprinted or recounted in volumes compiled by Brininstool,[14] Graham,[15] Hutton,[16] and others. Equally useful are compilations of Walter Mason Camp's archived research notes and papers like those edited by Richard G. Hardorff[17] and Kenneth Hammer.[18] Camp was the editor of a railroad magazine and an amateur historian keenly interested in the Indian Wars and especially the Custer fight. He published little on the battle itself but collected mounds of documents, photographs, and other forms of relevant evidence. He also kept copious notes of the scores of interviews he conducted with Native American and white battle participants as well as on his own thoughts and analyses of the material.

Another resource of immeasurable value is the proceedings of the Reno Court of Inquiry, either as meticulously reported by the Chicago press in 1879 or in the official record compiled by Graham.[19] But even the official proceedings require critical evaluation because there is much to suggest that the 7th Cavalry survivors and attached personnel, including some of Custer's harshest detractors, closed ranks to protect themselves, their comrades, and the honor of the regiment. That is not to say that everyone who testified held Custer accountable; many survivors blamed Reno and Benteen for what happened. And while some of the survivors were relentless critics of Custer others were loyal supporters. In an article originally published in *Century Magazine*,[20] then General Godfrey (a captain in 1876), for example, filled in the details of the battle story in a way that reflected particularly well on Custer. Godfrey devoted much of his post-battle life to safeguarding Custer's reputation. He also campaigned hard against the inclusion of Reno's name on a memorial erected at the siege site and championed Mrs. Custer's pet cause, which was to have a museum built at the site of the last stand to memorialize her darling Autie and the soldiers who died with him.

Soldiers of lesser rank also contributed moving accounts of their experiences to the accumulating battle literature, among them enlisted men like Sergeant Charles Windolph.[21] Despite the steadily growing volume of first-hand accounts, many of them told by men who were highly critical of or bore a grudge against Custer, a conspiracy of silence soon developed surrounding the battle. Out of respect for Libbie Custer's feelings, there was general agreement among the battle survivors that the harshest of their criticisms should remain unspoken so long as she was alive. Libbie finally died in 1933 at the age of ninety-three, having outlived nearly all of her husband's detractors. As a result, they took whatever secrets they held and criticisms they had to the grave with them.

Over time a great many Native American eyewitness accounts became public. Some of them were first recorded by the battle participants themselves but many more resulted from a process in which the warriors, scouts, and people in the village told their stories to non-Indian interlocutors through translators. Much of this Native testimony is reprinted in the volumes already mentioned but several other books have it as their exclusive focus. In 1920 Orin G. Libby published a valuable set of battle stories obtained from the Arikara scouts.[22] Jerome Greene[23] later compiled Lakota and Cheyenne narratives in a single volume while

Richard G. Hardorff[24] produced separate books for Lakota and Cheyenne recollections of the battle. More recently Herman J. Viola has brought an interesting selection of accounts from members of all the tribes present at the Greasy Grass together in a single heavily illustrated and attractive volume.[25] Other accounts are to be found embedded in book-length life histories of battle participants. Particularly noteworthy are those for Wooden Leg,[26] Black Elk,[27] White Man Runs Him,[28] and Sitting Bull.[29] Not to be overlooked is the unique perspective offered in Kate Bighead's story as originally recorded by Thomas Marquis.[30] In the Cheyenne camp circle at the time of the battle, Kate Bighead did not flee as some of the women did but watched the fight from close at hand. Consequently, she was able to vividly describe what transpired on the battlefield as well as in the village.

But even these Native eyewitness accounts are not without their problems. Many of the warriors and other Lakota and Cheyenne observers were reluctant to tell their stories to outsiders out of fear of reprisals and the scouts may have felt a need to justify or re-frame their actions in the face of criticism from other Native peoples. When these reluctant battle participants finally shared their experiences, it was usually many years later, often though a translator, and frequently in direct response to specific questions posed by the interviewer. Such factors inevitably introduced scope for distortion and inaccuracy. That is not to say, however, that the Native testimony should not be taken seriously. It is merely to remind readers that, like any other primary source, it must be critically evaluated and matched against other evidence.

The eyewitness accounts just listed, along with the official documents and archaeological evidence, are mother's milk to Custer buffs and other students of the battle, who pore over them in search of new insights into *exactly* what happened on that hot June day in 1876. They then publish finely argued, richly substantiated analyses and counter-analyses and spend hours and hours happily debating their differences of opinion. For many decades most of them dismissed the Native testimony as unreliable because they could not easily reconcile it with other sources and because it contradicted their own key assumptions about the battle and preferred ways of telling the story. During that time, there was a strong tendency to focus on the cavalry side of the story and to use the primary documents to address critical or controversial questions. Few of those questions had much at all to do with the Native American participants. Did Custer disobey orders? How big was the village and how badly outnumbered were the soldiers? Were they out-gunned by the Lakotas and Cheyennes and handicapped by weapon malfunctions? Who was to blame for what happened? Could Reno and Benteen have saved Custer's battalion? Did

Custer try to cross the river and was he wounded or killed there? How long did the last stand last? Was Custer a "glory hunter" with presidential aspirations? Did he make tactical errors and exercise bad judgment? What were the causes of the Sioux Campaign? Which soldier did exactly what, when, where, and why? Custerphobes and Custerphiles have differed in their answers to those questions but both have found ample support for their points of view in the primary documents.

Only after Native Americans launched their struggle to reclaim the battle story in the late 1960s and early 1970s—and particularly after events over the 1976 battle centennial highlighted imbalances in conventional renderings of the story and triggered debate over whose story should be told at the battlefield—did increasing numbers of researchers and writers begin to take the Native testimony seriously. Their efforts to do so resulted in some insightful reinterpretations of the available evidence. Richard A. Fox,[31] for example, used Native testimony in his synthesis and reanalysis of the data generated by archaeological research undertaken after a fire swept across the battlefield in 1983. His findings challenged conventional understandings of what had transpired at the Greasy Grass/Little Bighorn and thereby lent credence to the Native testimony by demonstrating that the warrior accounts often coincided with the archaeological data.

It is largely due to these developments, and the changing sensibilities they reflect, that recent book-length treatments of the battle have tended toward a more balanced telling of the story and dispassionate look at Custer and what motivated him to make the decisions that he did. Since the 1990s, most writers on the topic have incorporated both Indian and non-Indian views and experiences and have woven together the praise and criticism heaped on Custer. Three recent volumes are particularly noteworthy for their balanced and skillful marshaling of evidence derived from primary documents. Drawing together information from many of the sources mentioned, James Donovan[32] has crafted a particularly detailed account of the events that led up to the battle, the battle itself, and the aftermath. Much as Buchholtz[33] did for the Little Bighorn Battlefield National Monument, Michael A. Elliott[34] has also drawn on these materials in his study of how the different places that Custer lived and served register the Custer story and memorialize the man. Although he focuses particular attention on Custer and Sitting Bull, Nathaniel Philbrick[35] avoids attributing the battle to the actions of these two men by using primary documents to contextualize and flesh out the events that led up to the battle and the battle itself. Given that the mystery and ambiguity remains and that the Greasy Grass/Little Bighorn battle still speaks to diverse people in meaningful ways, one can expect the story to be told again and again in the coming years.

Documents

Fort Laramie Treaty (1868)

*I*n *forging the 1868 Fort Laramie Treaty, government negotiators hoped to end the series of attacks against settlers, travelers, soldiers, and army installations known as Red Cloud's War and thereby bring peace to the Powder River country of southern Montana and northeastern Wyoming. Only after the army halted traffic on the Bozeman Trail and closed the three posts it had created to protect travelers did Red Cloud sign the treaty and lay down his weapons. Eventually he and his people settled near the Red Cloud Agency on the Platte River. Red Cloud never again took up arms against the wasichus.*

The treaty also defined the territorial boundaries between different tribes and established the Great Sioux Reservation but it nonetheless failed to achieve peace. Some people did not sign the treaty nor did they acknowledge its legitimacy or the tribal boundaries it imposed. These so-called non-treaty Indians, bands led by Sitting Bull and other traditionalists, continued to roam as they always had and to launch attacks against both the white intruders and such long-time adversaries as the Crow. Both Indians and whites soon breached the provisions of the treaty, which led to mounting frustration, heightened tension, and escalating violence. The promises made in this treaty are typical of others forged with the Plains tribes, as were the breaches that followed. They also paved the way for years of legal wrangling over the Black Hills of South Dakota.

ARTICLES OF A TREATY MADE AND CONCLUDED BY AND BETWEEN

Lieutenant General William T. Sherman, General William S. Harney, General Alfred H. Terry, General O. O. Augur, J. B. Henderson, Nathaniel G. Taylor, John G. Sanborn, and Samuel F. Tappan, duly appointed commissioners on the part of the United States, and the different bands of the Sioux Nation of Indians, by their chiefs and headmen, whose names are hereto subscribed, they being duly authorized to act in the premises.

ARTICLE I.

From this day forward all war between the parties to this agreement shall forever cease. The government of the United States desires peace, and its honor is hereby pledged to keep it. The Indians desire peace, and they now pledge their honor to maintain it.

If bad men among the whites, or among other people subject to the authority of the United States, shall commit any wrong upon the person or property of the Indians, the United States will, upon proof made to the agent, and forwarded to the Commissioner of Indian Affairs at Washington city, proceed at once to cause the offender to be arrested and punished according to the laws of the United States, and also reimburse the injured person for the loss sustained.

If bad men among the Indians shall commit a wrong or depredation upon the person or property of any one, white, black, or Indian, subject to the authority of the United States, and at peace therewith, the Indians herein named solemnly agree that they will, upon proof made to their agent, and notice by him, deliver up the wrongdoer to the United States, to be tried and punished according to its laws, and, in case they willfully refuse so to do, the person injured shall be reimbursed for his loss from the annuities, or other moneys due or to become due to them under this or other treaties made with the United States; and the President, on advising with the Commissioner of Indian Affairs, shall prescribe such rules and regulations for ascertaining damages under the provisions of this article as in his judgment may be proper, but no one sustaining loss while violating the provisions of this treaty, or the laws of the United States, shall be reimbursed therefor.

ARTICLE II.

The United States agrees that the following district of country, to wit, viz: commencing on the east bank of the Missouri river where the 46th parallel of north latitude crosses the same, thence along low-water mark down said east bank to a point opposite where the northern line of the State of Nebraska strikes the river, thence west across said river, and along the northern line of Nebraska to the 104th degree of longitude west from Greenwich, thence north on said meridian to a point where the 46th parallel of north latitude intercepts the same, thence due east along said parallel to the place of beginning; and in addition thereto, all existing reservations of the east bank of said river, shall be and the same is, set apart for the absolute and undisturbed use and occupation of the Indians herein named, and for such other friendly tribes or individual Indians as from time to time they may be willing, with the consent of the United States, to admit amongst them; and the United States now solemnly agrees that no persons, except those herein designated and authorized so to do, and except such officers, agents, and employees of the government as may be authorized to enter upon Indian reservations in discharge of duties enjoined by law, shall ever be permitted to pass over, settle upon, or reside in the territory described in this article, or in such territory as may be added to this reservation for the use of said Indians, and henceforth they will and do hereby relinquish all claims or right in and to any portion of the United States or Territories, except such as is embraced within the limits aforesaid, and except as hereinafter provided.

ARTICLE III.

If it should appear from actual survey or other satisfactory examination of said tract of land that it contains less than 160 acres of tillable land for each person who, at the time, may be authorized to reside on it under the provisions of this treaty, and a very considerable number of such persons shall be disposed to commence cultivating the soil as farmers, the United States agrees to set apart, for the use of said Indians, as herein provided, such additional quantity of arable land, adjoining to said reservation, or as near to the same as it can be obtained, as may be required to provide the necessary amount.

ARTICLE IV.

The United States agrees, at its own proper expense, to construct, at some place on the Missouri river, near the centre of said reservation where timber and water may be convenient, the following buildings, to wit, a warehouse, a store-room for the use of the agent in storing goods belonging to the Indians, to cost not less than $2,500; an agency building, for the residence of the agent, to cost not exceeding $3,000; a residence for the physician, to cost not more than $3,000; and five other buildings, for a carpenter, farmer, blacksmith, miller, and engineer—each to cost not exceeding $2,000; also, a school-house, or mission building, so soon as a sufficient number of children can be induced by the agent to attend school, which shall not cost exceeding $5,000.

The United States agrees further to cause to be erected on said reservation, near the other buildings herein authorized, a good steam circular saw-mill, with a grist-mill and shingle machine attached to the same, to cost not exceeding $8,000.

ARTICLE V.

The United States agrees that the agent for said Indians shall in the future make his home at the agency building; that he shall reside among them, and keep an office open at all times for the purpose of prompt and diligent inquiry into such matters of complaint by and against the Indians as may be presented for investigation under the provisions of their treaty stipulations, as also for the faithful discharge of other duties enjoined on him by law. In all cases of depredation on person or property he shall cause the evidence to be taken in writing and forwarded, together with his findings, to the Commissioner of Indian Affairs, whose decision, subject to the revision of the Secretary of the Interior, shall be binding on the parties to this treaty.

ARTICLE VI.

If any individual belonging to said tribes of Indians, or legally incorporated with them, being the head of a family, shall desire to commence farming, he shall have the privilege to select, in the presence and with the assistance of the agent then in charge, a tract of land within said reservation, not exceeding three hundred and twenty acres in extent, which tract, when so selected, certified, and recorded in the "Land Book" as herein directed, shall cease to be held in common, but the same may be occupied and held in the exclusive possession of the person selecting it, and of his family, so long as he or they may continue to cultivate it.

Any person over eighteen years of age, not being the head of a family, may in like manner select and cause to be certified to him or her, for purposes of cultivation, a quantity of land, not exceeding eighty acres in extent, and thereupon be entitled to the exclusive possession of the same as above directed.

For each tract of land so selected a certificate, containing a description thereof and the name of the person selecting it, with a certificate endorsed thereon that the same has been recorded, shall be delivered to the party entitled to it, by the agent, after the same shall have been recorded by him in a book to be kept in his office, subject to inspection, which said book shall be known as the "Sioux Land Book."

The President may, at any time, order a survey of the reservation, and, when so surveyed, Congress shall provide for protecting the rights of said settlers in their improvements, and may fix the character of the title held by each. The United States may pass such laws on the subject of alienation and descent of property between the Indians and their descendants as may be thought proper. And it is further stipulated that any male Indians over eighteen years of age, of any band or tribe that is or shall hereafter become a party to this treaty, who now is or who shall hereafter become a resident or occupant of any reservation or territory not included in the tract of country designated and described in this treaty for the permanent home of the Indians, which is not mineral land, nor reserved by the United States for special purposes other than Indian occupation, and who shall have made improvements thereon of the value of two hundred dollars or more, and continuously occupied the same as a homestead for the term of three years, shall be entitled to receive from the United States a patent for one hundred and sixty acres of land including his said improvements, the same to be in the form of the legal subdivisions of the surveys of the public lands. Upon application in writing, sustained by the proof of two disinterested witnesses, made to the register of the local land office when the land sought to be entered is within a land district, and when the tract sought to be entered is not in any land district, then upon said application and proof being made to the Commissioner of the General Land Office, and the right of such Indian or Indians to enter such tract or tracts of land shall accrue and be perfect from the date of his first improvements thereon, and shall continue as long as he continues his residence and improvements and no longer. And any Indian or Indians receiving a patent for land under the foregoing provisions shall thereby and from thenceforth become and be a citizen of the United States and be entitled to all the privileges and immunities of such citizens, and shall, at the same time, retain all his rights to benefits accruing to Indians under this treaty.

ARTICLE VII.

In order to insure the civilization of the Indians entering into this treaty, the necessity of education is admitted, especially of such of them as are or may be settled on said agricultural reservations, and they, therefore, pledge themselves to compel their children, male and female, between the ages of six and sixteen years, to attend school, and it is hereby made the duty of the agent for said Indians to see that this stipulation is strictly complied with; and the United States agrees that for every thirty children between said ages, who can be induced or compelled to attend school, a house shall be provided, and a teacher competent to teach the elementary branches of an English education shall be furnished, who will reside among said Indians and faithfully discharge his or her duties as a teacher. The provisions of this article to continue for not less than twenty years.

ARTICLE VIII.

When the head of a family or lodge shall have selected lands and received his certificate as above directed, and the agent shall be satisfied that he intends in good faith to commence cultivating the soil for a living, he shall be entitled to receive seeds and agricultural implements for the first year, not exceeding in value one hundred dollars, and for each succeeding year he shall continue to farm, for a period of three years more, he shall be entitled to receive seeds and implements as aforesaid, not exceeding in value twenty-five dollars. And it is further stipulated that such persons as commence farming shall receive instruction from the farmer herein provided for, and whenever more than one hundred persons shall enter upon the cultivation of the soil, a second blacksmith shall be provided, with such iron, steel, and other material as may be needed.

ARTICLE IX.

At any time after ten years from the making of this treaty, the United States shall have the privilege of withdrawing the physician, farmer, blacksmith, carpenter, engineer, and miller herein provided for, but in case of such withdrawal, an additional sum thereafter of ten thousand dollars per annum shall be devoted to the education of said Indians, and the Commissioner of Indian Affairs shall, upon careful inquiry into their condition, make such rules and regulations for the expenditure of said sums as will best promote the education and moral improvement of said tribes.

ARTICLE X.

In lieu of all sums of money or other annuities provided to be paid to the Indians herein named under any treaty or treaties heretofore made, the United States agrees to deliver at the agency house on the reservation herein named, on or before the first day of August of each year, for thirty years, the following articles, to wit:

    For each male person over 14 years of age, a suit of good substantial woollen clothing, consisting of coat, pantaloons, flannel shirt, hat, and a pair of home-made socks.

For each female over 12 years of age, a flannel shirt, or the goods necessary to make it, a pair of woollen hose, 12 yards of calico, and 12 yards of cotton domestics.

For the boys and girls under the ages named, such flannel and cotton goods as may be needed to make each a suit as aforesaid, together with a pair of woollen hose for each.

And in order that the Commissioner of Indian Affairs may be able to estimate properly for the articles herein named, it shall be the duty of the agent each year to forward to him a full and exact census of the Indians, on which the estimate from year to year can be based.

And in addition to the clothing herein named, the sum of $10 for each person entitled to the beneficial effects of this treaty shall be annually appropriated for a period of 30 years, while such persons roam and hunt, and $20 for each person who engages in farming, to be used by the Secretary of the Interior in the purchase of such articles as from time to time the condition and necessities of the Indians may indicate to be proper. And if within the 30 years, at any time, it shall appear that the amount of money needed for clothing, under this article, can be appropriated to better uses for the Indians named herein, Congress may, by law, change the appropriation to other purposes, but in no event shall the amount of the appropriation be withdrawn or discontinued for the period named. And the President shall annually detail an officer of the army to be present and attest the delivery of all the goods herein named, to the Indians, and he shall inspect and report on the quantity and quality of the goods and the manner of their delivery. And it is hereby expressly stipulated that each Indian over the age of four years, who shall have removed to and settled permanently upon said reservation, one pound of meat and one pound of flour per day, provided the Indians cannot furnish their own subsistence at an earlier date. And it is further stipulated that the United States will furnish and deliver to each lodge of Indians or family of persons legally incorporated with them, who shall remove to the reservation herein described and commence farming, one good American cow, and one good well-broken pair of American oxen within 60 days after such lodge or family shall have so settled upon said reservation.

ARTICLE XI.

In consideration of the advantages and benefits conferred by this treaty and the many pledges of friendship by the United States, the tribes who are parties to this agreement hereby stipulate that they will relinquish all right to occupy permanently the territory outside their reservations as herein defined, but yet reserve the right to hunt on any lands north of North Platte, and on the Republican Fork of the Smoky Hill river, so long as the buffalo may range thereon in such numbers as to justify the chase. And they, the said Indians, further expressly agree:

1st. That they will withdraw all opposition to the construction of the railroads now being built on the plains.

2d. That they will permit the peaceful construction of any railroad not passing over their reservation as herein defined.

3d. That they will not attack any persons at home, or travelling, nor molest or disturb any wagon trains, coaches, mules, or cattle belonging to the people of the United States, or to persons friendly therewith.

4th. They will never capture, or carry off from the settlements, white women or children.

5th. They will never kill or scalp white men, nor attempt to do them harm.

6th. They withdraw all pretence of opposition to the construction of the railroad now being built along the Platte river and westward to the Pacific ocean, and they will not in future object to the construction of railroads, wagon roads, mail stations, or other works of utility or necessity, which may be ordered or permitted by the laws of the United States. But should such roads or other works be constructed on the lands of their reservation, the government will pay the tribe whatever amount of damage may be assessed by three disinterested commissioners to be appointed by the President for that purpose, one of the said commissioners to be a chief or headman of the tribe.

7th. They agree to withdraw all opposition to the military posts or roads now established south of the North Platte river, or that may be established, not in violation of treaties heretofore made or hereafter to be made with any of the Indian tribes.

ARTICLE XII.

No treaty for the cession of any portion or part of the reservation herein described which may be held in common, shall be of any validity or force as against the said Indians unless executed and signed by at least three-fourths of all the adult male Indians occupying or interested in the same, and no cession by the tribe shall be understood or construed in such manner as to deprive, without his consent, any individual member of the tribe of his rights to any tract of land selected by him as provided in Article VI of this treaty.

ARTICLE XIII.

The United States hereby agrees to furnish annually to the Indians the physician, teachers, carpenter, miller, engineer, farmer, and blacksmiths, as herein contemplated, and that such appropriations shall be made from time to time, on the estimate of the Secretary of the Interior, as will be sufficient to employ such persons.

ARTICLE XIV.

It is agreed that the sum of five hundred dollars annually for three years from date shall be expended in presents to the ten persons of said tribe who in the judgment of the agent may grow the most valuable crops for the respective year.

ARTICLE XV.

The Indians herein named agree that when the agency house and other buildings shall be constructed on the reservation named, they will regard said reservation their permanent home, and they will make no permanent settlement elsewhere; but they shall have the right, subject to the conditions and modifications of this treaty, to hunt, as stipulated in Article XI hereof.

ARTICLE XVI.

The United States hereby agrees and stipulates that the country north of the North Platte river and east of the summits of the Big Horn Mountains shall be held and considered to be unceded Indian territory, and also stipulates and agrees that no white person or persons shall be permitted to settle upon or occupy any portion of the same; or without the consent of the Indians, first had and obtained, to pass through the same; and it is further agreed by the United States, that within ninety days after the conclusion of peace with all the bands of the Sioux nation, the military posts now established in the territory in this article named shall be abandoned, and that the road leading to them and by them to the settlements in the Territory of Montana shall be closed.

ARTICLE XVII.

It is hereby expressly understood and agreed by and between the respective parties to this treaty that the execution of this treaty and its ratification by the United States Senate shall have the effect, and shall be construed as abrogating and annulling all treaties and agreements heretofore entered into between the respective parties hereto, so far as such treaties and agreements obligate the United States to furnish and provide money, clothing, or other articles of property to such Indians and bands of Indians as become parties to this treaty, but no further.

[signatures omitted]

Source: 15 Stats., 635, available in Charles J. Kappler, comp. and ed., *Indian Affairs: Laws and Treaties, Vol. II: Treaties* (Washington, DC: GPO, 1904), 998–1007.

General Terry's June 27, 1876 Telegram to General Philip H. Sheridan

Official Report

*G*eneral Terry's official report of what transpired on the Little Bighorn, which he submitted by telegram, was written with not only his superiors in Washington in mind but also the general public. This accounts for its terse and matter-of-fact style. The telegram was delayed in transit and reached Washington after his more damning confidential report to Sheridan had fallen into the hands of the press and become public. Note that his official report emphasizes the unprecedented size of the village and the rugged terrain the Montana column had to traverse as it moved toward the agreed-upon rendezvous point.

Headquarters Dept. of Dakota
Camp on Little Big Horn River, July 6, 1876
June 27th

To Adjutant Gen. of Military
Division of the Missouri at
Chicago, Ill.

It is my painful duty to report that day before yesterday, the 25th inst., a great disaster overtook Gen. Custer & the troops under his command. At 12 o'clock of the 22nd he started with his whole regiment & a strong detachment of scouts & guards from the mouth of the Rosebud. Proceeding up that river about twenty miles he struck a very heavy Indian trail, which had previously been discovered, & pursuing it, found that it led, as it was supposed that it would lead, to the Little Big Horn River. Here he found a village of almost unexampled *(sic)* extent, & at once attacked it with that portion of his force which was immediately at hand. Major Reno, with three companies, A, G & M, of the regiment, was sent into the valley of the stream at the point where the trail struck it. General Custer, with five companies, C, E, F, I & L, attempted to enter it about three miles lower down. Reno, forded the river, charged down its left bank, dismounted & fought on foot until finally completely overwhelmed by numbers he was compelled to mount, recross the river & seek a refuge on the high bluffs which overlooked its right bank. Just as he recrossed, Captain Benteen, who, with three companies, D, H & K, was some two miles to the left of Reno when the action commenced, but who had been ordered by Genl Custer to return, came to the river & rightly concluding that it was useless for his force to attempt to renew the fight in the valley, he joined Reno on the bluffs. Capt. McDougall with his company B was at first some distance in the rear with a train of pack mules. He also came up to Reno. Soon this united force was nearly surrounded by Indians, many of whom armed with rifles, occupied positions which commanded the ground held by the cavalry, ground from which there was no escape. Rifle pits were dug & the fight was maintained, though with heavy loss, from about half past two o'clock of the twenty fifth till six o'clock of the twenty sixth, when the Indians withdrew from the valley, taking with them their village. Of the movements of Gen. Custer & the five companies under his immediate command, scarcely anything is known from those who witnessed them; for no officer or soldier who accompanied him has yet been found alive. His trail from the point where Reno crossed the stream, passes along & in the rear of the crest of the bluffs on the right bank for nearly or quite three miles then it comes down to the bank of the river, but at once diverges from it, as if he had unsuccessfully attempted to cross then turns upon itself, almost completing a circle & closes. It is marked by the remains of his officers & men, the bodies of his horses some of them bobbed along the path, others heaped where halts appeared to have been made. There is abundant evidence that a gallant resistance was offered by the troops, but they were beset on all sides by overpowering numbers. The officers known to be killed are Gen. Custer, Captains Keogh, Yates & Custer, and Lieuts. Cook, Smith, McIntosh, Calhoun, Porter, Hodgson, Sturgis & Reilly of the cavalry. Lieut. Crittenden of the Twelfth Infantry & Acting Assistant Surgeon D. E. Wolf, Lieut. Harrington of the Cavalry, and Asst. Surgeon Lord are missing. Capt. Benteen & Lieut. Varnum of the cavalry are slightly wounded. Mr. Boston Custer, a brother, & Mr. Reed, a nephew, of Genl. Custer, were with him & were killed. No other officers than those whom I have named are among the killed, wounded & missing. It is impossible yet to obtain a nominal list of the enlisted men killed & wounded but the number of killed, including officers, must reach two hundred & fifty. The number of wounded is fifty-one. At the mouth of the Rosebud I informed Genl. Custer that I should take the supply steamer Far West up the Yellowstone to ferry Genl. Gibbon's column over the river, that I shall personally accompany that column & that it would in all probability reach the mouth of the Little Big Horn on the twenty sixth instant. The steamer reached Genl. Gibbon's troops near the mouth of the Big Horn early in the morning on the twenty fourth & at four o'clock in the afternoon all his men & animals were across the Yellowstone. At five o'clock the column consisting of five companies of the Seventh Infantry, four companies of the Second Cavalry & a battery of three Gatling Guns marched out to & across Tullocks Creek. Starting soon after five o'clock in the morning of the twenty fifth the infantry made a march of twenty two miles over the most difficult country which I have ever seen in order that scouts might be sent into the valley of the Little Big Horn. The cavalry with the battery was then pushed on thirteen or fourteen miles further reaching camp at midnight. The scouts were set out at half past four in the morning of the twenty-sixth. The scouts discovered three Indians who were at first supposed to be Sioux but when overtaken they proved to be Crows who had been with Gen. Custer. They brought the first intelligence of the battle. Their story was not credited. It was supposed that some fighting, perhaps severe fighting, had taken place but it was not believed that disaster could have overtaken so large a force as twelve companies of cavalry. The infantry which had broken camp very early soon came up & the whole column entered & moved up the valley of the Little Big Horn. During the afternoon efforts were made to send scouts through to what was supposed to be Gen. Custer's position & to obtain information of the condition of affairs but those who were sent out were driven back by parties of Indians who in increasing numbers were seen hovering in Genl. Gibbon's front. At twenty minutes before nine o'clock in the evening the infantry had marched between twenty nine and thirty miles. The men were very weary & daylight was fading. The column was therefore halted for the night at a point about eleven miles in a straight line above the mouth of the stream. This morning the movement was resumed & after a march of about nine miles Major Reno's entrenchment position was reached. The withdraw of the Indians from around Reno's command and the valley was undoubtedly caused by the appearance of Genl. Gibbon's troops. Major Reno and Capt. Benteen, both of who are officers of great experience accustomed to seeing large masses of mounted men estimate the number of Indians engaged at not less than twenty five hundred. Other officers think that the number was greater than this. The village in the valley was about three miles in length & about a mile in width. Besides the lodges proper a great number of temporary brush wood shelter was found. In it indicating that many men besides its proper inhabitants had gathered together there. Major Reno is very confident that there were a number of white men fighting with the Indians. It is believed that the loss of the Indians was larger. I have as yet received no official reports in regard to the battle. But what is stated in is gathered from the officers who were on the ground then & from those who have been over it since.

Alfred H. Terry
Brig. Gen.

Transcribed from *http://arcweb.archives.gov*. Abridged transcript available in Message from the President of the United States in compliance with a July 7, 1876 Senate resolution, read and ordered printed 13 July 1876, Senate Executive Document No. 81, 44th Cong., 1st Sess., Serial Volume 1664.

General Terry's July 2, 1876 Telegram to General Philip H. Sheridan

Confidential Report

*T*he confidential report General Terry submitted to General Sheridan was not meant for public release. Having read the report, Sheridan sent it by messenger to the Secretary of War. Unbeknownst to him, that messenger was a newspaper reporter who promptly forwarded it on to the press. Terry's criticisms of Custer thus became public, although that was never his intention. In focusing on the deviations Custer made from the agreed battle plan and from Terry's orders to him, the report raises the question of whether Custer had disobeyed orders or had merely exercised the legitimate discretion accorded a commander in the field. Such questions, in turn, factored in the debates that raged over who was to blame for the debacle. They were picked up by newspaper reporters and Custer critics and have since been rehashed ad nauseam by students of the battle. Some of them read Terry's confidential report as a callous attempt to deflect any criticism from himself to Custer while others read his official report as an honorable attempt to shield the dead Custer from criticism.

Confidential
Headquarters Department of Dakota
Camp on Yellowstone,
near Big Horn River, Montana
July 2, 1876

I think I owe it to myself to put you more fully in possession of the facts of the late operations. While at the mouth of the Rosebud I submitted my plan to General Gibbon and to General Custer. They approved it heartily. It was that Custer with his whole regiment should move up the Rosebud till he should meet a trail which Reno had discovered a few days before but that he should not follow it directly to the Little Big Horn; that he should send scouts over it and keep his main force further to the south so as to prevent the Indians from slipping in between himself and the mountains. He was also to examine the headwaters of Tullock's creek as he passed it and send me word of what he found there. A scout was furnished him for the purpose of crossing the country to me. We calculated it would take Gibbon's column until the twenty-sixth to reach the mouth of the Little Big Horn and that the wide sweep which I had proposed Custer should make would require so much time that Gibbon would be able to cooperate with him in attacking any Indians that might be found on that stream. I asked Custer how long his marches would be. He said they would be at first about thirty miles a day. Measurements were made and calculation based on that rate of progress. I talked with him about his strength and at one time suggested that perhaps it would be well for me to take Gibbon's cavalry and go with him. To this suggestion he replied that without reference to the command he would prefer his own regiment alone. As a homogeneous body, as much could be done with it as with the two combined and he expressed the utmost confidence that he had all the force that he could need, and I shared his confidence. The plan adopted was the only one that promised to bring the Infantry into action and I desired to make sure of things by getting up every available man. I offered Custer the battery of Gatling guns but he declined it saying that it might embarrass him: that he was strong enough without it. The movements proposed for General Gibbon's column were carried out to the letter and had the attack been deferred until it was up I cannot doubt that we should have been successful. The Indians had evidently nerved themselves for a stand, but as I learn from Captain Benteen, on the twenty-second the cavalry marched twelve miles; on the twenty-third, thirty-five miles; from five a.m. till eight p.m. on the twenty-fourth, forty-five miles and then after night ten miles further; then after resting but without unsaddling, twenty-three miles to the battlefield. The proposed route was not taken but as soon as the trail was struck it was followed. I cannot learn that any examination of Tullock's creek was made. I do not tell you this to cast any reflection upon Custer. For whatever errors he may have committed he has paid the penalty and you cannot regret his loss more than I do, but I feel that our plan must have been successful had it been carried out, and I desire you to know the facts. In the action itself, so far as I can make out, Custer acted under a misapprehension. He thought, I am confident, that the Indians were running. For fear that they might get away he attacked without getting all his men up and divided his command so that they were beaten in detail. I do not at all propose to give the thing up here but I think that my troops require a little time and in view of the strength which the Indians have developed I propose to bring up what little reinforcement I can get. I should be glad of any that you can send me. I can take two companies of Indians from Powder River and there are a few recruits and detached men whom I can get for the cavalry. I ought to have a larger mounted force than I now have but I fear cannot be obtained. I hear nothing from General Crook's operations. If I could hear I should be able to form plans for the future much more intelligently.

I should very much like instructions from you, or if not instructions your views on the situation based as they might be on what has taken place elsewhere as well as here.

I shall refit as rapidly as possible and if at any time I should get information showing that I can act in conjunction with General Crook, or independently, with good results, I shall leave at once.

I send in another dispatch a copy of my written orders to Custer, but these were supplemented by the distinct understanding that Gibbon could get to the Little Big Horn before the evening of the 26th.

Alfred H. Terry
Brigadier General

Reno's Official Report

*R*eno's accounting of what happened at the Greasy Grass/Little Bighorn leaves as much out as it includes but provides a fairly accurate time-line for the sequence of events at the southern end of the battlefield. It is nonetheless an obvious attempt by Reno to justify and put the most positive spin possible on his actions, perhaps in anticipation of forthcoming criticism from his subordinates. Note in particular his abbreviated description of his command's retreat to the bluff tops and later movement north along the bluffs toward the sound of the guns. Both suggest a degree of leadership that others said he failed to exhibit. Although his troops were confronted by an overwhelming number of warriors, Reno almost certainly exaggerates that number in his report as he does the degree of support he enjoyed from his officers.

HEADQUARTERS SEVENTH UNITED STATES CAVALRY,

Camp on Yellowstone River, July 5, 1876
E. W. Smith,
A. D. C. and A. A. A. Gen.:

The command of the regiment having developed upon me as the senior surviving officer from the battle of the 25th and 26th of June, between the Seventh Cavalry and Sitting Bull's band of hostile Sioux, on the Little Big Horn River, I have the honor to submit the following report of its operations from the time of leaving the main column until the command was united in the vicinity of the Indian village:

The regiment left the camp at the mouth of the Rosebud River, after passing in review before the department commander, under command of

Bvt. Maj. Gen. G. A. Custer, lieutenant-colonel, on the afternoon of the 22nd day of June, and marched up the Rosebud 12 miles and encamped; 23rd, marched up the Rosebud, passing many old Indian camps, and following a very large pole-trail, but not fresh, making 33 miles; 24th, the march was continued up the Rosebud, the trail and signs freshening with every mile, until we had made 28 miles, and we then encamped and waited for information from the scouts. At 9:25 p.m. Custer called the officers together and informed us that beyond a doubt the village was in the valley of the Little Big Horn, and in order to reach it it was necessary to cross the divide between the Rosebud and the Little Big Horn, and it would be impossible to do so in the day-time without discovering our march to the Indians; that we would prepare to march at 11 p.m. This was done, the line of march turning from the Rosebud to the right up one of its branches which headed near the summit of the divide. About 2 a.m. on the 25th the scouts told him that he could not cross the divide before daylight. We then made coffee and rested for three hours, at the expiration of which time the march was resumed, the divide crossed, and about 8 a.m. the command was in the valley of one of the branches of the Little Big Horn. By this time Indians had been seen and it was certain that we could not surprise them, and it was determined to move at once to the attack. Previous to this, no division of the regiment had been made since the order had been issued on the Yellowstone annulling wing and battalion organizations, but Custer informed me that he would assign commands on the march.

I was ordered by Lieut. W. W. Cooke, adjutant, to assume command of Companies M, A, and G; Captain Benteen of Companies H, D, and K. Custer retained C, E, F, I, and L under his immediate command, and Company B, Captain McDougall, in rear of the pack-train.

I assumed command of the companies assigned to me, and, without any definite orders, moved forward with the rest of the column, and well to its left.

I saw Benteen moving farther to the left, and, as they passed, he told me he had orders to move well to the left, and sweep everything before him. I did not see him again until about 2.30 p.m. The command moved down to the creek toward the Little Big Horn Valley, Custer with five companies on the right bank, myself and three companies on the left bank, and Benteen farther to the left, and out of sight.

As we approached a deserted village, and in which was standing one tepee, about 11 a.m., Custer motioned me to cross to him, which I did, and moved nearer to his column until about 12.30 a.m. [p.m.?] when Lieutenant Cook, adjutant, came to me and said the village was only two miles above, and running away; to move forward at as rapid a gait as prudent, and to charge afterward, and that the whole outfit would support me. I think those were his exact words. I at once took a fast trot, and moved down about two miles, when I came to a ford of the river. I crossed immediately, and halted about ten minutes or less to gather the battalion, sending word to Custer that I had everything in front of me, and that they were strong. I deployed, and, with the Ree scouts on my left, charged down the valley, driving the Indians with great ease for about two and a half miles. I, however, soon saw that I was being drawn into some trap, as they would certainly fight harder, and especially as we were nearing their village, which was still standing; besides, I could not see Custer or any other support, and at the same time the very earth seemed to grow Indians, and they were running toward me in swarms, and from all directions. I saw I must defend myself and give up the attack mounted. This I did. Taking possession of a front of woods, and which furnished, near its edge, a shelter for the horses, dismounted and fought them on foot, making headway through the woods. I soon found myself in the near vicinity of the village, saw that I was fighting odds of at least five to one, and that my only hope was to get out of the woods, where I would soon have been surrounded, and gain some high ground. I accomplished this by mounting and charging the Indians between me and the bluffs on the opposite side of the river. In this charge, First Lieut. Donald McIntosh, Second Lieut. Benjamin H. Hodgson, Seventh Cavalry, and Acting Assistant Surgeon J. M. De Wolf, were killed.

I succeeded in reaching the top of the bluff, with a loss of three officers and twenty-nine enlisted men killed and seven wounded. Almost at the same time I reached the top, mounted men were seen to be coming toward us, and it proved to be Colonel Benteen's battalion, Companies H, D, and K. We joined forces, and in a short time the pack-train came up. As senior, my command was then A, B, D, G, H, K, and M, about three hundred and eighty men, and the following officers: Captains Benteen, Weir, French and McDougall, First Lieutenants Godfrey, Mathey, and Gibson, and Second Lieutenants Edgerly, Wallace, Varnum, and Hare, and Acting Assistant Surgeon Porter.

First Lieutenant De Rudio was in the dismounted fight in the woods, but, having some trouble with his horse, did not join the command in the charge out, and hiding himself in the woods, joined the command after night-fall on the 26th.

Still hearing nothing of Custer, and, with this re-enforcement, I moved down the river in the direction of the village, keeping on the bluffs.

We had heard firing in that direction and knew it could only be Custer. I moved to the summit of the highest bluff, but seeing and hearing nothing sent Captain Weir with his company to open communication with him. He soon sent word by Lieutenant Hare that he could go no farther, and that the Indians were getting around him. At this time he was keeping up a heavy fire from his skirmish line. I at once turned everything back to the first position I had taken on the bluffs, and which seemed to me the best. I dismounted the men and had the horses and mules of the pack-train driven together in a depression, put the men on the crests of the bluffs, and had hardly done so when I was furiously attacked. This was about 6 p.m. We held our ground, with a loss of eighteen enlisted men killed and forty-six wounded, until the attack ceased, about 9 p.m. As I knew by this their overwhelming numbers, and had given up any support from that portion of the regiment with Custer, I had the men dig rifle pits, barricade with dead horses and mules, and boxes of hard bread, the opening of the depression toward the Indians in which the animals were herded, and made every exertion to be ready for what I saw would be a terrific assault the next day. All this night the men were busy, and the Indians holding a scalp-dance underneath us in the bottom and in our hearing. On the morning of the 26th I felt confident that I could hold my own, and was ready, as far as I could be, when at daylight, about 2.30 a.m., I heard the crack of two rifles. This was the signal for the beginning of a fire that I have never equaled. Every rifle was handled by an expert and skilled marksman, and with a range that exceeded our carbines, and it was simply impossible to show any part of the body before it was struck. We could see, as the day brightened, countless hordes of them pouring up the valley from the village and scampering over the high points toward the places designated for them by their chiefs, and which entirely surrounded our position. They had sufficient numbers to completely encircle us, and men were struck from opposite sides of the lines from where the shots were fired. I think we were fighting all the Sioux Nation, and also all the desperadoes, renegades, half-breeds, and squaw-men between the Missouri and the Arkansas and east of the Rocky Mountains, and they must have numbered at least twenty-five hundred warriors.

The fire did not slacken until about 9.30 a.m., and then we found they were making a last desperate effort and which was directed against the lines held by Companies H and M. In this charge they came close enough to use their bows and arrows, and one man lying dead within our lines was touched with the coup-stick of one of the foremost Indians. When I say the stick was only ten or twelve feet long, some idea of the desperate and reckless fighting of these people may be understood.

This charge of theirs was gallantly repulsed by the men on that line, lead by Colonel Benteen. They also came close enough to send their arrows into the line held by Companies D and K, but were driven away by a like charge of the line, which I accompanied. We now had many wounded, and the question of water was vital, as from 6 p.m. the previous evening until now, 10 a.m., about sixteen hours, we had been without.

A skirmish line was formed under Colonel Benteen to protect the descent of volunteers down the hill in front of his position to reach the water. We succeeded in getting some canteens, although many of the men were hit in doing so. The fury of the attack was now over, and to our astonishment the Indians were seen going in parties toward the village. But two solutions occurred to us for this movement; that they were going for something to eat, more ammunition, (as they had been throwing arrows,) or that Custer was coming. We took advantage of this lull to fill all vessels with water, and soon had it by camp-kettles full. But they continued to withdraw, and all firing ceased save occasional shots from sharp-shooters sent to annoy us about the water. About 2 p.m. the grass in the bottom was set on fire and followed up by Indians who encouraged its burning, and it was evident to me it was done for a purpose, and which purpose I discovered later on to be the creation of a dense cloud of smoke behind which they were packing and preparing to move their village. It was between 6 and 7 p.m. that the village came out from behind the dense clouds of smoke and dust. We had a close and good view of them as they filed away in the direction of the Big Horn Mountains, moving in almost perfect military order. The length of the column was full equal to that of a large division of the cavalry corps of the Army of the Potomac as I have seen it in its march.

We now thought of Custer, of whom nothing had been seen and nothing heard since the firing in his direction about 6 p.m. on the eve of the 25th, and we concluded that the Indians had gotten between him and us and driven him toward the boat at the mouth of the Little Big Horn River. The awful fate that did befall him never occurred to any of us as within the limits of possibility.

During the night I changed my position in order to secure an unlimited supply of water, and was prepared for their return, feeling sure they would do so as they were in such numbers; but early in the morning of the 27th, and while we were on the qui vire for Indians, I saw with my glass a dust some distance down the valley. There was no certainty for some time what they were, but finally I satisfied myself they were cavalry, and, if so, could only be Custer, as it was ahead of the time that I understood that General Terry could be expected. Before this time, however, I had written a communication to General Terry, and three volunteers were to try and reach him. (I had no confidence in the Indians with me, and could not get them to do anything.) If this dust were Indians it was possible they would not expect any one to leave. The men started, and were told to go as near as it was safe to determine whether the approaching column was white men, and to return at once in case they found it so, but if they were Indians to push on to General Terry. In a short time, we saw them returning a note from Terry to Custer saying Crow scouts had come to camp saying he had been whipped, but that it was not believed. I think it was about 10.30 a.m. when General Terry rode into my lines, and the fate of Custer and his brave men was soon determined by Captain Benteen proceeding to the battle-ground, and where was recognized the following officers, who were surrounded by the dead bodies of many of their men; Gen G.A. Custer, Col. W.W. Cook, adjutant; Capts. M.W. Keogh, G.W. Yates, and T.W. Custer; First Lieuts. A.E. Smith, James Calhoun; Second Lieuts. W.V. Reily, of the Seventh Cavalry and J.J. Crittenden, of the Twelfth Infantry, temporarily attached to this regiment. The bodies of Lieut. J.E. Porter and Second Lieuts. H.M. Harrington and J.G. Sturgis, Seventh Cavalry, and Asst. Surg. G. W. Lord, U. S. A., were not recognized; but there is every reasonable probability they were killed. It was more certain that the column of five companies with Custer had been killed.

The wounded in my lines were, during the afternoon and evening of the 27th, moved to the camp of General Terry, and at 5 a.m. of the 28th I proceeded with the regiment to the battle-ground of Custer, and buried 204 bodies, including the following-named citizens: Mr. Boston Custer, Mr. Reed (a young nephew of General Custer,) and Mr. Kellogg, (a correspondent for the New York Herald.) The following-named citizens and Indians who were with my command were also killed: Charles Reynolds, guide and hunter; Isaiah Dorman, (colored,) interpreter; Bloody Knife, who fell from immediately by my side; Bobtail Bull, and Stab, of the Indian scouts.

After traveling over his trail, it was evident to me that Custer intended to support me by moving farther down the stream and attacking the village in flank; that he found the distance greater to ford than he anticipated; that he did charge, but his march had taken so long, although his trail shows that he had moved rapidly, that they were ready for him; that Companies C and I, and perhaps part of E, crossed to the village or attempted it; at the charge were met by a staggering fire, and that they fell back to find a position from which to defend themselves, but they were followed too closely by the Indians to permit time to form any kind of a line.

I think had the regiment gone in as a body, and from the woods from which I fought advanced upon the village, its destruction was certain. But he was fully confident they were running away, or he would not have turned from me. I think (after the great number of Indians that were in the village,) that the following reasons obtain for the misfortune: His rapid marching for two days and one night before the fight; attacking in the day-time at 12 m., and when they were on the qui vire, instead of early morning; and lastly, his unfortunate division of the regiment into three commands.

During my fight with Indians, I had the heartiest support from officers and men, but the conspicuous services of Bvt. Col. F.W. Benteen I desire to call attention to especially, for if ever a soldier deserved recognition by his Government for distinguished services he certainly does. I enclose herewith his report of the operations of his battalion from the time of leaving the regiment until we joined commands on the hill. I also enclose an accurate list of casualties, as far as it can be made at the present time, separating them into two lists: A, those killed in General Custer's command; B, those killed and wounded in the command I had.

The number of Indians killed can only be approximated until we hear through the agencies. I saw the bodies of eighteen, and Captain Ball, Second Cavalry, who made a scout of thirteen miles over their trail, says that their graves were many along their line of march. It is simply impossible that numbers of them should not be hit in the several charges they made so close to my lines. They made their approaches through the deep gulches that led from the hill-top to the river, and, when the jealous care with which the Indian guards the bodies of killed and wounded is considered, it is not astonishing that their bodies were not found. It is probable that the stores left by them and destroyed the next two days was to make room for many of these on their travois. The harrowing sight of the dead bodies crowning the height on which Custer fell, and which will remain vividly in my memory until death, is too recent for me not to ask the good people of this country whether a policy that sets opposing parties in the field, armed, clothed, and equipped by one and the same Government should not be abolished.

All of which is respectfully submitted.

M.A. RENO,
Major Seventh Cavalry, Commanding Regiment.

Source: *Annual Report of the Secretary of War*, 1876, 44th Congr., 1st Sess., House Executive Document No. 1, Serial Vol. 1742, pp. 476–480.

DOCUMENT 5

Benteen's Official Report

*L*ike Reno, Benteen uses his official report to head off potential criticism. In it
he describes his frustrating reconnaissance of the bluffs to the south in such
sterile language as to convey what, in his mind, was its obvious futility. He also
defends himself against charges that he had failed to comply with orders contained
in the note delivered by Trumpeter Martin by observing that the trumpeter had
told him the Indians had "skedaddled." He further defends his decision to remain
with Reno's command rather than fetch the pack train (and, by implication, continue
on with it to Custer's position as ordered) by asserting that the significant action
was taking place at Reno's position.

3 Bb.—REPORT OF CAPT. F.W. BENTEEN.

Camp Seventh Cavalry, July 4, 1876

Sir:

In obedience to verbal instructions received from you, I have the honor
to report the operations of my battalion, consisting of Companies D, H,
and K, on the 25th ultimo.

The directions I received from Lieutenant-Colonel Custer were, to move
with my command to the left, to send well-mounted officers with about six
men who should ride rapidly to a line of bluffs about five miles to our left
and front, with instructions to report at once to me if anything of Indians
could be seen from that point. I was to follow the movement of this
detachment as rapidly as possible. Lieutenant Gibson was the officer selected,
and I followed closely with the battalion at times getting in advance of the
detachment. The bluffs designated were gained, but nothing seen but other
bluffs quite as large and precipitous as were before me. I kept on to those and
the country was the same, there being no valley of any kind that I could see

on any side, I had then gone about fully ten miles; the ground was terribly hard on horses, so I determined to carry out the other instructions, which were, that if in my judgment there was nothing to be seen of Indians, valleys, &c., in the direction I was going, to return with the battalion to the trail the command was following. I accordingly did so, reaching the trail just in advance of the pack-train. I pushed rapidly on, soon getting out of sight of the advance of the train, until reaching a morass, I halted to water the animals, who had been without water since about 8 p.m. of the day before. This watering did not occasion the loss of fifteen minutes, and when I was moving out the advance of the train commenced watering from that morass. I went at a slow trot until I came to a burning lodge with the dead body of an Indian in it on a scaffold. We did not halt. About a mile farther on I met a sergeant of the regiment with orders from Lieutenant Colonel Custer to the officer in charge of the rear-guard and train to bring it to the front with as great rapidity as was possible. Another mile on I met Trumpeter Morton, of my own company, with a written order from First Lieut. W.W. Cook to me which read: "Benteen, come on. Big village. Be quick. Bring pacs. W.W. Cook P. Bring pac's." I could then see no movement of any kind in any direction; a horse on the hill, riderless, being the only living thing I could see in my front. I inquired of the trumpeter what had been done, and he informed [me] that the Indians had "skedaddled," abandoning the village. Another mile and a half brought me in sight of the stream and plain in which were some of our dismounted men fighting, and Indians charging and recharging them in great numbers. The plain seemed to be alive with them. I then noticed our men in large numbers running for the bluffs on right bank of stream. I concluded at once that those had been repulsed, and was of the opinion that if I crossed the ford with my battalion, that I should have had it treated in like manner; for from long experience with cavalry, I judge there were 900 veteran Indians right there at that time, against which the large element of recruits in my battalion would stand no earthly chance as mounted men. I then moved up to the bluffs and reported my command to Maj. M. A. Reno. I did not return for the pack-train because I deemed it perfectly safe where it was, and we could defend it, had it been threatened, from our position on the bluff; and another thing, it savored too much of coffee-cooling to return when I was since a fight was progressing in the front, and deeming the train as safe without me.

Very respectively,
F.W. BENTEEN,
Captain Seventh Cavalry
Lieut. Geo. D. Wallace,
Adjutant Seventh Cavalry

Source: *Annual Report of the Secretary of War*, 1876, 44th Congr., 1st Sess., House Executive Document No. 1, Serial Vol. 1742, pp. 479–480.

DOCUMENT 6

Gall's Account as Told on the Battlefield on the Tenth Anniversary of the Battle

In June 1886 army and Indian veterans met on the battlefield to mark the tenth anniversary of the battle. Representing the army were such notables as Major Benteen, Captain Godfrey, Captain McDougall, and Dr. Porter. Among those representing the Indians were the Hunkpapa warrior Gall and the Crow scout Curley. Many warriors refused to talk about the battle but Gall willingly shared his recollections. He did so through an interpreter as he and a small party walked the battlefield. Newspapers across the country published his story.

The writer of the version included here credited Gall with telling the truth but for a long time serious students of the battle found his testimony difficult to reconcile with other accounts, the physical evidence, and their own assumptions about what had happened. Failing to realize that different people participated in or saw different parts of the action, they discounted it and similar Native American eyewitness accounts as unreliable. Only after new evidence produced by archaeological research conducted on the battlefield in the 1980s and 1990s suggested a different understanding of how the battle had unfolded were scholars like Richard Fox able to square Native testimony like Gall's with other accounts and the physical evidence.

THE STORY OF CHIEF GALL

Fuller Details of the Recent Visit to the Custer Battlefield—The Old Chief Told the Truth

---

Many Erroneous Impressions Corrected—A Lucky Escape for Those Who Failed to Get There

---

Fort Custer, Mont., Special Correspondence, July 14.—Much of the history connected with the true fate of Gen. Custer and those who marched with him into the valley of the Little Big Horn on that fateful June morning ten years ago would no doubt forever have remained a mystery had not Gall, the great Sioux Chief who commanded on that day, consented to revisit the scene of the terrible disaster, and tell all he knew of it according to the red man's side of the case.

. . .

He Told the Truth

Any one present with Gall at the Custer battlefield on the morning of June 25 last could see at a glance that the chief was telling the truth, the whole truth, and nothing but the truth. When he stood on the spot from which Custer had gazed his last on earth, and glanced up and down the valley of the Little Big Horn, once tenanted with thousands of lodges belonging to his people, one could readily see that the old man was visibly affected, by his solemn mien and the suspicion of moisture in his dark, glittering eye. His gaze remained long and fixed on the little grove of timber which marked the point where Reno made his unsuccessful attack on the upper end of the village.

"What is it, Gall?" inquired one of the officers present. "Why do you look so earnestly in that direction?"

"My two squaws and three children were killed there by the pale-faced warriors, and it made my heart bad. After that I killed all my enemies with the hatchet."

. . .

Some of Gall's Statements

The following are a few of the questions put to Gall as he rode over the field, with the answers given verbatim by him.

"How long before all the soldiers were killed?"

The chief made the sign of the white man's dinner time which means noon, and then with his finger cut a half, which would signify half an hour consumed in slaughtering everybody.

"Did the red men shoot guns or arrows?"

"Both. We soon shot all our cartridges, and then shot arrows and used our war clubs."

"Did the soldiers have plenty of ammunition?"

"No. They shot away all they had. The horses ran away, carrying in the saddle pockets a heap more. The soldiers threw their guns aside and fought with little guns." (Pistols.)

"Who got the horses?"

"The Cheyenne women. A lot of horses got into the river and I jumped in and caught them."

The chief's mind seemed to dwell particularly upon the number of horses they captured rather than the terrible slaughter which took place.

"Did the Indians fight standing up?"

"No. The soldiers did, but the braves fired from behind their horses. A lot of Indians fell over and died."

"When the soldiers had no more cartridges what did the Indians do?"

"The braves ran up to the soldiers and killed them with hatchets."

"How many Indians were killed?"

"Eleven down in that creek, (now called Reno Creek) four over there and two in that coulee."

"How many were killed altogether?"

"Forty-three in all. A great many crossed the river and died in the rushes. They died every day. Nearly as many died each day as were killed in the fight. We buried them in trees and on scaffolds going up Lodge Pole Creek toward the White Rain Mountains."

"How many different tribes were in the fight?"

"Uncpapa, Minneconjou, Ogalalla, Brule, Teton, Santee and Yanktonnais Sioux, Blackfeet, Cheyennes, Arapahoes, and a few Gros Ventres."

"Who fought first, Custer or Reno?"

"Reno was whipped first and then all with Custer were killed."

Of course the chief did not understand the names Custer and Reno, but he indicated by pointing and other signs whom he meant.

"How soon after Reno charged did Custer come down the valley?"

"We saw all at one time before they separated. When Reno charged, the women and children were moved downstream: and when the Sioux bucks drove Reno on top of the bluffs, everybody came down and fought Custer. All the Indians were mixed up then."

"How soon after Reno charged was Custer attacked?"

No satisfactory answer could be gotten to this important question; but it would seem that as soon as Reno was lodged safely on the hill the whole village massed on Custer at once and annihilated him.

"Did Custer get near the river?"

"No."

"Then how came the dead bodies of soldiers on the river's bank where we think the white chief crossed or attempted to cross?"

Gall's answer came without a moment's hesitation.

"They were soldiers who fled down another coulee, crossed the river lower down, were chased upstream again toward the village, driven back into the river, and killed on this side."

"Where was Custer first attacked?"

This and other questions have been answered in the narrative above.

"Did the soldiers fight on horseback or on foot?"

"They fought on foot. One man held the horses while the others shot the guns. We tried to kill the holders, and then by waving blankets and shouting we scared the horses down into that coulee, where the Cheyenne women caught them."

"Did you kill any soldiers?"

"Yes, I killed a great many. I killed them all with the hatchet; I did not use a gun."

"Who had command of all the red men?"

"I held command of those down stream."

"Who was the first one killed with Reno?"

"I don't know; but some of the Sioux say it was a Crow scout named Bloody Knife."

"Where was Sitting Bull all this time while the white soldiers were being killed?"

"Back in his tepee making medicine."

"Did he fight at all?"

"No; he made medicine for us."

"Did you fight Reno?"

"No; I only fought the white men soldiers down this way."

"Then you know nothing of what happened at the upper end of the village?"

No, I was down among the Cheyennes looking after horses when the first attack was made on our village."

"Did the old men and boys fight too?"

"Yes, and the squaws fought with stone clubs and hatchet knives. The squaws cut off the boot legs."

"Were there any white men or breeds in your camp?"

"No; we had only Indians."

"Did the soldiers have swords?"

"No, there was only one long knife with them, and he was killed too."

"Who had the long knife?"

"I don't know."

"Did you see Curley on that day?" (Pointing out the Crow scout who is the only survivor of all who marched with Custer into the Little Big Horn valley.)

"No; but my braves say he ran away early and did not fight at all."

"Did you take any prisoners, and if so what did you do with them?"

This question was put to find out if possible the true fate of Lieutenants Harrington, Jack Sturgis, Dr. Lord, and about fourteen others whose bodies were not found on the field, nor has anything been heard of them since the morning when the command was divided.

"No, we took no prisoners. Our hearts were bad, and we cut and shot them all to pieces."

"Do you remember seeing Custer, the big chief, after the fight?"

"I saw the big chief riding with the orderly before we attacked. He had glasses to his face (field glasses). During the fight there were too many soldiers scattered all around for me to see him."

"Did any of the soldiers get away?"

"No, all were killed. About fourteen (indicating the number with his fingers) started toward the Wolf Mountains, but the young braves got on their trail and all were killed."

No doubt Harrington, Sturgis, Lord and the other missing ones were of the party endeavoring to escape toward the Wolf Mountains.

"What did you do after all Custer's soldiers were killed?"

"We went back to fight the soldiers on the hill who were digging holes in the ground. We staid there until big dust was seen down the river, when we all moved up Lodge Pole Creek toward the White Rain Mountains." (Big Horn.)

Source: *St. Paul Pioneer Press*, July 18, 1886.

Two Moon's Account as Told to Hamlin Garland

*L*ike Gall, the Northern Cheyenne chief Two Moon participated in the Custer *fight. While Gall focused primarily on the battle itself, Two Moon also described the events that preceded it as well as what his people did in the immediate aftermath. He was thereby able to shed light on the movements of his people, how it is that the Cheyenne and Lakota came to be together at the Greasy Grass, their general frame of mind at the time of the battle, and what happened during the fight itself. Like Gall, he shared his views well after the fact and through an interpreter. And just the same as Gall's, his story was largely ignored until supported by evidence generated by archaeological research on the battlefield.*

GENERAL CUSTER'S LAST FIGHT AS SEEN BY TWO MOON
The Battle Described by a Chief Who Took Part In It
[Translated to Hamlin Garland, by Wolf Voice,
a Cheyenne interpreter.]

"Two Moon does not like to talk about the days of fighting; but since you are to make a book, and the agent says you are a friend to Grinnell, I will tell you about it—the truth. It is now a long time ago, and my words do not come quickly.

"That spring [1876] I was camped on Powder River with fifty lodges of my people—Cheyennes. The place is near what is now Fort McKinney. One morning soldiers charged my camp. They were in command of Three Fingers [Colonel McKenzie]. We were surprised and scattered, leaving our ponies. The soldiers ran all our horses off. That night the soldiers slept, leaving the horses one side; so we crept up and stole them back again, and then we went away.

"We traveled far, and one day we met a big camp of Sioux at Charcoal Butte. We camped with the Sioux, and had a good time, plenty grass, plenty game, good water. Crazy Horse was head chief of the camp. Sitting Bull was camped a little ways below, on the Little Missouri River.

"Crazy Horse said to me, 'I'm glad you are come. We are going to fight the white man again.'

"The camp was already full of wounded men, women, and children.

"I said to Crazy Horse, 'All right. I am ready to fight. I have fought already. My people have been killed, my horses stolen; I am satisfied to fight'."

Here the old man paused a moment and his face took a lofty and somber expression.

"I believed at that time the Great Spirits had made Sioux, put them here," he drew a circle to the right—"white men and Cheyenne here,"—indicating two places to the left—"expecting them to fight. The Great Spirits I thought liked to see the fight; it was to them all the same like playing. So I thought then about fighting." As he said this, be made me feel for one moment the power of a sardonic god whose drama was the wars of men.

"About May, when the grass was tall and the horses strong, we broke camp and started across the country to the mouth of the Tongue River. Then Sitting Bull and Crazy Horse and all went up the Rosebud. There we had a big fight with General Crook, and whipped him. Many soldiers were killed—few Indians. It was a great fight, much smoke and dust.

"From there we all went over the divide, and camped in the valley of the Little Horn. Everybody thought, 'Now we are out of the white man's country. He can live there, we will live here.' After a few days, one morning I was in camp north of Sitting Bull, a Sioux messenger rode up and said, 'Let everybody paint up, cook, and get ready for a big dance.'

"Cheyennes then went to work to cook, cut up tobacco, and get ready. We all thought to dance all day. We were very glad to think we were far away from the white man.

"I went to water my horses at the creek, and wash them off with cool water, then took a swim myself. I came back to the camp afoot. When I got near my lodge, I looked up the Little Horn towards Sitting Bull's camp. I saw a great dust rising. It looked like a whirlwind. Soon Sioux horsemen can rushing into camp shouting: 'Soldiers come! Plenty white soldiers.'

"I ran into my lodge and said to my brother–in–law, 'Get your horses; the white man is coming. Everybody run for horses.'

"Outside, far up the valley, I heard the battle cry, *Hay-ay, hay-ya*! I heard shooting, too, this way [clapping his hands very fast]. I couldn't see any Indians. Everybody was getting horses and saddles. After I had caught my horse, a Sioux warrior came again and said, 'Many soldiers are coming.'

"Then he said to the women, 'Get out of the way, we are going to have a hard fight.'

"I said, 'All right, I am ready'

"I got on my horse, and rode out into my camp. I called out to the people all running about: 'I am Two Moon, your chief. Don't run away. Stay here and fight. You must stay and fight the white soldiers. I shall stay even if I am to be killed.'

"I rode swiftly toward Sitting Bull's camp. There I saw the white soldiers fighting in a line [Reno's men]. Indians covered the flat. They began to drive the soldiers all mixed up—Sioux, then soldiers, then more Sioux, and all shooting. The air was full of smoke and dust. I saw the soldiers fall back and drop into the river-bed like buffalo fleeing. They had no time to look for a crossing. The Sioux chased them up the hill, where they met more soldiers in wagons, and then messengers came saying more soldiers were going to kill the women, and the Sioux turned back. Chief Gall was there fighting. Crazy Horse also.

"I then rode toward my camp, and stopped squaws from carrying off lodges. While I was sitting on my horse I saw flags come up over the hill to the east like that [he raised his finger-tips]. Then the soldiers rose all at once, all on horses, like this [he put his fingers behind each other to indicate that Custer appeared marching in columns of fours]. They formed into three bunches.' [squadrons] with a little ways between them. Then a bugle sounded, and they all got off horses, and some soldiers led the horses back over the hill.

"Then the Sioux rode up the ridge on all sides, riding very fast. The Cheyennes went up the left way. Then the shooting was quick, quick. Pop—pop—pop very fast. Some of the soldiers were down on their knees, some standing. Officers all in front. The smoke was like a great cloud, and everywhere the Sioux went the dust rose like smoke. We circled all around them—swirling like water round a stone. We shoot, we ride fast, we shoot again. Soldiers drop, and horses fall on them. Soldiers in line drop, but one man rides up and down the line—all the time shouting. He rode a sorrel horse with white face and white fore-legs. I don't know who he was. He was a brave man.

"Indians keep swirling round and round, and the soldiers killed only a few. Many soldiers fell. At last all horses killed but five. Once in a while some man would break out and run toward the river, but he would fall. At last about a hundred men and five horsemen stood on the hill all bunched together. All along the bugler kept blowing his commands. He was very brave too. Then a chief was killed. I hear it was Long Hair [Custer], I don't know; and then the five horsemen and the bunch of men, maybe so forty, started toward the river. The man on the sorrel horse led them, shouting all the time. He wore a buckskin shirt, and had long black hair and mustache. He fought hard with a big knife. His men were all covered with white dust. I couldn't tell whether they were officers or not. One man all alone ran far down toward the river, then round up over the hill. I thought he was going to escape, but a Sioux fired and hit him in the head. He was the last man. He wore braid on his arms [sergeant].

"All the soldiers were now killed, and the bodies were stripped. After than no one could tell which were officers. The bodies were left where they fell. We had no dance that night. We were sorrowful.

"Next day four Sioux chiefs and two Cheyennes and I, Two Moon, went upon the battlefield to count the dead. One man carried a little bundle of sticks. When we came to dead men, we took a little stick and gave it to another man, so we counted the dead. There 388. There were thirty-nine Sioux and seven Cheyennes killed, and about a hundred wounded.

"Some white soldiers were cut with knives, to makes sure they were dead; and the war women had mangled some. Most of them were left just where they fell. We came to the man with big mustache; he lay down the hill towards the river. The Indians did not take his buckskin shirt. The Sioux said, 'That is a big chief. That is Long Hair.' I don't know. I had never seen him. The man on the white-faced horse was the bravest man.

"That day as the sun was getting low our young men came up the Little Horn riding hard. Many white soldiers were coming in a big boat, and when we looked we could see the smoke rising. I called my people together, and we hurried up the Little Horn, into Rotton Grass Valley. We camped there three days, and then rode swiftly back over our old trail to the east. Sitting Bull went back into the Rosebud and down the Yellowstone, and away to the north. I did not see him again.

. . . "That was a long time ago. I am now old, and my mind has changed. I would rather see my people living in houses and singing and dancing. You have talked with me about fighting, and I have told you of the long time ago. All that is past. I think of these things now: First, that our reservation shall be fenced and the white settlers kept out and our young men kept in. Then there will be no more trouble. Second, I want to see my people raising cattle and making butter. Last, I want to see my people going to school to learn the white man's way. That is all."

Source: Hamlin Garland, "General Custer's Last Fight as Seen by Two Moon," *McClure's Magazine* XI, no. 5 (September, 1898).

The Revenge of Rain-in-the-Face by Henry Wadsworth Longfellow

The Hunkpapa warrior Rain-in-the-Face first fought the wasichus in 1866. He fought them many more times in the years to come. In 1874 Tom Custer arrested him for the murder of an army veterinarian and transferred him to Fort Abraham Lincoln, where he was jailed. Rain-in-the-Face eventually escaped (or was released by a sympathetic jailer) and by the spring of 1876 had joined Sitting Bull's band. While he fought the 7th Cavalry at the Greasy Grass/Little Bighorn, he denied doing any of the things attributed to him by Longfellow in this widely read poem. The poem depicts Rain-in-the-Face ripping out Tom Custer's heart in an act of savage vengeance. Although Tom's body was mutilated almost beyond recognition, his comrades nonetheless buried him with his heart intact.

As the source of the myth of Rain-in-the Face's revenge, this poem exemplifies the disconnect so common between popular culture treatments of the battle and what is actually known about it with a reasonable degree of certainty. It also illustrates how popular culture can influence public sensibilities.

In that desolate land and lone,
Where the Big Horn and Yellowstone
Roar down their mountain path,
By their fires the Sioux Chiefs
Muttered their woes and griefs
And the menace of their wrath.

"Revenge!" cried Rain-in-the-Face,
"Revenge upon all the race
Of the White Chief with yellow hair!"
And the mountains dark and high
From their crags re-echoed the cry
Of his anger and despair.

In the meadow, spreading wide
By woodland and river-side
The Indian village stood;
All was silent as a dream,
Save the rushing of the stream
And the blue-jay in the wood.

In his war paint and his beads,
Like a bison among the reeds,
In ambush the Sitting Bull
Lay with three thousand braves
Crouched in the clefts and caves,
Savage, unmerciful!

Into the fatal snare
The White Chief with yellow hair
And his three hundred men
Dashed headlong, sword in hand;
But of that gallant band
Not one returned again.

The sudden darkness of death
Overwhelmed them like the breath
And smoke of a furnace fire:
By the river's bank, and between
The rocks of the ravine,
They lay in their bloody attire.

But the foemen fled in the night,
And Rain-in-the-Face, in his flight,
Uplifted high in air
As a ghastly trophy, bore
The brave heart, that beat no more,
Of the White Chief with yellow hair.

Whose was the right and the wrong?
Sing it, O funeral song,
With a voice that is full of tears,
And say that our broken faith
Wrought all this ruin and scathe,
In the Year of a Hundred Years.

Source: *The Complete Poetic Works of Henry Wadsworth Longfellow* (1878; repr., Boston, MA, 1880).

Rain-in-the-Face's Story as Told to Charles Eastman

*N*ear the end of his life Rain-in-the-Face outlined his career as a warrior to Dr. Charles Eastman, a Lakota physician. That story is included here. In it he recounted his early fights with the wasichus, detailed his arrest and escape, and described what he did and saw at the Greasy Grass. While he knew that some people claimed he killed Custer and others said he ripped out Tom Custer's heart, he credibly denied doing either. A comparison of his own account of his actions that day with that offered by Longfellow further illustrates the problematic relationship between events on the ground and popular culture renditions of them.

RAIN-IN-THE-FACE

"I had been on many warpaths, but was not especially successful until about the time the Sioux began to fight with the white man. One of the most daring attacks that we ever made was at Fort Totten, North Dakota, in the summer of 1866.

"Hohay, the Assiniboine captive of Sitting Bull, was the leader in this raid. Wapaypay, the Fearless Bear, who was afterward hanged at Yankton, was the bravest man among us. He dared Hohay to make the charge. Hohay accepted the challenge, and in turn dared the other to ride with him through the agency and right under the walls of the fort, which was well garrisoned and strong.

"Wapaypay and I in those days called each other "brother-friend." It was a life-and-death vow. What one does the other must do; and that meant that I must be in the forefront of the charge, and if he is killed, I must fight until I die also!

"I prepared for death. I painted as usual like an eclipse of the sun, half black and half red.""

His eyes gleamed and his face lighted up remarkably as he talked, pushing his black hair back from his forehead with a nervous gesture.

"Now the signal for the charge was given! I started even with Wapaypay, but his horse was faster than mine, so he left me a little behind as we neared the fort. This was bad for me, for by that time the soldiers had somewhat recovered from the surprise and were aiming better.

"Their big gun talked very loud, but my Wapaypay was leading on, leaning forward on his fleet pony like a flying squirrel on a smooth log! He held his rawhide shield on the right side, a little to the front, and so did I. Our warwhoop was like the coyotes singing in the evening, when they smell blood!

"The soldiers' guns talked fast, but few were hurt. Their big gun was like a toothless old dog, who only makes himself hotter the more noise he makes," he remarked with some humor.

"How much harm we did I do not know, but we made things lively for a time; and the white men acted as people do when a swarm of angry bees get into camp. We made a successful retreat, but some of the reservation Indians followed us yelling, until Hohay told them that he did not wish to fight with the captives of the white man, for there would be no honor in that. There was blood running down my leg, and I found that both my horse and I were slightly wounded.

"Some two years later we attacked a fort west of the Black Hills [Fort Phil Kearny, Wyoming]. It was there we killed one hundred soldiers." [The military reports say eighty men, under the command of Captain Fetterman—not one left alive to tell the tale!] "Nearly every band of the Sioux nation was represented in that fight—Red Cloud, Spotted Tail, Crazy Horse, Sitting Bull, Big Foot, and all our great chiefs were there. Of course such men as I were then comparatively unknown. However, there were many noted young warriors, among them Sword, the younger Young-Man-Afraid, American Horse [afterward chief], Crow King, and others.

"This was the plan decided upon after many councils. The main war party lay in ambush, and a few of the bravest young men were appointed to attack the woodchoppers who were cutting logs to complete the building of the fort. We were told not to kill these men, but to chase them into the fort and retreat slowly, defying the white men; and if the soldiers should follow, we were to lead them into the ambush. They took our bait exactly as we had hoped! It was a matter of a very few minutes, for every soldier lay dead in a shorter time than it takes to annihilate a small herd of buffalo.

"This attack was hastened because most of the Sioux on the Missouri River and eastward had begun to talk of suing for peace. But even this did not stop the peace movement. The very next year a treaty was signed at Fort Rice, Dakota Territory, by nearly all the Sioux chiefs, in which it was agreed on the part of the Great Father in Washington that all the country north of the Republican River in Nebraska, including the Black Hills and the Big Horn Mountains, was to be always Sioux country, and no white man should intrude upon it without our permission. Even with this agreement Sitting Bull and Crazy Horse were not satisfied, and they would not sign.

"Up to this time I had fought in some important battles, but had achieved no great deed. I was ambitious to make a name for myself. I joined war parties against the Crows, Mandans, Gros Ventres, and Pawnees, and gained some little distinction.

"It was when the white men found the yellow metal in our country, and came in great numbers, driving away our game, that we took up arms against them for the last time. I must say here that the chiefs who were loudest for war were among the first to submit and accept reservation life. Spotted Tail was a great warrior, yet he was one of the first to yield, because he was promised by the Chief Soldiers that they would make him chief of all the Sioux. Ugh! he would have stayed with Sitting Bull to the last had it not been for his ambition.

"About this time we young warriors began to watch the trails of the white men into the Black Hills, and when we saw a wagon coming we would hide at the crossing and kill them all without much trouble. We did this to discourage the whites from coming into our country without our permission. It was the duty of our Great Father at Washington, by the agreement of 1868, to keep his white children away.

"During the troublesome time after this treaty, which no one seemed to respect, either white or Indian [but the whites broke it first], I was like many other young men—much on the warpath, but with little honor. I had not yet become noted for any great deed. Finally, Wapaypay and I waylaid and killed a white soldier on his way from the fort to his home in the east.

"There were a few Indians who were liars, and never on the warpath, playing 'good Indian' with the Indian agents and the war chiefs at the forts. Some of this faithless set betrayed me, and told more than I ever did. I was seized and taken to the fort near Bismarck, North Dakota [Fort Abraham Lincoln], by a brother [Tom Custer] of the Long-Haired War Chief, and imprisoned there. These same lying Indians, who were selling their services as scouts to the white man, told me that I was to be shot to death, or else hanged upon a tree. I answered that I was not afraid to die.

"However, there was an old soldier who used to bring my food and stand guard over me—he was a white man, it is true, but he had an Indian heart! He came to me one day and unfastened the iron chain and ball with which they had locked my leg, saying by signs and what little Sioux he could muster:

"'Go, friend! take the chain and ball with you. I shall shoot, but the voice of the gun will lie.'

"When he had made me understand, you may guess that I ran my best! I was almost over the bank when he fired his piece at me several times, but I had already gained cover and was safe. I have never told this before, and would not, lest it should do him an injury, but he was an old man then, and I am sure he must be dead long since. That old soldier taught me that some of the white people have hearts, he added, quite seriously.

"I went back to Standing Rock in the night, and I had to hide for several days in the woods, where food was brought to me by my relatives. The Indian police were ordered to retake me, and they pretended to hunt for me, but really they did not, for if they had found me I would have died with one or two of them, and they knew it! In a few days I departed with several others, and we rejoined the hostile camp on the Powder River and made some trouble for the men who were building the great iron track north of us [Northern Pacific].

"In the spring the hostile Sioux got together again upon the Tongue River. It was one of the greatest camps of the Sioux that I ever saw. There were some Northern Cheyennes with us, under Two Moon, and a few Santee Sioux, renegades from Canada, under Inkpaduta, who had killed white people in Iowa long before. We had decided to fight the white soldiers until no warrior should be left."

At this point Rain-in-the-Face took up his tobacco pouch and began again to fill his pipe.

"Of course the younger warriors were delighted with the prospect of a great fight! Our scouts had discovered piles of oats for horses and other supplies near the Missouri River. They had been brought by the white man's fire-boats. Presently they reported a great army about a day's travel to the south, with Shoshone and Crow scouts.

"There was excitement among the people, and a great council was held. Many spoke. I was asked the condition of those Indians who had gone upon the reservation, and I told them truly that they were nothing more than prisoners. It was decided to go out and meet Three Stars [General Crook] at a safe distance from our camp.

"We met him on the Little Rosebud. I believe that if we had waited and allowed him to make the attack, he would have fared no better than Custer. He was too strongly fortified where he was, and I think, too, that he was saved partly by his Indian allies, for the scouts discovered us first and fought us first, thus giving him time to make his preparations. I think he was more wise than brave! After we had left that neighborhood he might have pushed on and connected with the Long-Haired Chief. That would have saved Custer and perhaps won the day.

"When we crossed from Tongue River to the Little Big Horn, on account of the scarcity of game, we did not anticipate any more trouble. Our runners had discovered that Crook had retraced his trail to Goose Creek, and we did not suppose that the white men would care to follow us farther into the rough country.

"Suddenly the Long-Haired Chief appeared with his men! It was a surprise."

"What part of the camp were you in when the soldiers attacked the lower end?" I asked.

"I had been invited to a feast at one of the young men's lodges [a sort of club]. There was a certain warrior who was making preparations to go against the Crows, and I had decided to go also," he said.

"While I was eating my meat we heard the war cry! We all rushed out, and saw a warrior riding at top speed from the lower camp, giving the warning as he came. Then we heard the reports of the soldiers' guns, which sounded differently from the guns fired by our people in battle.

"I ran to my teepee and seized my gun, a bow, and a quiver full of arrows. I already had my stone war club, for you know we usually carry those by way of ornament. Just as I was about to set out to meet Reno, a body of soldiers appeared nearly opposite us, at the edge of a long line of cliffs across the river.

"All of us who were mounted and ready immediately started down the stream toward the ford. There were Ogallalas, Minneconjous, Cheyennes, and some Unkpapas, and those around me seemed to be nearly all very young men.

"'Behold, there is among us a young woman!' I shouted. 'Let no young man hide behind her garment!' I knew that would make those young men brave.

"The woman was Tashenamani, or Moving Robe, whose brother had just been killed in the fight with Three Stars. Holding her brother's war staff over her head, and leaning forward upon her charger, she looked as pretty as a bird. Always when there is a woman in the charge, it causes the warriors to vie with one another in displaying their valor," he added.

"The foremost warriors had almost surrounded the white men, and more were continually crossing the stream. The soldiers had dismounted, and were firing into the camp from the top of the cliff."

"My friend, was Sitting Bull in this fight?" I inquired.

"I did not see him there, but I learned afterward that he was among those who met Reno, and that was three or four of the white man's miles from Custer's position. Later he joined the attack upon Custer, but was not among the foremost.

"When the troops were surrounded on two sides, with the river on the third, the order came to charge! There were many very young men, some of whom had only a war staff or a stone war club in hand, who plunged into the column, knocking the men over and stampeding their horses.

"The soldiers had mounted and started back, but when the onset came they dismounted again and separated into several divisions, facing different ways. They fired as fast as they could load their guns, while we used chiefly arrows and war clubs. There seemed to be two distinct movements among the Indians. One body moved continually in a circle, while the other rode directly into and through the troops.

"Presently some of the soldiers remounted and fled along the ridge toward Reno's position; but they were followed by our warriors, like hundreds of blackbirds after a hawk. A larger body remained together at the upper end of a little ravine, and fought bravely until they were cut to pieces. I had always thought that white men were cowards, but I had a great respect for them after this day.

"It is generally said that a young man with nothing but a war staff in his hand broke through the column and knocked down the leader very early in the fight. We supposed him to be the leader, because he stood up in full view, swinging his big knife [sword] over his head, and talking loud. Some one unknown afterwards shot the chief, and he was probably killed also; for if not, he would have told of the deed, and called others to witness it. So it is that no one knows who killed the Long-Haired Chief [General Custer].

"After the first rush was over, coups were counted as usual on the bodies of the slain. You know four coups [or blows] can be counted on the body of an enemy, and whoever counts the first one [touches it for the first time] is entitled to the 'first feather.'

"There was an Indian here called Appearing Elk, who died a short time ago. He was slightly wounded in the charge. He had some of the weapons of the Long-Haired Chief, and the Indians used to say jokingly after we came upon the reservation that Appearing Elk must have killed the Chief, because he had his sword! However, the scramble for plunder did not begin until all were dead. I do not think he killed Custer, and if he had, the time to claim the honor was immediately after the fight.

"Many lies have been told of me. Some say that I killed the Chief, and others that I cut out the heart of his brother [Tom Custer], because he had caused me to be imprisoned. Why, in that fight the excitement was so great that we scarcely recognized our nearest friends! Everything was done like lightning. After the battle we young men were chasing horses all over the prairie, while the old men and women plundered the bodies; and if any mutilating was done, it was by the old men.

"I have lived peaceably ever since we came upon the reservation. No one can say that Rain-in-the-Face has broken the rules of the Great Father. I fought for my people and my country. When we were conquered I remained silent, as a warrior should. Rain-in-the-Face was killed when he put down his weapons before the Great Father. His spirit was gone then; only his poor body lived on, but now it is almost ready to lie down for the last time. Ho, hechetu! [It is well.]"

Source: Charles A. Eastman (Ohiyesa), *Indian Heroes and Great Chieftains* (Boston, MA: Little, Brown & Co., 1918).

Sioux Agreement (1876)

Black Hills Cession

*A*fter *the Greasy Grass/Little Bighorn battle, the Lakota were coerced into ceding the Black Hills and relinquishing their right to hunt in the unceded territory to the west of the Great Sioux Reservation. Under the terms of the agreement reprinted here, they also consented to draw their annuities and rations at whatever agency deemed suitable for them by the federal government, to become self-sufficient farmers, and to adopt the ways of civilization, which entailed among other things individual ownership of their lands and the education of their children by white missionaries and schoolteachers. These were significant conditions in that they set the stage for breaking the Great Sioux Reservation into several smaller units, eroding tribalism by curtailing the power of traditional leaders, ending the communal ownership and exploitation of key resources, and interfering with their traditional way of life. Because the government negotiators failed to secure the requisite number of signatures on the document but Congress nonetheless ratified it, the Sioux Agreement of 1876 led to many decades of land claims and lawsuits. Many of issues stemming from this agreement remain unresolved.*

19 Stat., 254
40th congr., 2nd sess.
An act to ratify an agreement with certain bands of the Sioux Nation of Indians and also with the Northern Arapaho and Cheyenne Indians.

Be it enacted by the Senate and House of Representatives of the United States of America in Congress assembled, That a certain agreement made by George W. Manypenny, Henry B. Whipple, Jared W. Daniels, Albert G. Boone, Henry C. Bulis, Newton Edmunds, and Augustine S. Gaylord, commissioners on the part of the United States, with the different bands of the Sioux Nation of Indians, and also the Northern Arapaho and Cheyenne Indians, be, and the same is hereby, ratified and confirmed: *Provided*, That nothing in this act shall be construed to authorize the removal of the Sioux Indians to the Indian Territory and the President of the United States is hereby directed to prohibit the removal of any portion of the Sioux Indians to the Indian Territory until the same shall be authorized by an act of Congress hereafter enacted, except article four, except also the following portion of article six: "And if said Indians shall remove to said Indian Territory as herein before provided, the Government shall erect for each of the principal chiefs a good and comfortable dwelling-house" said article not having been agreed to by the Sioux Nation; said agreement is in words and figures following, namely: Articles of agreement made pursuant to the provisions of an act of Congress entitled "An act making appropriations for the current and contingent expenses of the Indian Department, and for fulfilling treaty stipulations with various Indian tribes, for the year ending June thirtieth, eighteen hundred and seventy-seven, and for other purposes," approved August 15, 1876, by and between George W. Manypenny, Henry B. Whipple, Jared W. Daniels, Albert G. Boone, Henry C. Bulis, Newton Edmunds, and Augustine S. Gaylord, commissioners on the part of the United States, and the different bands of the Sioux Nation of Indians, and also the Northern Arapahoes and Cheyennes, by their chiefs and headmen, whose names are hereto subscribed, they being duly authorized to act in the premises.

ARTICLE 1.

The said parties hereby agree that the northern and western boundaries of the reservation defined by article 2 of the treaty between the United States and different tribes of Sioux Indians, concluded April 29, 1868, and proclaimed February 24, 1869, shall be as follows: The western boundaries shall commence at the intersection of the one hundred and third meridian of longitude with the northern boundary of the State of Nebraska; thence north along said meridian to its intersection with the South Fork of the Cheyenne River; thence down said stream to its junction with the North Fork; thence up the North Fork of said Cheyenne River to the said one hundred and third meridian; thence north along said meridian to the South Branch of Cannon Ball River or Cedar Creek; and the northern boundary of their said reservation shall follow the said South Branch to its intersection with the main Cannon Ball River, and thence down the said main Cannon Ball River to the Missouri River; and the said Indians do hereby relinquish and cede to the United States all the territory lying outside the said reservation, as herein modified and described, including all privileges of hunting; and article 16 of said treaty is hereby abrogated.

ARTICLE 2.

The said Indians also agree and consent that wagon and other roads, not exceeding three in number, may be constructed and maintained, from convenient and accessible points on the Missouri River, through said reservation, to the country lying immediately west thereof, upon such routes as shall be designated by the President of the United States; and they also consent and agree to the free navigation of the Missouri River.

ARTICLE 3.

The said Indians also agree that they will hereafter receive all annuities provided by the said treaty of 1868, and all subsistence and supplies which may be provided for them under the present or any future act of Congress, at such points and places on the said reservation, and in the vicinity of the Missouri River, as the President of the United States shall designate.

ARTICLE 4.

The Government of the United States and the said Indians, being mutually desirous that the latter shall be located in a country where they may eventually become self-supporting and acquire the arts of civilized life, it is therefore agreed that the said Indians shall select a delegation of five or more chiefs and principal men from each band, who shall, without delay, visit the Indian Territory under the guidance and protection of suitable persons, to be appointed for that purpose by the Department of the Interior, with a view to selecting therein a permanent home for the said Indians. If such delegation shall make a selection which shall be satisfactory to themselves, the people whom they represent, and to the United States, then the said Indians agree that they will remove to the country so selected within one year from this date. And the said Indians do further agree in all things to submit themselves to such beneficent plans as the Government may provide for them in the selection of a country suitable for a permanent home, where they may live like white men.

ARTICLE 5.

In consideration of the foregoing cession of territory and rights, and upon full compliance with each and every obligation assumed by the said Indians, the United States does agree to provide all necessary aid to assist the said Indians in the work of civilization; to furnish to them schools and instruction in mechanical and agricultural arts, as provided for by the treaty of 1868. (Also to provide the said Indians with subsistence consisting of a ration for each individual of a pound and a half of beef, (or in lieu thereof, one half pound of bacon,) one-half pound of flour, and one-half pound of corn; and for every one hundred rations, four pounds of coffee, eight pounds of sugar, and three pounds of beans, or in lieu of said articles the equivalent thereof, in the discretion of the Commissioner of Indian Affairs. Such rations, or so much thereof as may be necessary, shall be continued until the Indians are able to support themselves.) Rations shall, in all cases, be issued to the head of each separate family; and whenever schools shall have been provided by the Government for said Indians, no rations shall be issued for children between the ages of six and fourteen years (the sick and infirm excepted) unless such children shall regularly attend school. Whenever the said Indians shall be located upon lands which are suitable for cultivation, rations shall be issued only to the persons and families of those persons who labor, (the aged, sick, and infirm excepted;) and as an incentive to industrious habits the Commissioner of Indian Affairs may provide that such persons be furnished in payment for their labor such other necessary articles as are requisite for civilized life. The Government will aid said Indians as far as possible in finding a market for their surplus productions, and in finding employment, and will purchase such surplus, as far as may be required, for supplying food to those Indians, parties to this agreement, who are unable to sustain themselves; and will also employ Indians, so far as practicable, in the performance of Government work upon their reservation.

ARTICLE 6.

Whenever the head of a family shall, in good faith, select an allotment of said land upon such reservation and engage in the cultivation thereof, the Government shall, with his aid, erect a comfortable house on such allotment; [and if said Indians shall remove to said Indian Territory as hereinbefore provided, the Government shall erect for each of the principal chiefs a good and comfortable dwelling-house.

ARTICLE 7.

To improve the morals and industrious habits of said Indians, it is agreed that the agent, trader, farmer, carpenter, blacksmith, and other artisans employed or permitted to reside within the reservation belonging to the Indians, parties to this agreement, shall be lawfully married and living with their respective families on the reservation; and no person other than an Indian of full blood, whose fitness, morally or otherwise, is not, in the opinion of the Commissioner of Indian Affairs, conducive to the welfare of said Indians, shall receive any benefit from this agreement or former treaties, and may be expelled from the reservation.

ARTICLE 8.

The provisions of the said treaty of 1868, except as herein modified, shall continue in full force, and, with the provisions of this agreement, shall apply to any country which may hereafter be occupied by the said Indians as a home; and Congress shall; by appropriate legislation, secure to them an orderly government; they shall be subject to the laws of the United States, and each individual shall be protected in his rights of property, person, and life.

ARTICLE 9.

The Indians, parties to this agreement, do hereby solemnly pledge themselves, individually and collectively, to observe each and all of the stipulations herein contained, to select allotments of land as soon as possible after their removal to their permanent home, and to use their best efforts to learn to cultivate the same. And they do solemnly pledge themselves that they will at all times maintain peace with the citizens and Government of the United States; that they will observe the laws thereof and loyally endeavor to fulfill all the obligations assumed by them under the treaty of 1868 and the present agreement, and to this end will, whenever requested by the President of the United States, select so many suitable men from each band to co-operate with him in maintaining order and peace on the reservation as the President may deem necessary, who shall receive such compensation for their services as Congress may provide.

ARTICLE 10.

In order that the Government may faithfully fulfill the stipulations contained in this agreement, it is mutually agreed that a census of all Indians affected hereby shall be taken in the month of December of each year, and the names of each head of family and adult person registered; said census to be taken in such manner as the Commissioner of Indian Affairs may provide.

ARTICLE 11.

It is understood that the term reservation herein contained shall be held to apply to any country which shall be selected under the authority of the United States as the future home of said Indians.

This agreement shall not be binding upon either party until it shall have received the approval of the President and Congress of the United States.

(signatures omitted)
Approved, February 28, 1877.

Source: 19 Stat., 254, available in Charles J. Kappler, comp. and ed., *Indian Affairs: Laws and Treaties, Vol. I: Treaties* (Washington, DC: GPO, 1904), 168–172.

Notes

1 The Road to War

1 Timothy Braatz, "Clash of Cultures as Euphemism: Avoiding History at the Little Bighorn," *American Indian Culture and Research Journal* 28, no. 4 (2004): 107–130.

2 Russell Thornton, *American Indian Holocaust and Survival* (Norman: University of Oklahoma Press, 1990), 95–99.

3 John D. Unruh, Jr., *The Plains Across: The Overland Emigrants and Trans-Mississippi West, 1840–1860* (Champaign: University of Illinois Press, 1979), 119–120.

4 Quoted in David W. Smits, "The Frontier Army and the Destruction of the Buffalo: 1865–1883," *The Western Historical Quarterly* 25, no. 3 (1994): 323.

5 Frank B. Linderman, *Plenty-Coups: Chief of the Crows* (1930; repr., Lincoln: University of Nebraska Press, 1962), 311.

6 Smits, "Frontier Army," 338.

7 Frederick E. Hoxie, *Parading Through History: The Making of the Crow Nation in America, 1805–1935* (Cambridge: Cambridge University Press, 1995).

8 Francois Antoine Larocque, *Journal of Larocque from the Assiniboine to the Yellowstone, 1805*, ed. by L.J. Burpee, Publications of the Canadian Archives, no. 3 (Ottawa: Government Printing Bureau, 1910).

9 Linderman, *Plenty-Coups*, 154.

10 John H. Moore, *The Cheyenne* (London: Blackwell Publishers, 1996).

11 U.S. Office of Indian Affairs, *Annual Report of the Commissioner of Indian Affairs Accompanying the Annual Report of the Secretary of the Interior for the Year 1859* (Washington, DC: George W. Bowman, 1860), 138–139.

12 Guy Gibbon, *Sioux: The Dakota and Lakota Nations* (London: Blackwell Publishers, 2003).

13 Richard White, "The Winning of the West: The Expansion of the Western Sioux in the Eighteenth and Nineteenth Centuries," *Journal of American History* 65 (1978): 319–345.

14 Nathaniel Philbrick, *The Last Stand: Custer, Sitting Bull and the Battle of the Little Bighorn* (London: Vintage Books, 2010), 29.

15 Eleanor Hinman, "Oglala Sources on the Life of Crazy Horse," *Nebraska History* 57, no. 1 (1976): 31.

16   W.W. Newcomb, Jr., "A Re-Examination of the Causes of Plains Indian Warfare," *American Anthropologist* 52 (1950): 229.

17   U.S. Department of Commerce, *Historical Statistics of the United States, 1789–1954* (Washington, DC: GPO, 1949), 25.

18   U.S. Department of Homeland Security, *Yearbook of Immigration Statistics: 2004* (Washington, DC: Office of Immigration Statistics, 2006), 5.

19   John O'Sullivan, "Annexation," *The United States Magazine and Democratic Review* 17, no. 1 (1845): 5–10.

20   Brian W. Dippie, "Its Equal I Have Never Seen: Custer Explores the Black Hills in 1874," *The Magazine of Northwest History* 15 (2005).

2 Battle of the Greasy Grass/Little Bighorn

1   U.S. Senate, "Message from the President of the United States," *Senate Executive Document* No. 81, Serial Vol. 1164, 44th Cong., 2nd Sess. (Washington, DC: GPO, July 13, 1876).

2   Ibid.

3   Elizabeth Bacon Custer, *"Boots and Saddles", or Life in Dakota with General Custer* (Norman: University of Oklahoma Press, 1885), 263–264.

4   Orin Grant Libby, ed., *The Arikara Narrative of Custer's Campaign and the Battle of the Little Bighorn* (Cedar Rapids, IA: Torch Press, 1920), 75. http://www.archive.org/stream/collectionsofsta06stat/collectionsofsta06stat_djvu.txt.

5   Mrs. Fanny (Wiggins) Kelly, *Narrative of My Captivity among the Sioux Indians, with a Brief Account of General Sully's Indian Expedition in 1864* (Hartford, CT: Mutual Publishing Company, 1871).

6   Thomas B. Marquis, *Wooden Leg: A Warrior Who Fought Custer* (Minneapolis, MN: The Midwest Company, 1931), 199.

7   Ibid., 200–201.

8   Robert P. Higheagle, comp. and trans., "Twenty-five Songs Made by Sitting Bull, with Translations" (manuscript, 1929), 158. http://digital.libraries.ou.edu/whc/nam/manuscripts/Campbell_WS_104_18.pdf.

9   Edward S. Godfrey, "Custer's Last Battle," *Century Magazine* 43, no. 3 (1892): 358–385.

10   Kenneth Hammer, ed., *Custer in '76: Walter Camp's Notes on the Custer Fight* (Norman: University of Oklahoma Press, 1990), 222.

11   Col. W.A. Graham, ed. and comp., *The Official Record of a Court of Inquiry Convened at Chicago, Illinois, January 13, 1879, by the President of the United States upon the Request of Major Marcus A. Reno, 7th U.S. Cavalry to Investigate His Conduct at the Little Big Horn, June 25–26, 187* (Pacific Palisades, CA: privately printed, 1951), 75. http://digital.library.wisc.edu/1711.dl/History.Reno.

12   Ibid., 561.

13   Libby, *Arikara Narrative*, 183.

14   Col. W.A. Graham, *The Custer Myth* (Harrisburg, PA: The Telegraph Press, 1953), 349.

15   Ibid., 103.

16   Richard Allan Fox, Jr., *Archaeology, History, and Custer's Last Battle: The Little Bighorn Re-examined* (Norman: University of Oklahoma Press, 1993).

17   Custer, *Boots and Saddles*, 268.
18   Kate Bighead (as told to Thomas Marquis), "She Watched Custer's Last Battle," in *The Custer Reader*, ed. Paul Andrew Hutton (Lincoln: University of Nebraska Press, 1992), 376–377.
19   Ibid., 374.
20   Graham, *Custer Myth*, 220.
21   Ibid.
22   Ibid., 146.
23   Ibid.
24   Ibid., 376.
25   Ibid., 376–377.
26   Joseph Mills Hanson, *The Conquest of the Missouri: Being the Story of the Life and Exploits of Captain Grant Marsh* (Chicago, IL: A.C. McClurg & Co, 1916), 198. http://www.archive.org/stream/conquestmissour01hansgoog#page/n8/mode/2up.
27   Quoted in Lorna Thackery, "Far West Delivers News of 1876 Battle to 'Libbie' Custer, Other Widows: Dread then Sorrow at Fort Lincoln," *The Billing Gazette*, June 17, 2011. http://billingsgazette.com.
28   Custer, *Boots and Saddles*, 209.

3 Aftermath

1   Bighead, "She Watched," 372.
2   Marquis, *Wooden Leg*, 274.
3   Graham, *Custer Myth*, 103.
4   Robert Marshall Utley, *Little Bighorn Battlefield: A History and Guide to the Battle of the Little Bighorn,* Handbook 132 (Washington, DC: U.S. Department of the Interior, National Park Service, Division of Publications, 1994), 83.
5   Frederic F. van de Water, *Glory Hunter: A Life of General Custer* (New York, NY: The Bobbs-Merrill Company, 1934).
6   Utley, *Little Bighorn Battlefield*, 88.
7   Press release of Whittaker letter reprinted in Graham, *Official Record*, iii–iv.
8   Ibid., v.
9   Ibid., 555.
10   Utley, *Little Bighorn Battlefield*, 89.
11   U.S. House of Representatives, *Report of the Secretary of War Being Part of the Message and Documents Communicated to the Two Houses of Congress*, Vol. I. 44th Cong., 2nd Sess. (Washington, DC: GPO, 1876), 6. http://www.archive.org/stream/unitedstatescon575offigoog#page/n14/mode/2up.
12   U.S. Office of Indian Affairs, *Annual Report of the Commissioner of Indian Affairs to the Secretary of the Interior for the Year 1876* (Washington, DC: GPO, 1876), 334.
13   Ibid., 335.
14   Quoted in Robert Marshall Utley, *The Lance and the Shield: The Life and Times of Sitting Bull* (New York, NY: Henry Holt and Company, 1993), 232.
15   James McLaughlin, *My Friend the Indian* (Boston, MA: Houghton Mifflin, 1910), 180. http://ia700404.us.archive.org/5/items/myfriendindian00mcla/myfriendindian00mcla_bw.pdf.

16   Stanley Vestal, *New Sources of Indian History, 1850–1891* (Norman: University of Oklahoma Press, 1934), 280.

17   McLaughlin, *My Friend*, 184.

18   Robert Marshall Utley, *Custer and the Great Controversy: The Origin and Development of a Legend* (Lincoln: University of Nebraska Press, 1962), 99.

4 Reverberations

1   Utley, *Little Bighorn Battlefield*, 6.

2   Speech by Robert M. Utley, 24 June 1976, Custer Battlefield National Monument, copy in Medicine Crow Collection, box 12, folder 14, Little Big Horn College Archives, Crow Agency, MT.

3   George A. Custer, *My Life on the Plains* (New York, NY: Sheldon & Co., 1874), 18.

4   Frederick A. Whittaker, *A Complete Life of Gen. George A. Custer* (New York, NY: Sheldon & Company, 1876). http://www.archive.org/details/completelifeofge00whit.

5   Brian W. Dippie, *Custer's Last Stand: The Anatomy of an American Myth* (Lincoln: University of Nebraska Press, 1994), 12–61.

6   Quoted in ibid., 90.

7   Joseph K. Dixon, *The Vanishing Race* (Garden City, NY: Doubleday, Page and Company, 1913). http://www.gutenberg.org/ebooks/27616.

8   "The Custer Battle Celebration," *The Teepee Book* 2, no. 4 (1916): 34–35.

9   "Fortieth Anniversary Memorial," *The Teepee Book* 2, no. 6 (1916): 4–5.

10   Quoted in "Program for Custer Celebration: The 40th Anniversary," *Hardin Tribune*, May 26, 1916.

11   *Semi-Centennial of the Battle of the Little Big Horn*, issued by the Burlington Route, copy in Medicine Crow Collection, box 12, folder 26 (Crow Agency, MT: Little Big Horn College Archives).

12   *Carrying on for 50 Years with the Courage of Custer, 1876–1826* (Helena: Montana Department of Agriculture, Labor and Industry, n.d.).

13   Quoted in Douglas C. McChristian, "In Search of Custer Battlefield," *Montana, The Magazine of Western History* 42, no. 1 (1992): 64.

14   Quoted in Edward Tabor Linenthal, *Sacred Ground: Americans and Their Battlefields*, 2nd ed. (Urbana and Chicago: University of Illinois Press, 1993), 137.

15   Ibid., 132.

16   Ibid., 138.

17   Mrs. E.R. Burleigh, "Little Big Horn, 1876–1951," *Montana Treasure* 2, no. 3 (1952): 3.

18   Marjorie C. Matross, "Custer Memorial Museum will be Dedicated at Field Program," uncited newspaper article ca. 1952 in scrapbook (Billings, MT: Montana Room, Parmly Billings Library).

19   Harry B. Robinson, "The Custer Battlefield Museum," *Montana, The Magazine of Western History* 2, no. 3 (1952): 12.

20   Vine Deloria, Jr., *Custer Died for Your Sins: An Indian Manifesto* (New York, NY: Macmillan, 1969).

21 Jerome Greene, *Stricken Field: The Little Bighorn since 1876* (Norman: University of Oklahoma Press, 2008), 152.

22 Speech by Hal Stearns, 25 June 1976, Custer Battlefield National Monument, copy in Medicine Crow Collection, box 12, folder 25 (Crow Agency, MT: Little Big Horn College Archives).

23 John G. Neihardt, *Black Elk Speaks: Being the Life Story of a Holy Man of the Oglala Sioux* (1932; repr., Lincoln: University of Nebraska Press, 1961), 34.

24 Linenthal, *Sacred Ground*.

25 Ibid., 164.

26 Ibid., 145.

27 " 'Know the Power that is Peace,' Black Elk," *Hardin Herald*, August 5, 1976.

28 John Carroll, letter to the editor, *Little Big Horn Associates Newsletter* (Feb. 1983), 6–7.

29 Letter from John Carroll to James V. Court Letter, reprinted in *Little Big Horn Associates Newsletter* (Nov. 1978), 5.

30 *Little Big Horn Associates Newsletter* (April, 1983), 4–5.

31 *Little Big Horn Associates Newsletter* (May, 1983), 6–7.

32 "The Destruction of the Battlefield," *Custer/Little Bighorn Battlefield Advocate* (Winter, 1994), 11.

33 Quoted in Linenthal, *Sacred Ground*, 162.

34 Greene, *Stricken Field*, 148.

35 U.S. House of Representatives, *Custer Battlefield National Monument Indian Memorial: Hearing on HR 4600*, Subcommittee on National Parks and Public Lands of the Committee on Interior and Insular Affairs, 101st Cong., 2nd Sess. (Washington, DC: GPO, Sept. 4, 1990), 45.

36 Letter from Wells to Barbara Booher, reprinted in *Little Big Horn Associates Newsletter* (Feb. 1990), 4–5; "Booher Subject of News Articles," ibid., 4.

37 Little Bighorn Battlefield National Monument, *"Peace Through Unity": National Design Competition for an Indian Memorial* (U.S. Department of the Interior, National Park Service, July 1996), 2.

38 "Sabers and Tomahawks: Not Bread But a Stone," *Custer/Little Bighorn Battlefield Advocate* (Winter 1996–1997).

39 Tom Pream, "President's Message," *Battlefield Dispatch* (Spring, 1997), 3.

40 Linda Terrell, "Clear the Way: Some Dignity, Please," *Custer/Little Bighorn Battlefield Advocate* (Winter 1996–1997), 4.

41 *Custer/Little Bighorn Battlefield Advocate* (Winter 1994), 2.

42 Greene, *Stricken Field*, 232.

5 The Battle in Memory and History

1 Dippie, *Custer's Last Stand*, 144.

2 Debra Buchholtz, "Telling Stories: Making History, Place, and Identity on the Little Bighorn," *Journal of Anthropological Research* 67, no. 3 (2011).

3 Debra Buchholtz, "The Battle of the Little Bighorn: History, Identity, and Tourism in the 1990s," in *Tourism and Gaming on American Indian Lands*, ed. by Alan A. Lew and George Van Otten (New York, NY: Cognizant Communications Corporation, 1998), 113–127.

4   Debra Buchholtz, "Cultural Politics or Critical Public History? Battling on the Little Bighorn," *Journal of Tourism and Cultural Change* 3, no. 1 (2005): 18–35.

5   Douglas D. Scott, Richard A. Fox, Jr., Melissa A. Connor, and Dick Harmon, *Archaeological Perspectives on the Battle of the Little Bighorn* (Norman: University of Oklahoma Press, 1989).

6   Fox, *Archaeology, History*.

7   Dippie, *Custer's Last Stand*.

8   Andrew Paul Hutton, "From Little Bighorn to Little Big Man: The Changing Image of a Western Hero in Popular Culture," *Western Historical Quarterly* 7, no. 1 (1976): 19–45; "'Correct in Every Detail': General Custer in Hollywood," *Montana, The Magazine of Western History* 41, no. 1 (1991): 28–57.

9   John P. Langellier, *Custer: The Man, the Myth, the Movies* (Mechanicsburg, PA: Stackpole, 2000).

10   Marguerite Merington, *The Custer Story: The Life and Intimate Letters of General George A. Custer and His Wife Elizabeth* (New York, NY: Devin-Adair, 1950).

11   John Gibbon, "Last Summer's Expedition Against the Sioux and Its Great Catastrophe," *American Catholic Quarterly Review* 2, no. 6 (1877): 271–304; "Hunting Sitting Bull," *American Catholic Quarterly Review* 2, no. 8 (1877): 665–694.

12   John G. Bourke, *On the Border with Crook* (New York, NY: Charles Scribner's Sons, 1892).

13   Daniel O. Magnussen, *Peter Thompson's Narrative of the Little Bighorn Campaign, 1876: A Critical Analysis of an Eyewitness Account of the Custer Debacle* (Glendale, CA: Arthur H. Clark Co., 1974).

14   E.A. Brininstool, *Troopers with Custer: Historic Incidents of the Battle of the Little Big Horn* (Mechanicsburg, PA: Stackpole Books,1952).

15   Graham, *Custer Myth*.

16   Paul Andrew Hutton, ed., *Custer Reader* (Lincoln: University of Nebraska Press, 1992).

17   Richard G. Hardorff, ed. and comp., *On the Little Bighorn with Walter Camp: A Collection of Walter Mason Camp's Letters Notes and Opinions on Custer's Last Fight* (El Segundo, CA: Upton and Sons, 2002).

18   Hammer, *Custer in '76*.

19   Graham, *Official Record*.

20   Godfrey, "Custer's Last Battle."

21   Frazier Hunt and Robert Hunt, eds., *I Fought with Custer: The Story of Seargent Windolph, Last Survivor of the Battle of the Little Bighorn* (Lincoln: University of Nebraska Press, 1987).

22   Libby, *Arikara Narrative*.

23   Jerome Greene., ed. and comp., *Lakota and Cheyenne Indian Views of the Great Sioux War, 1876–1877* (Norman: University of Oklahoma Press, 1994).

24   Richard G. Hardorff, ed. and comp., *Lakota Recollections of the Custer Fight: New Sources of Indian-Military History* (Spokane, WA: Arthur H. Clarke & Co., 1991); *Cheyenne Memories of the Custer Fight* (Spokane, WA: Arthur H. Clarke & Co., 1995).

25   Herman J. Viola, *It is a Good Day to Die: Indian Eyewitnesses Tell the Story of the Battle Little Bighorn* (Norman: University of Oklahoma Press, 2002).

26   Marquis, *Wooden Leg*.

27   Neihardt, *Black Elk*.

28   Dennis W. Harcey and Brian R. Croone, with Joe Medicine Crow, *White-Man-Runs-Him: Crow Scout with Custer* (Evanston, IL: Evanston Publishing, 1991).

29   Utley, *Lance and Shield*; Stanley Vestal, *Sitting Bull: Champion of the Sioux* (1937; repr., Norman: University of Oklahoma Press, 1957).

30   Thomas B. Marquis, *She Watched Custer's Last Battle; Her Story Interpreted in 1927* (Hardin, MT: Herald Print, 1935).

31   Fox, *Archaeology, History*.

32   James Donovan, *A Terrible Glory: Custer and the Little Bighorn—The Last Great Battle of the West* (New York, NY: Little, Brown and Co., 2008).

33   Debra Buchholtz, "The Battle of the Little Bighorn: A Study in Culture, History and the Construction of Identity" (PhD diss., University of Minnesota, 2000).

34   Michael A. Elliott, *Custerology: The Enduring Legacy of the Indian Wars and George Armstrong Custer* (Chicago, IL: University of Chicago Press, 2007).

35   Philbrick, *Last Stand*.

Bibliography

Ambrose, Stephen E. *Crazy Horse and Custer: The Parallel Lives of Two American Warriors.* Garden City, NY: Doubleday & Company, 1975.

Bighead, Kate (as told to Thomas Marquis). "She Watched Custer's Last Battle." In *The Custer Reader,* edited by Paul Andrew Hutton, 363–377. Lincoln: University of Nebraska Press, 1992.

Bourke, John G. *On the Border with Crook.* New York, NY: Charles Scribner's Sons, 1892.

Braatz, Timothy. "Clash of Cultures as Euphemism: Avoiding History at the Little Bighorn." *American Indian Culture and Research Journal* 28, no. 4 (2004): 107–130.

Brininstool, E.A. *Troopers with Custer: Historic Incidents of the Battle of the Little Big Horn.* Mechanicsburg, PA: Stackpole Books, 1952.

Buchholtz, Debra. "The Battle of the Little Bighorn: A Study in Culture, History and the Construction of Identity." PhD diss., University of Minnesota, 2000.

Buchholtz, Debra. "The Battle of the Little Bighorn: History, Identity, and Tourism in the 1990s." In *Tourism and Gaming on American Indian Lands,* edited by Alan A. Lew and George Van Otten, 113–127. New York, NY: Cognizant Communications Corporation, 1998.

Buchholtz, Debra. "Cultural Politics or Critical Public History? Battling on the Little Bighorn." *Journal of Tourism and Cultural Change* 3, no. 1 (2005): 18–35.

Buchholtz, Debra. "Telling Stories: Making History, Place, and Identity on the Little Bighorn." *Journal of Anthropological Research* 67, no. 3 (2011): 421–445.

Calloway, Colin G. "'The Only Way Open to Us': The Crow Struggle for Survival in the Nineteenth Century." *North Dakota History* 53 (1986): 25–34.

Coward, John M. "Explaining the Little Bighorn: Race and Progress in the Native Press." *Journalism Quarterly* 71, no. 3 (1994): 540–549.

Custer, Elizabeth Bacon. *"Boots and Saddles", or Life in Dakota with General Custer.* Norman: University of Oklahoma Press, 1885.

Custer, George Armstrong. *My Life on the Plains, or Personal Experiences with Indians.* New York, NY: Sheldon & Co., 1874.

Deloria, Vine Jr. *Custer Died for Your Sins: An Indian Manifesto.* New York, NY: Macmillan, 1969.

Dippie, Brian W. *Custer's Last Stand: The Anatomy of an American Myth.* 1976; repr., Lincoln: University of Nebraska Press, 1994.

Dippie, Brian W. "Its Equal I Have Never Seen: Custer Explores the Black Hills in 1874." *The Magazine of Northwest History* 15 (2005). http://www.friendslittlebighorn.com/Georgecuster.htm.

Dixon, Joseph K. *The Vanishing Race.* Garden City, NY: Doubleday, Page and Company, 1913. http://www.gutenberg.org/ebooks/27616.

Donovan, James. *A Terrible Glory: Custer and the Little Bighorn-The Last Great Battle of the West.* New York, NY: Little, Brown and Co., 2008.

Elliott, Michael A. *Custerology: The Enduring Legacy of the Indian Wars and George Armstrong Custer.* Chicago, IL: University of Chicago Press, 2007.

Fox, Richard Allan, Jr. *Archaeology, History, and Custer's Last Battle: The Little Bighorn Re-examined.* Norman: University of Oklahoma Press, 1993.

Gibbon, Guy. *Sioux: The Dakota and Lakota Nations.* London: Blackwell Publishers, 2003.

Gibbon, John. "Hunting Sitting Bull." *American Catholic Quarterly Review* 2, no. 8 (1877): 665–694.

Gibbon, John. "Last Summer's Expedition Against the Sioux and Its Great Catastrophe." *American Catholic Quarterly Review* 2, no. 6 (1877): 271–304.

Godfrey, Edward S. "Custer's Last Battle." *Century Magazine* 43, no. 3 (1892): 358–385.

Graham, Col. W.A. *The Custer Myth.* Harrisburg, PA: The Telegraph Press, 1953.

Graham, Col. W.A., ed. and compiler. *The Official Record of a Court of Inquiry Convened at Chicago, Illinois, January 13, 1879, by the President of the United States upon the Request of Major Marcus A. Reno, 7th U.S. Cavalry to Investigate His Conduct at the Little Big Horn, June 25–26, 1876.* Pacific Palisades, CA: privately printed, 1951. http://digital.library.wisc.edu/1711.dl/History.Reno.

Greene, Jerome, ed. and comp. *Lakota and Cheyenne Indian Views of the Great Sioux War, 1876–1877.* Norman: University of Oklahoma Press, 1994.

Greene, Jerome. *Stricken Field: The Little Bighorn since 1876.* Norman: University of Oklahoma Press, 2008.

Hammer, Kenneth, ed. *Custer in '76: Walter Camp's Notes on the Custer Fight.* Norman: University of Oklahoma Press, 1990.

Hanson, Joseph Mills. *The Conquest of the Missouri: Being the Story of the Life and Exploits of Captain Grant Marsh.* Chicago, IL: A.C. McClurg & Co., 1916. http://www.archive.org/stream/conquestmissour01hansgoog#page/n8/mode/2up.

Harcey, Dennis W. and Brian R. Croone, with Joe Medicine Crow. *White-Man-Runs-Him: Crow Scout with Custer.* Evanston, IL: Evanston Publishing, 1991.

Hardorff, Richard G., ed. and comp. *Cheyenne Memories of the Custer Fight.* Spokane, WA: Arthur H. Clarke & Co., 1995.

Hardorff, Richard G. *Lakota Recollections of the Custer Fight: New Sources of Indian-Military History.* Spokane, WA: Arthur H. Clarke & Co., 1991.

Hardorff, Richard G. *On the Little Bighorn with Walter Camp: A Collection of Walter Mason Camp's Letters, Notes and Opinions on Custer's Last Fight.* El Segundo, CA: Upton and Sons, 2002.

Hoxie, Frederick E. *Parading Through History: The Making of the Crow Nation in America, 1805–1935.* Cambridge: Cambridge University Press, 1995.

Hunt, Frazier and Robert Hunt, eds. *I Fought with Custer: The Story of Seargent Windolph, Last Survivor of the Battle of the Little Bighorn.* Lincoln: University of Nebraska Press, 1987.

Hutton, Paul Andrew. "'Correct in Every Detail': General Custer in Hollywood." *Montana, The Magazine of Western History* 41, no. 1 (1991): 28–57.

Hutton, Paul Andrew. *Custer Reader.* Lincoln: University of Nebraska Press, 1992.

Hutton, Paul Andrew. "From Little Bighorn to Little Big Man: The Changing Image of a Western Hero in Popular Culture." *Western Historical Quarterly* 7, no. 1 (1976): 19–45.

Hutton, Paul Andrew. *Phil Sheridan and His Army.* Lincoln: University of Nebraska Press, 1985.

Langellier, John P. *Custer: The Man, the Myth, the Movies.* Mechanicsburg, PA: Stackpole, 2000.

Larocque, François Antoine. *Journal of Larocque from the Assiniboine to the Yellowstone, 1805,* edited by L.J. Burpee. Publications of the Canadian Archives, no. 3. Ottawa: Government Printing Bureau, 1910.

Lazarus, Edward. *Black Hills, White Justice: The Sioux Nation Versus the United States, 1775 to the Present.* New York, NY: HarperCollins, 1991.

Libby, Orin Grant, ed. *The Arikara Narrative of Custer's Campaign and the Battle of the Little Bighorn.* Cedar Rapids, IA: Torch Press, 1920. http://www.archive.org/stream/collectionsofsta06stat/collectionsofsta06stat_djvu.txt.

Linderman, Frank B. *Plenty-Coups: Chief of the Crows.* 1930; repr., Lincoln: University of Nebraska Press, 1962.

Linenthal, Edward Tabor. *Sacred Ground: Americans and Their Battlefields,* 2nd ed. Urbana and Chicago, IL: University of Illinois Press, 1993.

Magnussen, Daniel O. *Peter Thompson's Narrative of the Little Bighorn Campaign, 1876: A Critical Analysis of an Eyewitness Account of the Custer Debacle.* Glendale, CA: Arthur H. Clark & Co., 1974.

Marquis, Thomas B. *She Watched Custer's Last Battle; Her Story Interpreted in 1927.* Hardin, MT: Herald Print, 1935.

Marquis, Thomas B. *Wooden Leg: A Warrior Who Fought Custer.* Minneapolis, MN: The Midwest Company, 1931.

McChristian, Douglas C. "In Search of Custer Battlefield." *Montana, The Magazine of Western History* 42, no. 1 (1992): 75–76.

McGinnis, Anthony. *Counting Coup and Cutting Horses: Intertribal Warfare on the Northern Plains, 1738–1889.* Evergreen, CO: Cordillera Press, 1990.

McLaughlin, James. *My Friend the Indian.* Boston, MA: Houghton Mifflin, 1910. http://ia700404.us.archive.org/5/items/myfriendindian00mcla/myfriendindian00mcla_bw.pdf.

Merington, Marguerite. *The Custer Story: The Life and Intimate Letters of General George A. Custer and His Wife Elizabeth*. New York, NY: Devin-Adair, 1950.

Moore, John H. *The Cheyenne*. London: Blackwell Publishers, 1990.

Neihardt, John G. *Black Elk Speaks: Being the Life Story of a Holy Man of the Oglala Sioux*. 1932; repr., Lincoln: University of Nebraska Press, 1961.

Newcomb, W.W., Jr. "A Re-Examination of the Causes of Plains Indian Warfare." *American Anthropologist* 52 (1950): 317–330.

Philbrick, Nathaniel. *The Last Stand: Custer, Sitting Bull and the Battle of the Little Bighorn*. London: Vintage Books, 2010.

Rankin, Charles E., ed. *Legacy: New Perspectives on the Battle of the Little Bighorn*. Helena, MT: Montana Historical Society, 1996.

Robinson, Harry B. "The Custer Battlefield Museum." *Montana, The Magazine of Western History* 2, no. 3 (1952): 18–31.

Scott, Douglas D., Richard A. Fox, Jr., Melissa A. Connor, and Dick Harmon. *Archaeological Perspectives on the Battle of the Little Bighorn*. Norman: University of Oklahoma Press, 1989.

Smits, David D. "The Frontier Army and the Destruction of the Buffalo: 1865–1883." *The Western Historical Quarterly* 25, no. 3 (1994): 313–338.

Thornton, Russell. *American Indian Holocaust and Survival*. Norman: University of Oklahoma Press, 1990.

Unruh, John D. Jr. *The Plains Across: The Overland Emigrants and Trans-Mississippi West, 1840–1860*. Champaign: University of Illinois Press, 1979.

U.S. House of Representatives. *Custer Battlefield National Monument Indian Memorial: Hearing on HR 4600*. Subcommittee on National Parks and Public Lands of the Committee on Interior and Insular Affairs, 101st Cong., 2nd Sess., Washington, DC, September 4, 1990.

U.S. House of Representatives. *Report of the Secretary of War Being Part of the Message and Documents Communicated to the Two Houses of Congress*, Vol. I. 44th Cong., 2nd Sess., Washington, DC: GPO, 1876. http://www.archive.org/stream/unitedstatescon575offigoog#page/n14/mode/2up.

U.S. Office of Indian Affairs. *Annual Report of the Commissioner of Indian Affairs Accompanying the Annual Report of the Secretary of the Interior for the Year 1859*. Washington, DC: George W. Bowman, 1860.

U.S. Office of Indian Affairs. *Annual Report of the Commissioner of Indian Affairs to the Secretary of the Interior for the Year 1876*. Washington, DC: GPO, 1876.

U.S. Senate. "Message from the President of the United States." *Senate Executive Document* No. 81, Serial Volume 1164. 44th Cong., 2nd Sess., Washington, DC: GPO, July 13, 1876.

Utley, Robert Marshall. *Cavalier in Buckskin: George Armstrong Custer and the Western Military Frontier*. Norman: University of Oklahoma Press, 1988.

Utley, Robert Marshall. *Custer and the Great Controversy: The Origin and Development of a Legend*. Lincoln: University of Nebraska Press, 1962.

Utley, Robert Marshall. *Little Bighorn Battlefield: A History and Guide to the Battle of the Little Bighorn*. Handbook 132. Washington, DC: U.S. Department of the Interior, National Park Service, Division of Publications, 1994.

Utley, Robert Marshall. *The Lance and the Shield: The Life and Times of Sitting Bull.* New York: Henry Holt and Company, 1993.

van de Water, Frederic F. *Glory Hunter: A Life of General Custer.* New York: The Bobbs-Merrill Company, 1934.

Vestal, Stanley. *New Sources of Indian History, 1850–1891.* Norman: University of Oklahoma Press, 1934.

Vestal, Stanley. *Sitting Bull: Champion of the Sioux.* 1937; repr., Norman: University of Oklahoma Press, 1957.

Vestal, Stanley. *Warpath: The True Story of the Fighting Sioux Told in a Biography of Chief White Bull.* 1943; repr., Lincoln: University of Nebraska, 1964.

Viola, Herman J. *It is a Good Day to Die: Indian Eyewitnesses Tell the Story of the Battle of the Little Bighorn.* Norman: University of Oklahoma Press, 2002.

White, Richard. "The Winning of the West: The Expansion of the Western Sioux in the Eighteenth and Nineteenth Centuries." *Journal of American History* 65 (1978): 319–343.

Whittaker, Frederick. *A Complete Life of Gen. George A. Custer.* New York, NY: Sheldon & Company, 1876. http://www.archive.org/details/completelifeofge 00whit.

Index

acculturation 30, 102–03, 110, 117, 122

Allison Commission 32

allotment 9, 90, 96, 97, 99, 200–01

American bicentennial (*see* battle anniversaries)

American centennial 3, 34–5, 133, 134

American Horse 82

American Indian Movement (AIM) 115–16, 119–20, 142

Arapaho 14, 16, 20–2, 50, 120, 126

archaeology 60, 62–3, 144–45, 149, 179

Arikara 7–8, 12–13, 21, 125, 126, 133–34; scouts 13, 39, 41, 51, 53

assimilation 14–15, 129, 133; anniversary observances 109–10, 137; Grant's Peace Policy 102–03; Manypenny Commission 87–90; battle reenactments 141–43; Wanamaker expedition 107–08

Baker, Gerard 125–26, 129

battle anniversary 4, 113–14, 123, 126–29; tenth 106–07, **128**, 179–83; fortieth 108–09; semi-centennial 110–12; centennial 115–19

Battle of Cedar Creek 83–4

Battle of the Greasy Grass (*see* Battle of the Little Bighorn)

Battle of the Little Bighorn 1, **43**, 44–5, 55–66, **59**, 69–70, 163–66, 167–69, 170–76, 177–78; Battle of the Greasy Grass 64, 105, 133–34, 179–83,

194–96; blame for 74–8; Custer's Last Stand 2, 62–3, 105–06, 112–13, 134, 144; meaning of 5, 102–03, 106, 108–10, 112–13, 115–21, 123, 131–43, 145, 149; name of 2, 135

Battle of the Washita 16, 18–19, 142

battle story 2–6, 101–04, 109, 113–20, 122–23, 126–27, 131–43

Battle Where the Sister Saved Her Brother (*see* Rosebud Battle)

battlefield interpretation **59**, 102, 126, 129–30, 136–38; 144–45, 149; contention over 118–20; Luce and 113–14

Belknap, William 33, 75, 78

Benteen, Frederick W. 1, **59**, 60, 64–6, 138, 164, 168, 171–76; bitterness over Elliott affair 18–19, 52; blamed 76, 78, 112, 147–48; official report 177–78

Bighead, Kate 64, 72–3, 148

bison (*see* buffalo)

Black Elk 73–4; quotation, 117–19

Black Hills **43**, 146, 153–54, 192, 197–98; Cheyenne in 14, 32, 42; Crazy Horse 22–3; gold in 31–2, 137; Lakota in 32, 87–92; whites in 31–2

Black Hills Cession (*see* Sioux Agreement)

Black Hills Expedition 31–2

Black Kettle 15–16, 18

Blackfoot (*see* Lakota)

Bloody Knife 13, 53–4, 57

Boyer, Mitch 53–4
Bozeman Trail 9, 21–4, 153, 161
Bradley, James H. 39–40, 67–8
Brulé (*see* Lakota)
buffalo 7, 9–10, 20, 23, 94, 142, 180;
    buffalo culture 24–5; return of 97–8
Buffalo Calf Woman 49
burials 176; cavalry **59**, 68–9, 103–04,
    111–12, **139**, 144; Cheyenne 72–3;
    Lakota 41, 72–3, 86, 100

Calf Tail Woman 64
Calhoun, James 17, 31, 52, 61–2
Canada (Grandmother's Land) 74, 84–6,
    93–5
cemetery **59**, 61, 101, 103–04, 113, 122
Centennial Campaign (*see* Sioux
    Campaign)
Centennial Exhibition (*see* American
    centennial)
Cheyenne 1–4, 42, 79–81, 84–5, 92–3,
    103–05, 110, 116–18, 120–21, 123,
    125–27, 129, 133, 147–49;
    cooperation with the Lakota 19–24,
    30, 40, 44, 46–7, 49–51, 56, 61–6,
    68, 72–4, 83–4, 137–38; culture
    25–8, 32; history 10, 12, 13–16;
    Monasetah 18, 64, 142; Sand Creek
    16; Two Moon's story 184–87;
    Washita 16, 18–19, 142
Cheyenne break out (*see* Cheyenne)
citizenship 29, 103, 108, 111–12; fee
    patents and 97, 157; Indian
    Citizenship Act 110
Civil War 2, 9, 16, 31, 52, 133–34;
    Centennial Exhibition and 3, 34;
    Custer in 17–18
civilization 97, 104, 108, 140, 157–58,
    195, 199–200; Grant's Peace Policy
    21, 29–30, 34–5; Indian
    Appropriations Act (1876) 87–90;
    savagery and 5, 106, 109, 112, 132
clash of cultures 5, 109, 124, 136–37
Clymer Commission 33, 75
Cody, William Frederick "Buffalo Bill"
    79, 96, 107
Coinage Act (1873) 31
Cold War 113–15, 118

commemoration 104, 110–14, 119–22,
    126–29; bicentennial 115–17; fortieth
    anniversary 108–09; Last Great Indian
    Council 107–08, **139**; semi-
    centennial 77, 110–12; tenth
    anniversary 106–07;
Cooke, William W. 52, 55, 56, 58, 60,
    62, 65
counting coup 28, 140, 142; at the Greasy
    Grass 55, 173, 195; contemporary
    119–20, 125, 127
Crawler, Mary (*see* Moving Robe
    Woman)
Crazy Horse 21–3, 25–6, 28, 42, 84; at
    the Greasy Grass 62, 185–86; at Slim
    Buttes 81–2; surrender and death
    85–6
Crook, George 32–3, 37–9, **43**, 78, 80–1,
    84–5, 137; Crook's Starvation March
    81–2; General Terry on 169;
    Rosebud Battle 42–3, **43**, 47, 49–50,
    193–94
Crow 47, 49, 96, 107, 120, 123–25,
    133–34; Crow Reservation **59**, 93,
    102; culture 24–8, 105; history 7–8,
    10–12; observances 108–15, 126;
    scouts 24, 39–40, 51, 52–4, 58, 60,
    67–8, 70, **139**, 165, 175;
    reenactments 107–08, **139**–42;
    treaties 14, 21–2
Crow Foot 48, 95, 99
Crows Nest 53–4
Curley 40, 54, 70, **139**, 179, 182
Custer Battlefield (*see* Little Bighorn
    Battlefield National Monument)
Custer Battlefield Museum & Historical
    Association 4, 125
Custer Battlefield National Monument
    (*see* Little Bighorn Battlefield
    National Monument)
Custer National Cemetery (*see* Little
    Bighorn Battlefield National
    Monument)
Custer Battlefield Preservation Committee
    4, 102
Custer, Boston 41, 52, 60, 62
Custer buffs 4, 118–21, 124–29, 148–49
Custer descendants 110, 113, 117–18

Custer, Elizabeth "Libbie" Bacon: 17–18, 40, 71, 103, 113, 147; *Boots and Saddles* 63, 146

Custer, George Armstrong 30–1, 103, 118, 132–33, 134, 146; Belknap Affair 33–4; Black Hills Expedition 31–2; blamed 74–5, 147; Civil War 17–18; defended 76, 78, 116, 147; Little Bighorn 1, 40–44, **43**, 51–6, 57–64, **59**, 68–9, 137–38, 163–66, 167–69, 170–75, 177–78; orders to 45; popular culture, in 5, 79, 96, 105–07, 112–13, 115–16, 139–43, 182–83; views on the Indians 104; Washita 16, 18–19

Custer, Thomas 51–2, 58, 62–3; and Rain-in-the-Face 188, 190, 192, 195–96

Custer's Last Stand (*see* Battle of the Little Bighorn)

Dakota 15–16, 19–20, 50
Dakota column 33–4, 39, 40–4, **43**, 137
Dawes Act (*see* General Allotment Act)
Deep Ravine **59**, 62, 195
disease 7–8, 12–14, 20, 97–8
Dorman, Isaiah 41
Dull Knife 79, 84–5, 92–3

Edgerly, Winfield 65
Elliott, Joel 18–19, 66, 78
eyewitness accounts 2–3, 144, 147–49, 179

Far West 41, 43, 45, 67, 69–71, 74
Fetterman Massacre 21, 23, **43**, 191
Fools Crow, Frank 117
Fort Abraham Lincoln 18, 30–1, 33–4, 40, **43**, 63, 69–70, 71, 82, 192–93
Fort Laramie Treaty (1851) 12, 14–15, 20–1, 93
Fort Laramie Treaty (1868) 12, 22–4, 28, 32, 88–91, 93, 137, 141, 153–62; Sioux Agreement 198–201
Fort Robinson 22–3, 85–6, 92–3
Fort Wise Treaty (1861) 15
Fox, Richard A. 62–3, 144, 149, 179
Friends of the Indian 18, 36, 87, 114
fur trade 7, 10–13, 19–20

Gall 60–1, 74, 94, 106–07; eyewitness account 179–83
Gatling guns 39, 51, 75, 165, 168
General Allotment Act 97
Gerard, Fred 41, 55, 57, 69
Ghost Dance 48, 83, 97–100
Gibbon, John 38–41, 46, 51, 82, 146; as scapegoat 78; with Terry 41, 44–5, 67–8, 70, 137–38, 165, 167–69
Godfrey, Edward S. 65, 77–8; at anniversary events 106, 109, 111–12, 179; eyewitness account 41, 53–4, 61, 67–9, 147
gold 8–9, 31, 192; Black Hills 31–2, 90–1, 137; Montana 21
Grant, Ulysses S. 32–3, 34–5; Peace (Quaker) Policy 29–30, 35, 78, 80, 90–1, 103
Grattan Massacre 21, 23
Great Sioux Reservation 9, 23, 97, 99, 141, 197–98; Fort Laramie Treaty 153–55
guns 7–8, 14, 61–2, 79–80, 85, 93–4, 144, 180–81

Herendeen, George 44–5, 52–4
Hidatsa 8, 11–13
homesteading 15, 97, 99
horses 7–8, 14, 20, 56, 72–3, 79–80, 85, 94, 140, 142, 180–81; Comanche 69–70; in Plains Indian culture 24–8
Hunkpapa (*see* Lakota)

Indian Appropriations Act (1871) 30
Indian Appropriations Act (1876) 87
Indian memorial **59**, 115, 118, 120–25, **125**, 127, 129–30
Indian village 1, 18, 49–50, 55–6, **59**, 66, 72–3

Kanipe, Daniel 58, 65
Keogh, Myles W. 58, 61–2, 82
Kellogg, Mark 39, 69

Lakota 32, 41, 48–9, 85–6, 93–7, 105; Black Hills cession 87–92, 197–202; contemporary 116–17, 119–20, 126–29; cooperation with the

Cheyenne 1–2, 19–24, 30, 40, 46–7, 49–51, 56, 61–6, 68, 72–4, 81–5, 137–38; culture 25–8, 63–4; Ghost Dance 97–9; history 7–14, 19–24; on reservations 79–80; Rain-in-the-Face story 190–96; Reno fight 56–7; Wounded Knee 99–100

Lame Deer 85

Lame White Man 61–2, 121, 129

Last Great Indian Council 107–08, **139**

Last Stand Hill **59**, 61–3, 68–9, 103, 122, 141; commemorations on 106–07, 111–12, **128**; protests on 116, 119–20

Lewis and Clark Expedition 6–7, 141

Little Big Man 5, 115

Little Bighorn Battlefield National Monument **59**, 101–02, 104, 113–14; controversies at 115–30; story told at 136–38

Little Wolf 84–5, 92–3

lone tipi 49, 55, 65

Louisiana Purchase 6

McDougall, Thomas M. 54–5, 58, 164, 179

MacKenzie, Ranald S. 84–5, 184

Mangum, Neil C. 129–30

manifest destiny 3, 8, 29, 34, 110

Manypenny Commission 87–90, 197–202

markers, cavalry dead 69, 103–04, **139**, 144

markers, Indian dead 105, 121, 129

Martin, John (Giovanni Martini) 60, 65, 177–78

Means, Russell 116, 119–20

medicine 25–7

Medicine Crow, Joe 139–40

Medicine Lodge Treaty 16

Medicine Tail Coulee **59**, 58–60, 142

memorialization **59**, 136; Black Elk quotation 117–19; Crazy Horse 42; Custer Battlefield 103–05, **125**, 144; Indian memorial 115, 119–30, **139**; Reno-Benteen Battlefield 77–8, 112, 147

Me-o-tzi (*see* Monasetah)

Miles, Nelson A. "Bear Coat" 82–5, 92, 94, 99, 106

Mills, Anson 81–2

Minneconjou (*see* Lakota)

Minnesota Uprising (*see* Santee Sioux Uprising)

Monasetah 18, 64, 142

Montana column 38–45, **43**, 67–8, 70, 137–38

Moving Robe Woman 64, 194

museum (*see* Little Bighorn Battlefield National Monument)

mutilation 18, 63–4, 69, 124; of Tom Custer 188–89, 196

name change 113, 116, 120–23

National Park Service (NPS) 101–02, 113–14, 136–38; controversy involving 115–21, 123, 127–29

Native American activism 115–20, 125, 127, 129, 142

Native testimony 2, 49, 144, 146–49, 179

newspapers 87, 132, 145, 167; *Bismarck Tribune* 69, 71; *New York Herald* 33, 39, 60, 69, 78

non-treaty Indians 153, campaign against 32–4, 36–7, 85, 87, 133; depredations by 30, 40

North Shield Ventures 123

Northern Cheyenne (*see* Cheyenne)

Oglala (*see* Lakota)

Oregon Trail 8–9, 15, 20

paintings 106, 145

Pahá Sápa (*see* Black Hills)

patriotism 109–14, 117–18, 140; Native American patriots 49, 119,

Plainfeather, Mardell 120

Plains Indian culture 7, 24–9, 63, 97–8, 141–42

Plenty Coups 10, 12

poetry 145, 188–89

Poor Bear, Enos 123–24

popular culture 132, 134,; Buffalo Bill; film 5, 79, 112–13, 115; poetry 186–87; reenactments 139–43; Whittaker 105–06, 145–46 population, Native American 8, 12–13, 20, 104

population, United States 8–9, 29, 34

protests 115–20, 128–29

railroad 9, 23–4, 28, 31, 110, 160; attacks on 22, 30

Rain-in-the-Face 188–89, 190–96

Real Bird: reenactment 140–43; Richard 120, 142

Red Cloud Agency 85–6, 88, 93, 153

Red Cloud 21, 23–4, 28, 85–6, 153

Red Cloud's War 21–4, 141, 153, 191

Red Power (*see* Native American activism)

Red Tomahawk 48, 111–12

Reed, Harry Armstrong "Autie" 41, 52, 60, 62

reenactments 4, 106–08, 136, 138–43, **139**

Reno Court of Inquiry 57, 60–1, 76–7, 147

Reno, Marcus A. 52, 138, 164–66; blamed 76–8, 105, 112, 147; Court of Inquiry 76–7; official report 170–76; reconnaissance 41–2, **43**; siege 64–7; valley fight 55–9, **59**

Reno-Benteen Battlefield (*see* Little Bighorn Battlefield National Monument)

reservations 23, 79–80, 85–6; conditions on 15–16, 30, 32–3; Crow 102; exodus from 38–9, 47, 50, 52, 78–9; Fort Laramie Treaty 153–62; Northern Cheyenne 92–3; Sitting Bull on 95–9; Sioux Agreement 197–202

Reynolds, Joseph J. 38–9, 46

Rosebud Battle 42–4, **43**, 47, 50, 185, 193–94

Sand Creek Massacre 16

Sans Arc (*see* Lakota)

Santee (*see* Dakota)

Santee Sioux Uprising 15–16, 48, 50

savagery 5, 106, 109, 112

scouts, Indian 51, 84, 92; Arikara 13, 53–4, 57; Crow 12, 39–40, 53–4, 58, 60, 67–8, **139**, 165; Curley 70

scouts, white 44–5, 53–4, 146

Seventh Cavalry **43**, 44–5, 71, 110–12, 130, 137–38, 144–45; Black Hills Expedition 31–2; discord in 18–19; en route to Little Bighorn 39–42, 51–5; Little Bighorn 55–63, **59**, 64–9; official reports 163–66, 167–69, 170–76, 180–83; Washita 16; Wounded Knee 99–100; Yellowstone Expedition 30–1

Seventh Cavalry memorials 103–04, 112, 116, 118, 124, 127–28

Sheridan, Philip 3, 9, 16, 17, 36–9, 79–80

Sherman, William Tecumseh 3, 9, 33

siege 64–6, 69, 77–8, 170–76

Sioux 19–24, 91–2

Sioux Acts (1887, 1889) 97

Sioux Agreement (1876) 87–92, 197–202

Sioux Campaign 37–9, **43**, 133, 137

Sitting Bull 10, 28, 30, 48–51, 81–7; Canada 93–5; Ghost Dance 97–9; Little Bighorn 56, 60, 182; Standing Rock 95–7; Sun Dance vision 46–7, 50, 52

Slim Buttes 82

Southern Cheyenne (*see* Cheyenne)

Spotted Tail 85–6

Spotted Tail Agency 85–6, 88

Standing Rock Reservation **43**, 48, 94–9

Stearns, Hal 116–17

suicide boys 50, 62

Sun Dance 26–7, 142: Sitting Bull's 46–7, 50, 52, 141

Sutteer, Barbara (Booher) 120–21, 125–26

Terry, Alfred 33, 37, 39, 41–2, **43**, 70, 74–5, 94, 137–38; orders to Custer 44–5, 53, 55; telegrams 163–66, 167–69; with Crook 80–2; with Gibbon 67–8

Teton (*see* Lakota)

They Died With Their Boots On 5, 112–13

The Red Right Hand; Or Buffalo Bill's First Scalp for Custer 79

Thompson, Peter 58, 146

Two Kettles (*see* Lakota)

Two Moon 65, 84–5, 92–3, 109; eye
    witness account 62, 73, 184–87
Two Moon, Austin 116, 119, 123

ultimatum 33, 37, 46–7, 137
unceded territory 9, 23, 37, 87–8, 161,
    197–98
unity 117, 129–30, 140–41,143; Indian
    memorial 122–26; post-Civil War 34,
    133–34; reconciliation 108–14
Utley, Robert Marshall 100, 102, 116,
    117; official handbook by 74–6, 78,
    101

Vanishing Race 107–08
Varnum, Charles A. 53, 58–9
Vietnam 115, 118
Vision Quest 23, 26, 32, 142

wanderers (*see* non-treaty Indians)
warfare 7, 12, 19–21, 25, 27–8

Weir, Thomas B. 52, 65, 68–9, 138, 172
White Bull 111
White Man Runs Him 68, 109, 111,
    139
Whittaker, Frederick 76–7, 105,
    145–46
Wild West Show 79, 96, 107
Wooden Leg 49, 56
World War I 109–10, 112
World War II 5, 112–14, 140
Wounded Knee 129; massacre (1890)
    83, 99–100, 118; siege (1973) 115,
    118
Wyoming column 38–40, 42–4, 80–2;
    Battle of the Rosebud 46–7, 49–50

Yankton-Yanktonais (*see* Dakota)
Yates, George 60–2
Yellow Hair 79, 107
Yellowstone Column 80–1
Yellowstone Expedition 30